Getting Government Jobs

By the Partnership for Public Service

A member of Penguin Group (USA) Inc.

To all of the people out there willing to commit themselves to serving the public through government work.

ALPHA BOOKS

Published by the Penguin Group

Penguin Group (USA) Inc., 375 Hudson Street, New York, New York 10014, USA

Penguin Group (Canada), 90 Eglinton Avenue East, Suite 700, Toronto, Ontario M4P 2Y3, Canada (a division of Pearson Penguin Canada Inc.)

Penguin Books Ltd., 80 Strand, London WC2R 0RL, England

Penguin Ireland, 25 St. Stephen's Green, Dublin 2, Ireland (a division of Penguin Books Ltd.)

Penguin Group (Australia), 250 Camberwell Road, Camberwell, Victoria 3124, Australia (a division of Pearson Australia Group Pty. Ltd.)

Penguin Books India Pvt. Ltd., 11 Community Centre, Panchsheel Park, New Delhi—110 017, India

Penguin Group (NZ), 67 Apollo Drive, Rosedale, North Shore, Auckland 1311, New Zealand (a division of Pearson New Zealand Ltd.)

Penguin Books (South Africa) (Pty.) Ltd., 24 Sturdee Avenue, Rosebank, Johannesburg 2196, South Africa

Penguin Books Ltd., Registered Offices: 80 Strand, London WC2R 0RL, England

International Standard Book Number: 978-1-59257-979-2
Library of Congress Catalog Card Number: 2009938582

12 11 10 8 7 6 5 4 3 2 1

Interpretation of the printing code: The rightmost number of the first series of numbers is the year of the book's printing; the rightmost number of the second series of numbers is the number of the book's printing. For example, a printing code of 10-1 shows that the first printing occurred in 2010.

Printed in the United States of America

Publisher: *Marie Butler-Knight*
Editorial Director: *Mike Sanders*
Senior Managing Editor: *Billy Fields*
Acquisitions Editor: *Paul Dinas*
Development Editor: *Lynn Northrup*
Senior Production Editor: *Janette Lynn*
Copy Editor: *Andy Saff*
Cartoonist: *Steve Barr*
Cover Designer: *Kurt Owens*
Book Designer: *Trina Wurst*
Indexer: *Tonya Heard*
Layout: *Ayanna Lacey*
Proofreader: *John Etchison*

Contents at a Glance

Appendixes

Contents

Appendixes

Introduction

You know those romantic comedies where two people are clearly destined to be together, but keep missing one another? They stand in the same line for coffee, but don't meet. They sit in the same row on a plane, but are separated by one person who monopolizes the conversation. In these movies, there's a series of missed connections—right until the very end, when they finally (finally!) get together.

Well, that's you and your government job.

The federal government hires roughly 200,000 people each year—people from all backgrounds, majors, professional experiences, and regions of the country.

You, for whatever reason, are considering a career in government. Maybe you're looking for a change in careers. Maybe you lost your job in the economic downturn, maybe you've been inspired to give back through public service, or perhaps you've dreamed of a public service career since you were four years old.

It's already a match made in heaven.

The Complete Idiot's Guide to Getting Government Jobs will help you make the necessary connections the first time around—avoiding resumé faux pas, poor application etiquette, mismanaged expectations (and much, much more), so that you can land the government job of your dreams.

By the end of this book, you should be able to:

- Understand the federal hiring process.
- Find and apply for government jobs online.
- Network masterfully.
- Write an excellent KSA essay (don't worry, we'll explain what that is).
- Prepare for a stellar interview.
- Make it through the security clearance process without blowing a fuse.

We'll guide you along your journey, from searching for jobs to preparing for your first day of work—the moment in your movie that you and your government job finally (finally!) get together.

How This Book Is Organized

This book is here to guide you through what can be an intimidating and confusing process: finding and applying for government jobs. Here's a quick summary of the tips, tricks, and insider advice that you're about to read:

Part 1, "Government Jobs: Why, What, and Who," introduces you to employment with our federal government. What makes it a great employer? What are the benefits? What things should you consider? Find out where the jobs are (in the United States and overseas) and how you can increase your chances of success.

Part 2, "Navigating the System," explores the USAJOBS.gov website—your one-stop shop for federal jobs! Learn the ins and outs of the federal hiring process and how to get through your government background check. We'll also spill the secrets of successful networking, interviewing, and the rest of the application process.

Part 3, "Government Jobs at All Levels," will tell you what opportunities there are for students, entry-level, mid-career, and encore-career jobseekers. This section knows no age limits!

Part 4, "Other Ways to Work in Government," looks at opportunities in the legislative and judicial branches as well as state government jobs. We'll give you the inside scoop on political appointments, grantees, contracting jobs, and temporary jobs. You didn't think there was just one way to work in government, did you?

You'll also find five helpful appendixes: a federal agency list to learn about all the agencies and their missions, a glossary where you can look up unfamiliar terms, a list of helpful websites, an application checklist to keep you organized, and a list of government websites organized by state.

Extras

If we could be with you while you read this book, we would want to jump in every once in a while to explain things further, warn you about potential pitfalls, and share insider information. However, until this whole "space/time continuum" thing gets worked out, we'll have to settle for putting this information into sidebars. We've included four types of sidebars that will help you along the way:

Federal Facts

These are helpful and interesting nuggets of information about government and the application process.

def•i•ni•tion

Government is well known for its use of jargon. These explanations will help you understand what the heck they're talking about.

The Fine Print

Unfortunately, there are a few potential pitfalls in the government hiring process. As we go, we'll sound the warning bells for you, so that you can avoid any trouble.

Top Secret

A benefit of the work we do at the Partnership for Public Service is that we have access to hiring managers and human resources professionals across government. Don't tell anyone, but they have shared with us their most closely held insider information about getting government jobs—and in these sidebars, we share it with you!

Acknowledgments

First, the Partnership for Public Service would like to acknowledge all of the public servants who are working to deliver vital services to the American people. We appreciate that you are working on every major issue confronting our nation, and we thank you.

The Partnership would also like to thank Sally K. Smith, who served as primary author, project manager, and chief cat-herder-of-information for this book.

Of course, no effort of this kind is possible without a great team of folks behind it. Additional thanks goes to John Palguta and Tim McManus for sharing their vast expertise on the government hiring process. They taught us how to make sense of the things people in government often say, do, or write and why they do it that way—not always an easy task.

Thanks as well to Erin Creasy, Jenn Carignan, and Lindsey O'Keefe for their wonderful contributions to this book. We especially appreciate your adherence to deadlines.

To Melody Gilbert, research assistant, writer, editor, and wonderful gal. Even her cats, Susan B. Anthony and Mister President, underscore her commitment to honoring public servants.

To Bob Cohen for all of his edits, snarky comments, and general good company throughout the book-writing process.

To Bob Lavigna of the Partnership for Public Service and Leslie Scott of NASPE for all of their time and wisdom on state government jobs.

To Lara Shane, Vice President of Communications, for agreeing to take this project on and then having to review and edit every word.

To Max Stier, our fearless leader, whose unsurpassed enthusiasm for *our* government inspires us each and every day, except possibly at Monday morning staff meetings, which come too early for inspiration.

To the entire staff and team at the Partnership for Public Service for all that you have added not only to this book, but also to our dynamic, scrappy, dedicated organization. You make the Partnership what it is and we thank you for the work you do to revitalize our federal government.

Trademarks

Part 1

Government Jobs: Why, What, and Who

Impossible to get in. Endless rows of cubicles full of paper shufflers. Impenetrable bureaucracy. These myths—and many others—hold back many jobseekers from applying for the challenging and fulfilling careers in government that demand the best and the brightest of our country.

This part introduces you to employment with the *real* federal government. We'll let you in on what makes government a great employer, what the benefits of working for government are, and what things you should consider before applying. Use this part to find out where the jobs are (in the U.S. and overseas) and how you can increase your chances of getting in.

Chapter 1

Is Government Work Right for You?

In This Chapter

- What it means to work in government
- The pros and cons of public service
- The various ways that government hires employees
- The eligibility requirements for government jobs

What makes a job a good fit for you? Is it the salary or the fulfillment? The hours you work or the outcome of that work? Vacation or location?

No matter what your answer is, one thing is for certain: working for the federal government is like the professional version of having your cake and eating it too. You can get the paycheck and the fulfillment, the flexible hours, and the chance to make a difference. You can live in cities across the country and countries around the world. You can live out your career dreams, whatever they may be.

There is no better place to make a difference in our country than in our government, which touches all aspects of our lives, from the air we breathe, to the food we eat, to the roads we travel. Government employees are on the front lines of solving challenging and complex issues such as global warming, health care, and our economic health. As a civil servant, your work can have a positive impact on both our country and our world.

Government job options range from accountant to zoologist, and everything in between. After all, there are roughly 2 million civilian government jobs at more than 120 federal departments and agencies—and that doesn't include the U.S. Postal Service. You can find government work in all 50 states, the District of Columbia, and all U.S. territories, and in more than 140 foreign countries.

In our government, there are jobs for every type of person with every type of background, but the folks most likely to succeed are those who want to have a significant impact on people's lives and care deeply about good governance. They are "change agents"—optimistic, skilled people with a can-do attitude that is complemented by a sense of realism and practicality, recognizing that government changes come in small measures. These are smart individuals who are willing to challenge the status quo.

If this sounds like you, then you've found the right book—and the start to the right career.

What Do We Mean by Government Jobs?

What does it mean to work for the government? For the purpose of this book, we are dealing primarily with *civil service* jobs in the executive branch of the federal government, although we will touch on the legislative and judicial branches of government in Chapters 15 and 16.

If you're thinking that the executive branch consists of the President and the White House, you're right—but it's also much more.

def•i•ni•tion

The **civil service** is comprised of workers in the executive, judicial, and legislative branches of the government of the United States, except those in the military, political appointees, or elected officials.

You've probably heard of the President's Cabinet, which includes the secretaries of Defense, State, Energy, Treasury, Interior, Agriculture, Commerce, Labor, Health and Human Services, Housing and Urban Development, Transportation, Education, and Veteran's Affairs. There's also the administrator of the Environmental Protection Agency, the director of the Office of Management and Budget, and the attorney general, who oversees the Department of Justice.

All of these Cabinet members work with the President (and other Cabinet-level officers) to oversee our government's departments, agencies, programs, and workforce. There are also a number of independent agencies that report directly to the White House, such as the Corporation for National and Community Service and the National Aeronautics and Space Administration (NASA). (For a full list of agencies, see Appendix A.)

The Upside of Government Jobs

Good government starts with good people, which is why it's so important for great people like you to choose public service. The best thing about working in government is the chance to truly make a difference in people's lives, while doing interesting and challenging work.

You'll also find perks in government that you might not find in other sectors, including world-class health care, generous vacation days, and flexible work hours. Here are the top 10 pros of working in government:

1. **You need a job—and the government is hiring.** By 2015, the Office of Personnel Management (OPM) projects that more than 550,000 federal employees—one third of the entire full-time permanent workforce—will leave the government.

> **Federal Facts**
>
> Due to the imminent retirement wave of baby boomers in government (and all sectors), and the fact that new jobs are constantly being added, the government consistently hires 150,000 to 200,000 new employees each year.

2. **Make a difference.** The work of government employees impacts the lives of every American—and the lives of people around the world. You can play a vital role in addressing pressing issues, from homelessness to homeland security.
3. **Great benefits and competitive pay.** Average government salaries are competitive with the private and nonprofit sectors. Pay can also increase fairly quickly for top candidates with strong education and experience. Federal benefits—including health insurance, retirement and vacation—are extremely competitive with, if not superior to, other sectors.
4. **Location, location, location.** Where do you want to work and live? Whatever the answer, chances are you can find government work there. Most people think

that government jobs are all in Washington, but in fact 84 percent of government jobs are outside the D.C. area. Interested in immersing yourself in a culture outside of the United States? More than 50,000 government employees work abroad.

5. **Jobs for every interest.** There are federal jobs suited to every interest and skill, from art history to airplane mechanics to zoology. Government is also a great place to combine your skills with your interests. For example, you could use your mathematics background and your interest in the environment by working as an accountant at the Environmental Protection Agency (EPA), your engineering degree to improve airport security, or your biology degree and interest in medicine to conduct cutting-edge medical research at the National Institute of Health (NIH).

6. **Interesting and challenging work.** There's a stereotype that government buildings are filled with endless rows of drones shuffling paper in cubicles—basically doing a whole lot of nothing on the taxpayer's dime. This couldn't be further from the truth in today's civil service, where government workers are leading and innovating on issues such as developing vaccines for deadly diseases, fighting sexual and racial discrimination, keeping our massive systems of transportation safe, and navigating the diplomatic waters overseas.

7. **Work/life balance.** Flexible work schedules, including telework (working from home or a remote location), are a major plus for those with busy schedules or long commutes. And, of course, everyone's favorite: federal holidays (Columbus Day, anyone?), plus generous vacation and sick leave. All of these packaged together make government an attractive employer if you are looking to have a life outside of work.

8. **Opportunities to advance and move within government.** You will also have many opportunities to move up the ladder in government, but you will have to be proactive. Many agencies use Individual Development Plans (IDPs), an official format for working with your supervisor to plan your short- and long-term career goals within government. An internal Merit Promotion Program helps ensure that once you are in and doing a good job, you will have easy access to information about job openings within government.

Top Secret

Once you are a federal employee, it is relatively easy to switch jobs within your agency or to other agencies, all the while continuing to build your seniority, salary, vacation, and retirement.

9. **Opportunities for professional development.** Government managers understand the value of continuing education for their employees—not only to consistently improve the skills of the people already in government, but also as a way to entice people (like you) to apply for positions. The government offers excellent training and development opportunities and has human resources personnel to help you connect with these opportunities and choose which courses are right for your career path. See Appendix C for links to training opportunities.

10. **Job security**. We hate to encourage you to choose government for the sole purpose of obtaining job security, because there are so many other great reasons to become a public servant. But the fact remains that government work is steady and secure—an attractive selling point, especially when economic times are tough.

The Downside of Government Jobs

We're going to be straight with you: working in government isn't all blue skies and calm seas. By design, change doesn't happen overnight in government, which can be frustrating. Therefore, patience and commitment are virtues of a happy and successful government employee. However, you'll find pros and cons in every sector and every organization—and if you're willing to persevere, the pros far outweigh the cons of government work.

Here are the top five cons of working in government:

1. **Bureaucracy: it does exist.** For many people, the word *government* is synonymous with bureaucracy—evoking images of red tape, inefficiency, and waste. Sadly, there is some truth to this. Put simply, government is huge, and in order to manage all agencies, employees, and programs, there is a complex system of rules and procedures in place, which can be frustrating. However, by hiring people who are well matched to their jobs and who bring enthusiasm and a good work ethic to the office, the scope and impact of the bureaucracy can be minimized. However, we have to ask: have you ever seen a large company that *doesn't* have bureaucracy and red tape?

2. **The hiring process.** Before you even get a chance to experience government as an insider, you will get a taste of it as an outsider through the hiring process. During an "Extreme Hiring Makeover" project conducted by the Partnership for Public Service, a survey of one agency revealed that its hiring process consisted

of a whopping 114 steps (the good news is that the agency quickly cut the number of steps in half and is working to streamline the process even more). Some agencies are worse and many are better, but the hiring process is often cited as the biggest turn-off for would-be applicants (and would-be contributors to our government's important work). Luckily, there is a concerted government-wide effort under way to improve the hiring process, but job applicants will still need patience and persistence.

3. **You won't get rich working in government.** While many government job salaries are comparable to those in the private sector, you are not likely to become extraordinarily wealthy on your government salary, although this depends on your definition of "wealthy." Many of the government's top jobs pay annual salaries that range from $117,000 to $177,000, and starting salaries are often comparable to the private sector. Not too shabby.

4. **Revolving door of leadership.** One complaint that some government employees have is that, while government work is not inherently political, it is affected by politics. A political appointee's "here today, gone tomorrow" nature can be a challenge, even when they are well received by an agency's workforce. For example, when a President's political appointee comes in to an agency and does a good job, his or her peers are frustrated when he or she leaves, only to be replaced by another appointee with different priorities and a different idea of how things should be done. All of this can leave government workers feeling torn between their agency's mission and politically driven agendas. However, the number of political appointees is very small compared to the overall number of employees in the federal workforce, and most federal employees have little direct contact with political appointees.

5. **Making a difference: a marathon, not a sprint.** Many people go into government to get that much-desired balance of bringing home a nice paycheck, getting great benefits, *and* having the chance to make a difference. There may be no better place to give back than through government service—every job, in its essence, is intended to help our country and our world in some way. On the other hand, choosing this path can be tough if you are the kind of person who needs to see immediate results in order to be fulfilled. Real, lasting results are sometimes slow in the making. The process of "getting things done" takes patience, perseverance, and a positive attitude.

Federal Facts

There are many jobs that involve direct contact with the public that can in fact give you the immediate satisfaction of having made a difference—at least for one person or one family. Examples include providing care in a Veterans Administration hospital and helping individuals filing for Social Security benefits. In these and other direct-services jobs, you have the chance to make a real and immediate difference on a daily basis.

How Are Jobs Filled in Government?

One of the many ways that government employment is different from the private sector is how the government fills its jobs. There are several categories of hiring and terms you should know before getting started on your job search.

Competitive Service

Competitive civil service jobs are filled according to a merit system where the best-qualified candidates are chosen based on an application and interview process. Managers can hire a current federal employee (via promotion or transfer) or may choose to hire someone from outside the federal government. *Virtually all jobs discussed in this book are competitive service jobs unless otherwise stated.*

Non-Competitive Status

Some individuals can be hired without going through the full competitive process (which we get to in Chapter 7), frequently because they have earned their stripes in other government positions. For example, former federal employees who were highly regarded while in their government job and then left government may be non-competitively "reinstated" into a government position.

Another example involves individuals who choose to serve our country through certain programs, such as AmeriCorps VISTA and the Peace Corps. Upon completion of their service and for one year following their departure, those returning volunteers can also be hired non-competitively to a position in the federal government. In some cases, that eligibility can be extended for up to two more years if the person first goes into the military or an institution of higher learning after leaving the Peace Corps or VISTA.

Other special hiring programs also allow for the hiring of individuals without going through the full competitive process, including disabled veterans and non-veterans with severe physical disabilities. These individuals must still be qualified for the job, but federal agencies are empowered to recognize the special needs of some individuals and, in the case of eligible veterans, take into consideration their service to our country.

It should be noted that the term "non-competitive" does not imply an entitlement to a government job, nor does it imply that the individual hired non-competitively is not qualified for that job.

Excepted Service

Excepted service lets agencies use a streamlined hiring process rather than hiring through the traditional competitive process, allowing agencies to meet an unusual or special hiring need. Agencies use this to hire people with backgrounds in high-need or hard-to-recruit occupations, such as attorneys, chaplains, and medical doctors.

The excepted service authority is also used to fill jobs under a special circumstance—for example, when there is a part-time or temporary job in a remote location or when there is a critical hiring need. The U.S. Office of Personnel Management may also use a special hiring authority on a case-by-case basis to make a political appointment.

From a job applicant's point of view, the process used to fill a job in the excepted service versus the competitive service may seem very similar. Both typically use the same procedures, and requirements are similar. However, applicants hired in excepted service will likely be able to start their job sooner than if they had gone through the full competitive process.

The Fine Print

Excepted service positions are not required to be posted on USAJOBS.gov, government's website for jobseekers. (See Chapter 5 for a full rundown of how to use USAJOBS.gov.) As a result, it is important to look at individual agency websites for these job announcements.

Who Can Work in Government: Determining Your Eligibility

Being eligible to work in government is about more than having the qualifications for the career you want, although that is a critical component of getting any job. Compared to the private sector, the government has stricter requirements for who it can hire and how they get hired. Before you embark on your job search, make sure you read and understand this section on requirements for getting a government job.

Citizenship

Only on rare occasions will the U.S. government hire non-citizens for government jobs. If you are not a citizen of the United States and are looking to work for government, the best route is to contact the agency you want to work for and see what opportunities, if any, it has available for non-citizens and how you can apply for those positions.

Criminal Records

If you have a criminal history, don't cross government work off your wish list ... yet. Whether or not government considers you for a job depends on what you did and when you did it. For example, an arrest for reckless driving or one-time marijuana use may not disqualify you if the arrest was some time ago and you have had a clean record since. Of course, if you are applying to be a government driver or wish to work in the Drug Enforcement Agency, the type of offense has special relevance. You should be candid in your application about any arrests or convictions, and the agency will determine whether it is disqualifying. It is always disqualifying if you are found to have lied on your application. For more information on this, see Chapter 8.

Credit Score

Something you may not have considered (or ever heard about) is that your credit score can stand in the way of you and your government job. Why? Your credit score is based on such things as your payment history, your credit card debt, the length of your credit history, and more. In essence, your credit history acts as a character witness: if you pay your bills on time and have a small amount of debt, you are likely to be a dependable and responsible person. If not, well, you get the picture. As with past arrests and convictions, however, the circumstances surrounding a poor credit history will determine whether or not it presents a problem.

This is part of the background check for all federal employees, and it is discussed in depth in Chapter 8.

The Least You Need to Know

- The possibilities for government jobs and locations are practically endless.
- Although, like any profession, it has some drawbacks, working in government offers you the chance to earn a living while making a difference—and the job security doesn't hurt.
- The hiring process can be daunting, but, after all, that's why you picked up this book! We'll get you through it.
- Beware your history: things like your credit score and criminal history can stand between you and your government job.

Chapter 2

Choose Your Own Adventure

In This Chapter

- Why government is hiring hundreds of thousands of people
- Top three agencies with the most job openings
- Top five occupational areas with the most job opportunities
- Other areas you might be interested in

One of the best aspects of government work is that there are virtually limitless possibilities for what you can do. Astronaut? Check. Park ranger? Check. Social worker? Check. Nurse? Check. Attorney, engineer, diplomat? Check, check, check. (And the list goes on.)

The first thing you should do for your government job search is learn about all of your options and decide which agency or agencies and occupation or occupations you want to pursue. What's a good fit for you? You might want to start by looking at the list of federal agencies in Appendix A.

The next piece of good news is that the government is hiring more than half a million people. In fact, it's estimated that by 2012, government will hire nearly 600,000 people. That's almost one third of the current federal workforce! (However, it's important to note that government isn't growing significantly bigger historically. There are roughly 1.9 million civilian government workers—about the same number as in 1963, when there were 116 million fewer people.)

Of these 600,000 hires, more than 270,000 are for mission-critical jobs (those jobs that an agency needs to fill in order to meet its essential obligations to the American public) will need to be filled by September 2012, and we expect this trend to continue well after this date.

You can use this chapter to get a good idea of where the government is doing the majority of its hiring. As a straight numbers game, you will have a better chance of getting a job if you are qualified to (and want to) work in an area where the government is hiring lots of people.

This chapter will serve as your guide for learning about what kind of jobs are available, where they are, and how you can get them. For more information that is always up-to-date, check out the interactive site wherethejobsare.org, hosted by the Partnership for Public Service.

Why So Many Jobs in Government?

There are many reasons that government is hiring. First, across all sectors, as baby boomers retire, they are leaving a huge wake of jobs that need to be refilled. So, many of these job openings are not to expand the government workforce, but rather simply to fill these jobs.

Federal Facts

It is estimated that 241,428 federal employees will retire by 2012.

Changing times and political priorities are also contributing to the need for new hires. For example, energy and health care issues are coming to the forefront, as are increased demands for homeland security. The care of our veterans is also a driving force for more government hiring.

With the changing times and issues facing our nation, agency hiring needs change. For example, an increased need for diplomatic efforts and reconstruction in foreign countries has created increased hiring needs at the State Department.

Who's Hiring?

Nearly all federal agencies are hiring. Typically, the larger the agency, the larger the hiring need. Nearly 60 percent of federal employees work at three Cabinet-level departments:

- **The Department of Defense (DOD).** The DOD is our government's largest employer, and has many critical needs besides the obvious military personnel. DOD has tons of occupations with available jobs including health care, business and finance, language specialists, information technology (IT) specialists, contract managers, engineers, and more.
- **The Department of Veterans Affairs (VA).** The VA projects that it will need to hire more than 19,000 nurses and 8,500 physicians between fiscal year 2010 and 2012. In total, the VA will be looking to hire 48,159 employees over the next couple of years.
- **The Department of Homeland Security (DHS).** To protect our air travelers and secure our borders, DHS expects to hire tens of thousands of transportation security officers and border patrol agents. Issues such as terrorism and illegal immigration have fueled the need for many new hires over the next three years.

Intelligence officials have openly recognized a need to hire thousands of employees over the next several years due to continuing threats to national security.

Accounting and budgeting employees are needed across government. The Federal Deposit Insurance Corporation (FDIC) needs to hire more financial examiners, resolutions specialists, and attorneys to maintain the stability of the nation's financial institutions, and the Internal Revenue Service (IRS) needs to hire more agents and tax examiners to achieve its mission. The list goes on and on. With an aging and changing federal workforce, government has some big shoes to fill.

And we're really just touching the tip of the iceberg here. Whatever you are looking to do, the government is most likely hiring in that area.

Top Secret

Check out the Service to America Medals website (www.servicetoamericamedals.org) to see what cool things people are doing in government today.

Top Five Hiring Areas

The following areas are where jobseekers will find the highest concentration of available jobs in government. Think supply and demand: where government's demand is high, your odds as a jobseeker are higher if you have the skills for the job.

Medical and Public Health

According to a survey by the Partnership for Public Service titled *Where the Jobs Are* (released September 2009), "Medical and Public Health" is currently the top field for government hiring, with a projected 54,114 new hires from fiscal year 2010 to 2012.

Jobs in this field include:

- Physicians (all disciplines)
- Nurses
- Dieticians/nutritionists
- Occupational and rehabilitation therapists
- Radiologists
- Pharmacists
- Industrial hygienists
- Consumer safety specialists

The main agencies hiring in this field are:

- VA
- Health and Human Services (HHS)
- DOD

Security and Protection

Where the Jobs Are (2009) lists "Security Protection" as the second most in-demand occupational area in government, with a projected 52,077 hires between 2010 and 2012.

Jobs include:

- Intelligence analysts
- International relations (diplomats, etc.)
- Foreign affairs specialists
- Security administration
- Transportation security officers
- Park rangers
- Correctional officers
- Police officers

The main agencies hiring in this field are:

- DHS
- DOD
- Department of Justice (DOJ)
- Navy

- Army
- Air Force
- Department of the Interior

Compliance and Enforcement

Coming in at number three on the *Where the Jobs Are* survey is "Compliance and Enforcement," with 31,276 projected hires from 2010 to 2012.

Jobs include:

- Inspectors
- Investigators (including criminal)
- Customs and border patrol and protection agents
- Import specialists
- Customs inspection agents

The main agencies hiring in this field are:

- DHS
- DOJ
- United States Department of Agriculture (USDA)
- Department of Labor (DOL)
- DOD
- Environmental Protection Agency (EPA)
- Office of Personnel Management (OPM)

Legal

Number four on the *Where the Jobs Are* survey is "Legal," with 23,596 projected hires from fiscal year 2010 to 2012.

Jobs include:

- Attorneys
- Contact representatives
- Paralegals
- Passport/visa examiners
- Claims examining/assistance professionals

Main agencies hiring in this field:

- Social Security Administration (SSA)
- Department of Treasury
- DOJ
- VA
- Department of State
- DHS
- DOL
- Securities and Exchange Commission

Administration/Program Management

Rounding out the top five on the *Where the Jobs Are* survey is "Administration/ Program Management," with 17,287 projected hires from 2010 to 2012.

Jobs include:

- Human resources professionals
- Equal employment opportunity specialists
- Program managers and analysts

Main agencies hiring in this field:

- DOD
- Army
- DHS
- DOJ
- Navy
- Air Force
- USDA
- NASA
- Department of Housing and Urban Development (HUD)
- EPA
- HHS
- VA
- General Services Administration
- Government Accountability Office
- Department of Treasury
- Department of Education
- Department of Commerce

Other Jobs in Government

If you aren't drawn to or qualified for a job in one of the top five hiring areas, don't fret. We meant what we said: government is hiring in virtually all occupational areas.

Top Secret

There are even more jobs and job areas than we can list in this chapter. Check out Chapter 5 to learn how you can do job searches on USAJOBS.gov to find your perfect match!

Accounting and Budget

Overview: 16,661 jobs

Occupations include financial managers/administrators, accountants, auditors, revenue agents, tax specialists, and budget analysts.

The main agencies hiring in this field are the Department of Treasury, DOD, FDIC, the Department of the Army, the Department of the Navy, the U.S. Air Force, and DHS.

Biological Sciences

Overview: 4,886 jobs

Occupations include microbiologists, ecologists, zoologists, physiologists, entomologists, toxicologists, botanists, plant pathologists and physiologists, horticulturists, geneticists, soil scientists/conservationists, forestry professionals, fish and wildlife workers, animal scientists, rangers, and irrigation system operators.

The main agencies hiring in this field are USDA, DHS, HHS, the Department of the Interior, and EPA.

Business and Industry

Overview: 10,765 jobs

Occupations include contractors, property managers, trade specialists, loan specialists, and realty specialists.

The main agencies hiring in this field are the Department of the Army, the Department of Defense, the Department of the Navy, the General Services Administration (GSA), USDA, DHS, U.S. Air Force, and FDIC.

Engineering

Overview: 10,642 jobs

Occupational areas include all disciplines of engineering and architecture.

The main agencies hiring in this field are the Department of the Navy, the Department of the Army, the Department of Transportation (DOT), NASA, the U.S. Air Force, the Department of Energy (DOE), DHS, EPA, and the Nuclear Regulatory Commission (NRC).

Foreign Service

Overview: 5,027 jobs

Occupational areas include political, public diplomacy, management and economics, health, security, information technology, operations management, and training.

The main agencies hiring in this field are the Department of State and the Agency for International Development (USAID).

Information and Arts

Overview: 337 jobs

Occupations include public affairs specialists, writers/editors, audiovisual professionals, museum curators, and interior designers.

The main agency hiring in this field is the Broadcasting Board of Governors.

Information Technology

Overview: 11,549 jobs

Occupational areas include systems analysis, security, application software, data management, and network services.

The main agencies hiring in this field are the Department of the Army, the Department of the Navy, DOD, the Department of Treasury, DHS, HHS, and DOT.

Library and Archives

Overview: 534 jobs

Occupations include librarians and archivists.

The main agency hiring in this field is the National Archives and Records Administration.

Mathematics and Statistics

Overview: 1,620 jobs

Occupational areas include mathematics, actuarial science, statistics, and computer science.

The main agencies hiring in this field are the Department of the Navy and the Department of Commerce.

Physical Sciences

Overview: 2,645 jobs

Occupational areas include physics; chemistry; astronomy; geology; oceanography; food, textile, and forest products technology; and land surveying.

The main agencies hiring in this field are the Department of Commerce, EPA, and HHS.

Quality Assurance

Overview: 1,135 jobs

Occupational areas include inspection/quality assurance of materials, facilities, and process; and agricultural grading.

The main agency hiring in this field is DOD.

Social Sciences

Overview: 6,021 jobs

Occupational areas include economics, workforce training and development, social work, recreation activities, and public welfare and insurance programs (e.g., unemployment insurance); also, intelligence analysis, which this study lists under "Security and Protection."

The main agency hiring in this field is SSA.

Transportation

Overview: 10,560 jobs

Occupational areas include transportation analysis and safety, including air traffic control.

The main agency hiring in this field is DOT.

Veterinary Sciences

Overview: 215 jobs

Occupations include veterinarians.

The main agency hiring in this field is USDA.

The Least You Need to Know

- As baby boomers retire and national priorities change, the government will need to hire tens of thousands of new employees over the coming years in many areas.
- Nearly two thirds of the federal workforce is employed by the three largest agencies: DOD, VA, and DHS.
- The largest number of available jobs over the next few years will be in five areas: medical and public health, security and protection, compliance and enforcement, legal, and administration/program management.
- Don't worry if your dream job doesn't fall neatly into one of the categories listed in this chapter. These are where you will find the most available jobs, but there are jobs for virtually every field and interest.

Chapter 3

Overseas Jobs

In This Chapter

- The types of positions generally available overseas
- Where to find overseas jobs
- What requirements you must meet to be considered for overseas jobs
- What you should know about working abroad
- Agency-specific opportunities available abroad
- How to get a head start on the Foreign Service Exam

Have you always wanted to live in another country, immerse yourself in a new culture, and speak a foreign language? A great way to fulfill that dream could be to apply for a U.S. government position abroad.

Roughly 44,000 federal employees work overseas in more than 140 countries, doing everything from diplomacy to engineering to teaching. In addition, a classified but significant number of employees from U.S. intelligence agencies, such as the Central Intelligence Agency (CIA), are also stationed overseas.

What's Available?

Aside from foreign service officers, the positions that are most often available overseas are:

- Teachers
- IT personnel
- Clerks
- Assistants
- Management and program analysts
- Secretaries
- Customs and border protection workers
- Intelligence officers
- Human resources personnel
- Criminal investigators
- Social workers
- Engineers
- Budget analysts
- Nurses
- Attorneys
- Civil engineers
- Auditors
- Procurement officers
- Alcohol and drug abuse rehabilitation specialists
- Telecommunications specialists

How Are Overseas Jobs Filled?

Government jobs in foreign countries are extremely competitive—not only because so many people want to work and live abroad, but also because a lot of those jobs are filled with federal workers who have applied internally for jobs located outside the United States.

Many civilian overseas jobs are posted on USAJOBS.gov unless the position is excluded from regular posting requirements, such as those within the CIA, which are not posted for security reasons.

To start your search for a federal job overseas:

1. Go to USAJOBS.gov and search for the country and the general type of position you want.
2. If you see a job that is of interest, or close to what you're looking for, click the How to Apply tab.

3. Inquire with the agency contact about the job and ask whether there are other similar opportunities.

Since a relatively small number of federal agencies account for the majority of civilian employees working overseas—including the Department of Defense (DOD), the State Department, the U.S. Agency for International Development (USAID), the Department of Homeland Security (DHS), and the intelligence community—you'll want to visit their individual websites in addition to checking USAJOBS.gov. Also see Appendix A for information on agencies, including their websites.

Top Secret

If you don't get an overseas job right away, consider working in a U.S.-based government job; it will give you a leg up on trying to get an overseas job later in your career.

Are You Eligible?

Aside from being qualified for the overseas job of your dreams and passing any required tests, you will also need to pass physical exams to make sure you are in good health. If you have any major medical conditions, the truth is you will likely not be chosen for an overseas job. While this may seem discriminatory, the rule is in place only to protect you. For example, if you were to be assigned to a foreign country where there is limited access to medical supplies that you need, you may not be able to receive in a timely manner regular or emergency medical treatment that is unique to your needs.

However, if you have a disability, all government agencies must give you the same considerations as other applicants in accordance with federal law.

As with almost any federal job, you will be required to pass a background check (see Chapter 8 for details). In addition to the normal process, you should be aware that if you meet one or more of the following criteria, your background check will likely take longer than usual:

- You hold dual citizenship.
- You have had extensive travel, education, residence, and/or employment overseas.
- You have foreign contacts, a foreign-born spouse, or immediate family members or relatives who are not citizens of the United States.

What's Different About Working Overseas?

Aside from the fact that you will be living in a foreign country—and all the differences that come with that—there are several things you should consider before embarking on your overseas career:

- **Living expenses.** Your living expenses are generally covered by your agency, including your home, driver, and security. You may also receive a car, gas money, and other benefits for your family, such as education allowances.
- **Taxes.** Contrary to urban legend, as an overseas employee of our government, you will still pay taxes as if you were living in the United States.
- **Salary.** Salaries range depending on the job you have and your level of experience, but are generally the same as a similar position in the United States. However, the government frequently takes into account the cost of living, location, and safety of the country in which you are assigned and will adjust your pay to compensate you for the additional risk, expense, or burden that the location places on you or your family.
- **Vacation and travel.** Overseas employees receive additional days of vacation. Also, you will travel for free and the government will generally pay for you to come home to the United States in between jobs.
- **Additional benefits.** As an overseas employee, the government will pay for you to transport and store your possessions, as long as the expenses are under the limit determined by the government.

Agency-Specific Opportunities

When most people consider working abroad, they immediately think of America's ambassadors and diplomats, who are indeed a big part of our government's presence outside the United States. However, there are several agencies that have opportunities abroad.

Learning which agency and job is the best fit for you—and how to make yourself competitive for that job—is hugely important. In this section, take a look through these overseas programs to see which one is a good fit for you. (Remember, these are just a few overseas programs—many agencies not listed here also have jobs overseas, which you can find by searching on USAJOBS.gov.)

Department of Agriculture (USDA)

The Foreign Agricultural Service (FAS) offers employees the chance to work abroad on all things related to America's standing in the global agricultural marketplace (in other words, our buying, selling, growing, and providing of food outside the United States). FAS also provides assistance and aid in the form of food. While not all of the FAS jobs are based overseas, many of its employees do occasionally travel abroad.

You will be particularly competitive for an FAS job if you have a background in one or many of the following: agriculture, diplomacy, economic development, foreign languages, international trade/business, marketing, negotiating, program management, or strategic planning.

Department of Defense (DOD)

As the largest government employer of Americans working abroad, DOD has a variety of opportunities, for everything from teaching to clerical work.

For one of its overseas programs, DOD runs schools for about 50,000 children of military personnel overseas and is always looking for teachers. Salaries range from around $40,000 (if you are just getting started and have the equivalent of a Bachelor's degree) to nearly $90,000 (if you have earned a doctorate and have many years of teaching experience) and above for experienced personnel. DOD accepts applications each year from September through January 15 (positions start each fall).

Federal Facts

DOD employs more than 16,000 civilian (non military) employees overseas. The State Department and the Agency for International Development (USAID) have the next highest number of employees overseas, with over 13,000 each.

Department of Commerce (DOC)

The Foreign Commercial Service (FCS), a division of the Department of Commerce, is tasked with making America more competitive in the worldwide market. Employees work overseas to promote American exports and look after our commercial interests. Much like the State Department, which is discussed later in this chapter, the FCS has a rigorous oral and written test, and the program is extremely competitive. Unlike the State Department, the Department of Commerce offers its exam only once every two years.

Federal Facts

There are about 240 FCS officers working in more than 80 countries.

To qualify for the FCS, you must either have two years of experience in the field of international market analysis or one year of experience in addition to a Master's degree in a related field.

The Intelligence Community

So you want to be a spy? Want to collect intelligence vital to our nation's security and international interests? The intelligence community—and in particular the CIA—has a good number of employees working overseas on our nation's behalf. How many? Actually, nobody knows, because for the security of our nation and those employees, there is not a lot of public data available. If you're interested, check out intelligence.gov for career opportunities.

Peace Corps

One of the government's best-known overseas programs is the Peace Corps, which is designed to help people in underdeveloped countries. A term of service in the Peace Corps is 27 months, and participants, who must be at least 18 years old, are technically volunteers, although they do earn a small stipend. At any given time, there are roughly 7,000 Peace Corps volunteers serving around the world.

Working for the Peace Corps, you are assigned one of several areas:

- Education
- Youth and community development
- Business and information, and communication technology
- Agriculture
- Environment
- Food security
- Health
- HIV/AIDS

Top Secret

Joining the Peace Corps is a great way to get your foot in the door for other government jobs because Peace Corps volunteers earn special consideration when they apply for federal jobs.

The acceptance process takes between six and nine months and includes an application, an interview, and medical and legal clearance. Like all overseas programs and jobs, it's quite competitive—the Peace Corps receives roughly 10,000 applications each year for about 3,500 positions.

If you are interested in applying to be a Peace Corps volunteer, you will be particularly competitive if you have a Bachelor's degree or higher, speak French or Spanish, have volunteer experience, and are willing to work and live in Third World (read: tough) conditions for two years.

U.S. Agency for International Development (USAID)

Within the Agency for International Development, thousands of employees work overseas to support the mission of the agency.

Foreign Service Officer (FSO) with USAID

The main difference between USAID's Foreign Service program and that of the State Department is the mission. The State Department's mission for FSOs is to "strengthen peace and support prosperity as they promote our business interests and protect American citizens throughout the world." On the other hand, FSOs for USAID specifically work to oversee the United States' international aid work for developing countries.

Also, while the State Department employs about 6,500 FSOs (and another 5,000 Foreign Service specialists), USAID employs fewer than 1,000 people for these particular jobs.

Unlike the State Department, USAID does not require you to take the Foreign Service Exam (discussed later in this chapter), although the selection process is still rigorous.

To be competitive for an FSO position within USAID, you should have a background in international development, a graduate-level degree, and foreign-language proficiency.

Junior Officer

USAID's three-year Junior Officer program is designed to prepare entry-level candidates for the Foreign Service and includes one year in Washington, D.C., before going overseas. This is an especially great way to get into USAID's Foreign Service if you initially lack fluency in a foreign language, because it can be included in your training.

Department of State

While most jobs in the State Department are in the United States, roughly 20,000 of their employees work overseas in the foreign service.

Foreign Service Officer–State Department

One of the most popular—and competitive—overseas jobs is that of the State Department's Foreign Service Officer. "America's advocates," as the State Department calls them, "promote peace and support prosperity as they advance our interests and protect American citizens throughout the world." FSOs work in more than 250 embassies, consulates, and other diplomatic missions around the world.

To be a Foreign Service officer with the Department of State, you must be:

- A U.S. citizen
- Between the ages of 20 and 59
- Available to live and travel abroad

To be an FSO, you must first choose one of five career tracks: management officer, consular officer, economic officer, political officer, or public diplomacy officer. The political and public diplomacy tracks for FSOs have the most applicants, so you will have a greater chance of getting selected and assigned if you choose another track.

The Fine Print

Being an FSO can seem glamorous and exotic. However, you must be willing to go anywhere, possibly alone. In some cases, your family cannot accompany you due to security reasons.

Foreign Service Specialist

Another option with the State Department is that of Foreign Service specialist—someone who has a specialized skill that our government needs overseas. There are seven general categories of skill sets: administration, construction engineering, information technology, international information and English language programs, medical and health, office management, and security.

While Foreign Service specialists do not have to take the intensive, revered, and feared Foreign Service written exam, they do go through a selection process that includes an oral assessment, a writing exercise, a meeting with a qualifications review panel, and medical and security clearances.

Foreign Service Exam

The Foreign Service Exam is a required step to work in the Foreign Service for the State Department and is given several times a year in multiple cities across the country and around the world. The entire process—if you pass each stage—can take from 9 to 11 months. The good news is that the State Department is very clear about what the process is and notifies applicants along the way about whether or not they are still in contention.

It is similar to the bar exam that one must take to become a licensed lawyer. It's widely known to be difficult to pass, and a great deal of study is strongly recommended. In fact, up to 10,000 applicants take the test each time it is given, but only 25 to 30 percent will pass and move on to the next stage.

Why so tough? Think of the Foreign Service as being the military for peace: our brave men and women overseas who use brainpower to keep our place in the world strong and diplomatic relations peaceful. We need our FSOs to be the best and the brightest.

Preparing for the Exam

To ready yourself for the Foreign Service Exam, you will need to brush up on a variety of topics that will measure your readiness to represent the United States. These include:

- Current affairs, both domestic and international
- U.S. government
- U.S. history
- World history

It is also helpful to have knowledge of U.S. public and foreign policy, culture, psychology, economics and finance, and management theory.

In addition to reading the online "Guide to the Foreign Service Officer Selection Process" or purchasing the *Foreign Service Officer Test Study Guide* (we suggest doing both; see Appendix C for details), you will want to follow advice directly from the State Department and regularly read the following:

- *The Economist*
- *Newsweek*
- *The New York Times*
- *U.S. News and World Report*
- *The Wall Street Journal*

Top Secret

You will also be judged on your usage of the English language. The State Department is looking for proper usage, which you can study in *The Elements of Style* by William Strunk Jr. There are various editions of this classic writing guide; check online at www.amazon.com.

What the Exam Includes

The Foreign Service Exam is much more than a written test. In fact, that is only the first step in the process. If you pass the written test, you will be asked for a personal narrative and then undergo an oral assessment.

1. **A written test.** Divided into four sections, the written exam takes about three hours and is the second step (after choosing a career track) toward becoming a Foreign Service Officer. It includes an essay (you'll be able to use a computer), English expressions (basically a grammar test), job knowledge (a variety of questions on foreign and domestic policies, culture, government, and so on), and a biographic questionnaire (information about you).

2. **A personal narrative.** If you pass your written test, you move on to phase two: the personal narrative, which consists of answering five questions online. You'll have three weeks to submit your answers, so take your time to submit your best work. Answers are limited to 200 words each, so focus your responses on examples of your most impressive and outstanding experiences, whether they come from volunteer experiences, your college education, or a previous job. These are judged by the Qualifications Evaluation Panel, which is looking for work and life experience that would prepare you for the Foreign Service.

3. **An oral assessment.** To test you for certain qualities, including knowledge, skills, and abilities, the State Department conducts full-day oral assessments for candidates who have passed the written exam and have been approved by the Qualifications Review Committee.

4. **A final review.** If the State Department finds you suitable after the oral assessment, you still have to go through one more step: the final review. This is a more holistic look at everything you have to offer, from your medical history to your scores on the previously mentioned tests. They also consider whether you are up to snuff when it comes to things the tests can't measure: integrity and reliability.

   The final review panel most often dismisses candidates for drug and/or alcohol abuse, financial irresponsibility, criminal history, dishonesty at any point in the process, or a general demonstration of poor judgment. If you know that these things might show up in your background, understand they may be serious roadblocks to your selection.

Getting Hired

Once you make it through final review, you will be placed on a hiring register for your chosen career track. Here you will be given a ranking, which incorporates your test score as well as language skills and preferences for veterans. Hiring is based on two things: (1) the need for people in each chosen career track, and (2) your ranking on the register (top ranks are hired first).

The Least You Need to Know

- USAJOBS.gov is a great source for overseas jobs in general, but you may want to consider specific agency programs, such as the Foreign Service.
- Make sure you meet the eligibility requirements and that you have a fairly clean background before you go through the process.
- There are many types of jobs available overseas beyond the Peace Corps and the Foreign Service.
- The Foreign Service Exam is tough, but you can prepare by doing your homework and using the recommended study materials.

Chapter 4

Pay and Benefits

In This Chapter

- Salaries in the public versus private sectors
- The scales of government pay
- Health care, annual leave, and retirement benefits
- Student loan repayment and other potential bonuses

So you've read up on the pros and cons of government, what types of jobs are available, and where you can work, and you have decided that public service is still your perfect match. But one very important question remains: what sort of compensation will government offer you?

This chapter not only outlines the pay and benefits available to federal government employees, but also shows how the government is different from—and sometimes better than—the private sector when it comes to salary and benefits.

Your Salary

No matter where you want to work, considering the available salary is a part of your decision-making process. If you're considering working in government, the process is no different.

The stereotype that public-sector pay is significantly lower than private-sector pay is simply not true. The truth is, as you may suspect, there are situations where a private-sector job will pay more than a public position. But the differences might not be as great as you think.

For example, when looking at yearly salary averages for a lawyer, the government average is estimated at $111,304, while the nationwide average is $124,750. Using the same studies for a financial management position, the government average projects $101,022, where the nationwide average is $110,640.

Many federal government jobs actually pay better than their private-sector counterparts. Just look at the salary averages for a microbiologist: the government average of $87,206 surpasses the nationwide average of $70,150. Switching gears to architecture, the government average is significantly higher at $87,128, topping the wide range of nationwide averages from $64,000 to $76,750. A medical technician who works for the government makes about $59,840 a year, almost double that of the nationwide average of $33,170.

Federal Facts

The federal pay system tends to be less flexible than in the private sector, and therefore, less market-sensitive. If there is a talent shortage for a particular occupation, the private sector may quickly increase salaries to continue to attract the talent it needs. In the federal government, an adjustment to the General Schedule (GS) pay system may literally take an act of Congress!

If you are a *blue-collar worker* in the federal government—that is, a laborer who possesses a trade or craft and is paid by the hour—then there are actually standards established by the government that are designed to even out the differences between the sectors. One such structure is the Federal Wage System (FWS), which sets pay in a uniform manner for blue-collar workers. The FWS ensures that:

- If there are other jobs in the federal government similar to your job and within your pay range, your salary must be the same as these.
- Your salary will align with that of similar jobs in the private sector.

def•i•ni•tion

Blue-collar workers are generally categorized by the fact that they perform manual labor.

Aside from the FWS, there are several other pay measures that attempt to level the financial playing field between private and public employees. The types of pay systems include the General Schedule (GS) pay scale, banded systems, salary adjustment by region, and Cost of Living Allowance. Let's take a closer look at each pay system.

The General System Pay Scale

Where the FWS helps set standard pay rates for blue-collar federal workers, the GS pay scale is geared toward white-collar workers in administrative or professional roles. This system consists of 15 grades (or levels), starting at GS-1 and continuing up to GS-15, the highest level.

Within each grade, there are 10 steps that can increase your pay by approximately 3 percent for each step. This is in addition to annual pay adjustments in which the federal pay for all employees is increased in response to pay increases in the private sector. For example, at the end of 2008, most federal employees received a 2.9 percent pay increase and employees in some high cost of living areas received even more, and this was in addition to any within-grade increases.

On average, an individual paid by the GS system will receive a raise by moving up one step at a time within his or her respective grade. However, it's a one-year waiting period for the first three step increases, then two years for the next three increases, and then a three-year waiting period for the next step increases.

Additionally, even when a federal employee is in a two- or three-year waiting period, a federal supervisor can authorize a quality step increase (QSI) that provides an increase in pay for that person. Usually, a federal worker will move up one step per year, unless his or her performance at work is rated as outstanding.

In addition to pay increases for employees who stay at the same grade level, many positions have established "career ladders." For example, if a new college graduate accepts a GS-5-level job in the federal government, it's not uncommon that there will be a career ladder to at least the GS-11 level. This reflects the fact that new employees learn and grow on the job and are able to take on additional tasks and responsibilities that deserve higher levels of pay.

For many positions, the career ladder is at two-grade intervals to the GS-11 level. So a new hire could move from a GS-5 to a GS-7, then to a GS-9, and then a GS-11 level in as little as three years. A federal job announcement will usually indicate the "promotion potential" for this kind of fast-tracking.

The good news is that you will be able to use your experience and education to help place you at a higher grade before you even start working under the GS system. Remember, it's the grade level assigned to a job that determines the pay level for that job. If you apply and are selected for a position, you are entitled to the pay assigned to that job. In some cases, your qualifications or experience will qualify you for a higher grade.

For example, individuals with a bachelor's degree will qualify for many positions at the GS-5 level. But if you were in the top third of your graduating class, earned a 3.0 grade point average (GPA) or higher, or were part of an honor society, then you may qualify for Superior Academic Achievement, which will qualify you for a GS-7-level position. The hiring agency has the discretion to advertise and fill a job at whatever grade level it deems appropriate.

Banded Systems

Although most government agencies use the GS pay scale, there are other alternative pay systems that are being used throughout the public sector, such as a "pay banded" system, which combines some of the grades from the GS system together into a wider "band," or a "cluster" of grades. So instead of having different levels within 15 different grades (as in the GS system), you'll have just a few ranges of salary in a pay banded system.

Movement through the pay band tends to be more closely tied to your supervisor's appraisal of your performance than under the GS pay system. High performers under a pay banded system can advance more rapidly than their GS counterparts. Of course, the opposite is true for poor performers.

Federal Facts

The majority of federal employees are still paid under the GS pay system, but there are more than 30 federal agencies or agency subcomponents that operate alternative pay systems, most of which are pay banded systems. Some are controversial, such as the "pay for performance" system operated under the National Security Personnel System (NSPS) in the Department of Defense. In October 2009, Congress directed the Department of Defense to discontinue NSPS by 2012. The federal government, however, continues to search for ways to update the GS pay system to make it more market-sensitive and better able to reward high-performing employees. It's likely we'll see some major changes in the federal pay system in the next few years.

Where the GS system is uniform across the board for each agency that uses it, a pay banded system can vary a bit in its details from one agency to another.

Salary Adjustments by Region

The government realizes that the cost of living is not the same in each city in the United States. Therefore, the federal government issues "locality pay scales," which maintain a standard rate of government pay that is then adjusted according to a pay formula that takes into account pay levels provided by other nongovernment employers in the region. While this doesn't fully close the pay gap in high cost of living areas, it does help.

Cost of Living Allowance

In addition to regionalized pay, the government offers certain employees a Cost of Living Allowance (COLA). If you are a civilian, white-collar, federal worker residing in Alaska or Hawaii or if you live in the territories of the U.S. Virgin Islands, Puerto Rico, Guam, or the Northern Mariana Islands, then the U.S. government will give you a COLA.

To set the COLA rates, the Office of Personnel Management (OPM) evaluates the cost of living in each of these areas by assessing the value of hundreds of various everyday expenditures and comparing those values to the standard rates in Washington, D.C.

By law, the COLAs are limited to no more than 25 percent of an individual's base pay. The rates vary from 14 to 25 percent for the designated areas.

Health Care Benefits

In addition to salary, you should take into consideration the fact that the government provides its employees with a first-class benefits package. In fact, studies conducted by the Bureau of Labor Statistics reveal that the gap concerning benefits between the private and public sectors has been growing—in favor of the public sector.

Once you've been selected to be a part of the government team, you'll have access to first-class health care (and other) benefits.

Pick a Plan

The federal government offers a vast assortment of health care plans. There are more than 180 plans to choose from, although the actual number available to you will depend in part on your location and your agency. All of these options fall under the Federal Employees Health Benefits Program (FEHB).

While you will pay for a portion of the cost of the health care plan you select, the federal government pays the lion's share of the premium (typically between 70 and 75 percent, depending on the cost on the plan you select). Also, if you work in the federal government long enough to retire, you can continue to participate in the federal health benefits program at the subsidized rate indefinitely and the premiums can be deducted automatically from your retirement annuity.

Dental and Vision

The Federal Employees Dental and Vision Insurance Program (FEDVIP) offers three vision plans and seven dental plans. New employees are able to sign up for a plan during the first 60 days in their new job. Employees who select these options typically pay the full premium, but they are given a very competitive group rate.

Life Insurance

The government also offers life insurance to its employees. The Federal Employees Group Life Insurance (FEGLI) is made up of two parts. When you are officially entered into the pay cycle, you are automatically enrolled in Basic life insurance. This Basic life insurance is equal to your yearly salary and then rounded up $1,000. You also get an extra $2,000 with the Basic life insurance.

The second part of FEGLI involves three optional, additional life insurance plans. These options are not included with the Basic life insurance, and so you need to sign up for a specific option if you want it. If you do not select an option within 31 days after your start date, then you will not receive any of this coverage.

The three optional plans are:

- Standard (Option A) = $10,000
- Additional (Option B) = one to five times your yearly basic salary once you round up to the closest $1,000
- Family (Option C) = coverage for your spouse and any dependent children who are considered eligible

The federal government is responsible for paying one third of the total cost of the Basic life insurance, while you are responsible for paying the remaining two thirds. If you decide to have one of the optional plans, then you must pay the entire cost of that addition.

Long-Term Care

If you or any of your dependents require long-term care, you can apply for the Federal Long Term Care Insurance Program (FLTCIP). As an employer, the government understands that long-term care is not just for the elderly, but also for those recovering from an accident or who have continuing health problems. Long-term care can be given at home, in assisted living facilities, in adult day care facilities, or in any other location.

Flexible Spending

Another option within the main health care programs for federal employees is the Federal Flexible Spending Account Program (FSAFEDS). Flexible Spending Accounts are a little different because you can use pretax dollars to pay for additional health care and dependent care costs. This translates into a huge discount—up to 40 percent.

Work/Life Balance Benefits

Finding a challenging, well-paying job that you enjoy is important, but for many people it's just as vital to be able to have a life outside of work. In many positions, the culture of work in the federal government provides its employees with the flexibility to balance their work and home life.

Holidays and Leave

Starting a new job in the federal government, you'll get 13 days of vacation for the year, at the very least, depending on the number of hours you work. More senior employees who have been working at least three years will earn more leave time based on the amount of hours they work, and will usually double their leave time to 26 vacation days per year. Those who have been working in federal government more than 15 years can triple their leave time.

Top Secret

If you are coming into the government from the private sector, be sure to ask whether your years of experience count toward your allotted vacation time. Don't wait for the agency to offer such credit to you, because the agency might not.

You can also carry over up to 30 days of vacation time for the following year. On top of that, you'll get 10 days of paid holidays annually.

As a federal employee, you will also receive at least 13 sick days, which are earned at the rate of four hours for every two weeks of work. You are not limited to the amount of sick leave that adds up over time. Sick leave can count for any of your own medical needs, if you need to take care of anyone in your family, are having a child, or are going through an adoption process.

Child and Dependent Care

There are many different programs available to you for child and/or dependent care. It's best to talk to the human resources representatives at your particular agency to find out what specific child or elder care is available within your workplace.

Flexible Work Arrangements

To fit everyone's individual needs within the workplace, there are several programs for federal workers that allow a great deal of flexibility for work hours, location, leave, child care, and more. Here are some examples of the flexible programs that might be offered:

- **Flexible work schedules.** Workers can alter the hours they work so that they are able to have one day off every two weeks. This can be completed by working 80 hours in a time span of nine days, allowing a day off every other Friday.
- **Alternative work schedules.** When approved by their supervisor, workers can choose the time frame when they get to work and when they leave at the end of the day, depending on what is most convenient for them. This might help people who have long commutes or those who have families.
- **Telework.** Some agencies allow eligible employees to work from home or another location outside the workplace.
- **Family-friendly leave policies.** These are designated for emergency time off, whether it is to take care of a family member who is ill or to tend to some other type of emergency.

- **Job-sharing positions.** In some cases, one full-time job can be split between two part-time employees.

Retirement Savings

Now we all know that you can't work forever, no matter how much you love your government job. The public sector automatically provides you with the Federal Employees Retirement System (FERS), which consists of three different contributions to your retirement.

Social Security

As you progress along your public service career path, you will earn credit for your Social Security account and pay taxes for this program in full. But in the end, Social Security will supply you with many benefits once you turn 62, such as protection for your survivors, protection if you become disabled, and others.

Basic Benefits Plan

As a government employee, you must pay a small amount to your Basic Benefits Plan, and your employer will pay a sum for this plan that is equal to 1 percent of your annual pay for this plan. This happens each pay cycle. Similar to your Social Security benefits, this plan will protect you if you become disabled and can provide your survivors with benefits if you die. You will get these benefits under the Basic plan only if you have five or more years of public-sector work before your retirement.

Thrift Savings Plan (the Government's 401[k])

Similar to the typical 401(k) Plan used in many private business workplaces, a Thrift Savings Plan (TSP) enables you to control part of your own salary for retirement. Your agency helps by automatically giving you a sum that is equal to 1 percent of your typical salary each pay cycle. This 1 percent is literally "automatic" and the amount is not subtracted from your salary. Even if you don't put your own money into your TSP, your agency will give you this automatic (1 percent) contribution.

Additionally, your agency will match certain contributions that you personally make to your TSP. So for every dollar that you invest, your employer will contribute a dollar as well, up to 2 percent of your total salary (and 50 cents for every dollar you contribute from 2 to 5 percent of your salary).

The following table shows some examples of what the government will contribute to your TSP based on what you choose to contribute.

Your Salary	You Contribute	Government Contributes	Total Amount Added Annually to Your TSP
$50,000	$0	$500	$500
$50,000	$1,000 (2 percent of your salary)	$1,000	$2,000
$50,000	$2,500 (5 percent of your salary)	$1,750	$4,250
$50,000	$5,000 (10 percent of your salary)	$1,750	$6,750

Additional Benefits

For certain positions, you may be able to get additional benefits once you are offered the job, including student loan repayment, a recruitment bonus, and/or a relocation bonus. The availability of these bonus items generally depends on the agency's budget and whether or not yours is a hard-to-fill position (the harder it is to fill, the more likely the agency is to try to entice you and other candidates with additional bonuses).

Most agencies will mention in their job postings whether they are offering additional incentives. However, when you are offered a job in the federal government, or even during the interview process, you should feel free to ask about any additional benefits that they would be able to offer you.

Student Loan Repayment

If you have student loans, some agencies will help to repay those loans if you commit yourself to working for the agency for at least three years. Through the Student Loan Repayment Program, you can get a maximum of $10,000 for each year you work for the government, up to $60,000 total.

Some agencies conduct this program differently from others, so your eligibility requirements will depend on your employer. For example, the Department of Justice has a Student Loan Repayment Program specifically for lawyers. If you're looking to work for NASA, there is a different plan for each center (there are 10 space and research centers), so your student loan repayment requirements will depend on the field and location of your work.

The Fine Print

Be forewarned that if you are fired or if you quit before your three years are finished, you must pay back the whole amount of loans—completely.

Because the program varies across agencies, you might not be able to transfer your student loan repayment deal if you choose to change jobs, even if you stay within the federal government.

Recruitment Bonus

If your job is particularly hard to fill, your agency might offer a bonus of up to 25 percent of your basic pay before you even start. In special cases, you might even be offered a bonus of 50 percent of your basic pay. You may have to sign a contract committing to work for a minimum period of time for that employer.

The positions that can receive a recruitment bonus, if applicable, can be those appointed to the General Schedule (GS), scientific or professional (ST), or the Federal Bureau of Investigation and Drug Enforcement Administration (FBI/DEA), among other positions.

Relocation Bonus

Similar to the recruitment bonus, there is a relocation bonus that will pay up to 25 percent of your basic pay if you agree to move to a new location in order to work in a hard-to-fill position.

To qualify for this incentive, the job must be considered difficult to fill and you must be an employee of the public sector before you move. You must also rate "fully successful" in your job before relocating. For the most part, the same positions that are applicable for the recruitment bonus are also applicable for the relocation bonus.

The Least You Need to Know

- Depending on the position, many federal government jobs offer better pay than their private-sector counterparts.
- There are several different types of pay systems within the federal government, depending on where you work in government.
- Government provides a generous and comprehensive set of benefits, including world-class health insurance and retirement plans.
- Many health care plans are available to you as a federal employee. Find the plan that fits your needs.
- There are many other flexible benefits to being a civil servant—be sure to ask about them in order to take advantage of them.

Part 2

Navigating the System

There's a good chance that if you're reading this book, you've already started snooping around at government jobs online. There's also a good chance that you've come away thinking, "huh?" While many myths about government are untrue, the complexity of the hiring process is unfortunately very real.

This part explores the USAJOBS.gov website—your one-stop shop for federal jobs. We'll walk you through the ins and outs of the federal hiring process and teach you how to get through your government background check. We'll also spill the secrets of successful networking, interviewing, and the rest of the application process.

Chapter 5

Where to Find Government Jobs

In This Chapter

- USAJOBS.gov: your one-stop shop for finding government jobs
- Navigating your way around the site
- How to read and understand a job listing
- Where to find government jobs offline

Finding the government job of your dreams is a lot easier if you know where to look. (Online? Job fairs?) This chapter will equip you with the knowledge you need to begin your search.

We'll also walk you through some additional resources and creative ways to locate government jobs through tailored research. Keep in mind that this chapter is specific to federal government jobs. For more information on state government jobs, see Chapter 18.

USAJOBS.gov

USAJOBS.gov is the search engine/database for federal government jobs. This is where you will find virtually all government job openings (the government calls them *vacancy announcements*), complete with salary info, location, the kinds of qualifications that the agency is looking for in an applicant, and more.

As the one-stop shop for government jobs, USAJOBS.gov typically has roughly 30,000 vacancy announcements on the site at any given time. It's a treasure trove of information because 100 percent of all the competitive jobs—that is, the ones you can apply for—are listed there.

> **def•i•ni•tion**
>
> **Vacancy announcements** are government-speak for job postings or job openings.

Navigating USAJOBS.gov and understanding job listing information is half the battle. With a little help decoding all the government language used to describe the types of jobs that the government has available, you'll be well on your way.

Creating Your Account

To get started and gain full access to the site, you need to establish your own USAJOBS.gov account. Get started under the "My USAJOBS" tab as a new user, where you will provide standard personal information and create a username and account information.

Next you will go to your main personal page, where you can save multiple versions of your resumé as well as search, save, and track the status of your job applications on the site. You can also upload and store forms required for various federal applications. Also, by managing your basic account profile information, you can save a lot of time and energy by making sure you won't always have to duplicate your efforts.

Be sure to save your username and password so you can access your stored information as you continue your government job search.

Navigating the Site

Using the site is fairly simple. You can choose to search by location, agency, occupation, and more—or you can search using multiple criteria.

Keyword Search

Keyword search can help you narrow your job search to only those positions that fit your expertise and experience. If you're looking for a job with a specific title (such as engineer or writer), you can type that title into the keyword search box and the search will show you only those jobs that match your description.

There is often more than one way to describe the same job, industry, or skill set. You will get better results if you stretch your vocabulary and use search techniques such as (AND, OR, AND NOT, "", and *) to have USAJOBS.gov produce the results you're really looking for from the system.

For example:

- "____ AND ____" will give you results where both search criteria are found.
- "____ OR ____" will give you results where one or the other or both of the search criteria are found.
- "____ AND NOT ___" will give you results that exclude certain criteria from your search for the first item listed.

If you put quotation marks around the specific phrase you're looking for, then your results will reflect those words in that order. For example, a search for "marine biology" will produce specific results on this phrase and will not generate all the search results that just said "marine" or "biology" (either of which would bring up thousands of additional defense positions).

If you use the asterisk behind the root of a word, you can find results that you could be missing by just using a single word or phrase. For example, try **geo*** to find thousands of geography, geology, and similar jobs, but type in **geology** to get results with that term only.

Cracking the Job-Posting Code

So you've found a position that sounds interesting in your dream city of Kansas City, Missouri (or wherever your dream city may be). The next step is reading the actual job posting and deciding whether it's right for you. Although government job postings are not always easy to read and understand, this section should help you decode job postings.

Let's walk through a sample USAJOBS.gov job posting and find out what other information you need to pay attention to and what can be ignored to simplify your search.

Closing Date: 10/10/2012	Job Summary: Park Ranger	Agency: Interior, National	Location: US-AZ-Organ Pipe National Monument	Salary: $48,179+
	Organ Pipe Cactus National Monument is located in the Sonoran desert in Southwestern Arizona. Headquarters is 34 miles south of Ajo, Arizona, and 5 miles north of the Mexican border. [continues] Vacancy Ann #: AZSHRO-9-77 (MP/DEU)			
	Who May Apply: U.S. Citizens and Status Candidates			
	Pay Plan: GL-0025/09			
	Appointment Term: Permanent			
	Job Status: Full-Time			
	Opening Date: 09/27/2012			
	Salary Range: From $48,179 to $62,166 USD per year			

Closing Date

The closing date is the final date you can submit your full application for consideration for the job. If you do not apply by the closing date, you will not be considered for this specific job. However, some agencies use closing dates that are months away, so go ahead and apply as soon as possible—the agency might be looking at applicants in waves, and you'll want to be considered sooner rather than later.

The Fine Print

If there is less than a week between the opening date and the closing date, you may want to put your efforts elsewhere unless you know the job matches you perfectly. Small windows of opportunity can indicate that the agency has someone specifically in mind already and is only posting the job because it is required to do so.

Job Summary

The job summary is simply the title of the job posted.

Agency

The agency listed is the "company" within government that is hiring for the job posted.

Location

Be sure to check this carefully. There is often more than one location posted in job postings.

Salary

The salary range is the highest and lowest amounts that the government will pay to hire someone into this position. This range is mostly dependent on your level of experience.

Description

This is a general description of the job, which is often accompanied by information about the agency.

Vacancy Announcement Numbers

Vacancy announcement numbers generally won't make a lot of sense to the outsider, so don't waste any time trying to decode these. Just remember you may need to reference this in your cover letter or other documentation you submit with your application package.

Who May Apply

This information is critically important for you to understand. Don't waste your time applying for positions if you know you don't fit the basic description.

Rarely, you'll see something under "Who May Apply" about a commuting area. If you can see yourself getting to the job location daily from wherever you live, then consider yourself inside the commuting area. Also, if you will be moving or are open to moving to the commuting area, then indicate so, but understand that the agency will not pay for relocation (because the agency is expecting that it can find the new employee that it needs from within the commuting area).

Definitions for titles under "Who May Apply" include the following:

- **Status Candidates.** These are people who are current federal employees in permanent positions or who have been competitive service federal employees (see Chapter 1) for at least three years.
- **Public.** Any interested U.S. citizens.
- **U.S. Citizens.** Actual U.S. citizens by birth or naturalization. Generally, dual citizenship will be okay too (but not Green Card holders or permanent residents).
- **Agency Employees Only.** Only those already working at that agency will be considered.
- **All Groups of Qualified Individuals.** Everyone who meets job requirements (meaning any qualified candidates, status candidates, and agency employees).
- **CTAP.** This stands for Career Transition Assistance Program and is intended for employees who are being downsized from a government job and have been given special preference to find another government job in a different part of their agency.
- **ICTAP.** This stands for Interagency Career Transition Assistance Program and is intended for people who are being downsized from a government job and have been given special preference to find another government job at an agency that isn't downsizing its type of position.

Top Secret

Often agencies will advertise the same job twice: one listing for any citizen who meets the qualifications and the other for "status" applicants who are already federal employees or were previously federal employees. So be sure you're applying for the right listing of the job you want.

Pay Plan

Pay plan information is also very important. There are three main pieces of the pay plan. The first section, generally two letters, tells you what pay system is being used for the job. Many positions will say GS (for General Schedule) or WG/WS/WL (for blue-collar jobs), and these types of pay systems are used across lots of different agencies. However, you might also see other seemingly random letter combinations at the beginning of the pay plan information; that's because some agencies have permission to pay their employees on scales (pay bands) different from the General Schedule. A popular example is Foreign Service positions, but many agencies or specialized types of jobs have their own pay bands and you may need to check with the agency contact on the vacancy announcement if you can't find satisfactory pay information in the job description (under salary information, for example).

The second section is the "occupational series" information for the job. The Occupational Series Code is a number that corresponds with different categories of jobs available within the government. Employees at different agencies doing the same type of job will have the same number coded to represent their work.

For example:

Type of Job	Occupational Series Code
Mail and File Clerk	0305
Chaplain	0060
Information Technology Management	2210

The third section is the level of the position (frequently referred to as the grade or pay band). As you learned in Chapter 4, the standard GS system has bands 1 through 15, with 15 being the highest within the system. Many agencies, though, use bands or even sub-bands to determine the level of their positions, and you'll know this when you see different pay plans indicated in the job description.

Sometimes the largest number in a pay band is the most senior-level position, and sometimes the lowest number is the most senior level at the agency. Call the agency's Human Resources (HR) office if it's not clear from reading a few of the agency's job descriptions.

Also, if the GS level is not listed on an announcement, read closely within the Qualifications and Evaluations tab on USAJOBS.gov; sometimes the information in this section will reference GS levels even if the agency uses pay bands.

Also note that sometimes the same type of job is advertised at different levels under different vacancy announcement numbers. If you see a position with the right title for your interest, but you think you might be over- or underqualified, keep searching USAJOBS.gov for similar positions at different levels. For instance, if an agency needs to hire a few seasoned economists, but could also train less-experienced candidates to do the same job down the road, then that agency may post a few vacancy announcements for different experience and pay levels. If you think you're qualified for the senior positions, but would also be willing to take a less-senior position if it meant getting your foot in the door at that agency, then apply to both or multiple jobs and see how things go.

Appointment Term

The appointment term tells you how long the job will last. "Permanent" is the most common type of appointment term, which means the job is expected to be a continuing one. Other words that you might see here include "Temporary" and "Term," which indicate shorter assignments with the government. For more information on temporary and term appointments, see Chapter 17.

Job Status

Job status is usually one of two options: full-time or part-time. A full-time schedule is 40 hours per week and anything less is part-time (regularly defined as anything between 16 and 32 hours per week).

Opening Date

Opening date is the first day the position was posted on USAJOBS.gov.

Salary Range

Salary range provides a broad guide for compensation for the job. Generally the ranges are quite large to allow agencies to hire toward the bottom or middle of the salary range. In some cases, the range simply reflects the potential for salary increases after an employee is on the job, but the agency may be restricted to offering a starting salary at the lower end of the range. If offered the job, you can attempt to negotiate a higher starting salary, but the agency may or may not be allowed by law, regulation, or internal policy to increase its offer. The range generally reflects pay permitted to all people working within the pay band or GS level.

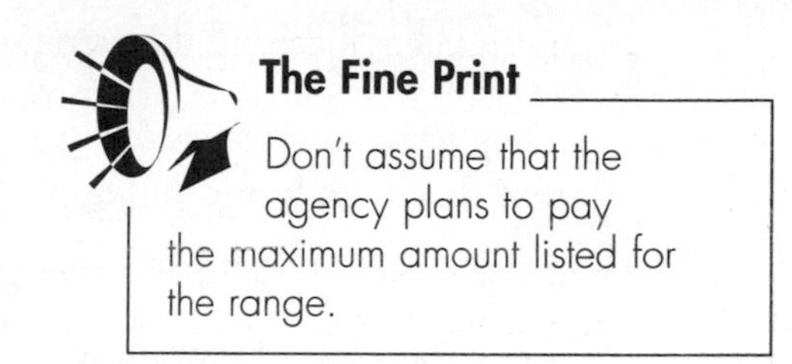

The Fine Print

Don't assume that the agency plans to pay the maximum amount listed for the range.

Human Resources

The Human Resources contact for each job is listed at the bottom of the "Overview" portion of the job posting on USAJOBS.gov. You should feel free to follow up directly with that person to ask questions about the job and the hiring timeline.

Other Places to Find Government Jobs

When trying to fill jobs, government recruiters often do more than post jobs on USAJOBS.gov. These active recruiting approaches are helpful to you as a jobseeker if you value personal interaction and real-time conversation with someone at the agency.

Agency Websites

Sometimes it pays to go straight to the source, especially if you're focusing your job search on a limited number of agencies. All agencies will have a Jobs, Careers, or Opportunities tab on their website. These sites may provide special instructions or have more detailed information about fellowship, internship, and coop programs. Regardless, if you have your heart set on one agency, you should make searching its site a priority early in the job search process. Information on different levels and career opportunities (and organization charts showing how the agency is structured) is spelled out on agency websites.

Job Fairs

Many job and career fairs are hosted by a variety of organizations, universities, and specialized groups of working professionals. Often, career fairs are attached to major conventions or produced as a series of events with a geographical or demographic focus (for example, nine executive diversity fairs in large cities over the course of a year, or economic development fairs on one academic campus each semester). Check your local convention center calendars, scour the newspaper, and look at career websites for local colleges and universities. Search for "federal career days" online.

Federal agencies are motivated to attend career fairs for four key reasons:

- They have many open positions and want to generate interest from jobseekers so that they'll go home and apply to their positions online.
- They're targeting a particular group (such as at a diversity job fair).
- They want to raise awareness about what their agency does and how people can get jobs down the road when the agency has more jobs available.
- They sometimes have a special permission to hire jobseekers tentatively into open positions right on the spot (this is the least frequent of the four reasons).

Federal Facts

One of the largest federal government job and internship fairs is hosted by the Partnership for Public Service (www.ourpublicservice.org) each summer in Washington, D.C., and usually has representatives from 60 to 80 agencies in attendance.

The trend these days is for federal agency reps to attend but *not* interview candidates at job fairs. Sometimes they won't even accept resumés, much to the jobseekers' frustration. You may find this confusing ("Why can't they just interview me at the job fair? What's the point of going when they are going to tell me to apply on USAJOBS.gov?"), but sometimes these are the best places to learn about what someone does in his or her government job and pick up on the details of how to navigate specific application processes, such as with the intelligence community, law enforcement, or international development.

Often, additional job information is shared during information sessions at job fairs. Keep an ear out for insider hints on hiring needs. Organizations who know they will be hiring a lot of people in the near future are often the ones who conduct info sessions, sit on panels, or otherwise reach a larger audience.

Pros to job fairs: You can make personal connections, and you may be identified as a top candidate on the spot.

Cons to job fairs: There are usually long lines, and you often still need to apply online after meeting a recruiter in person.

Newspapers

Yes, print media ads are the old-school way of recruiting for government jobs, but you can still find government job listings in most major newspapers. These ads usually target blue-collar and some white-collar positions (including administrative positions) in a local area that are hard to fill.

Generally these announcements will direct you to go through the same application processes as described on a USAJOBS.gov job posting for that same position, but some may announce special opportunities that are not posted online.

On occasion, agencies will also use newspapers, magazines, or journals to announce high-level and high-visibility postings in the government. If you have unique skills or a really accomplished skill set, look for these announcements in publications such as *The Economist*, *The Wall Street Journal*, or *The International Herald Tribune*.

Pros to newspaper job listings: There's a focus on local opportunities and immediate government needs.

Cons to newspaper job listings: They don't give you a leg up and still generally direct you to USAJOBS.gov.

Special Interest Sites

If you're searching for a specific profession, there may be sites already tailored to address your needs. For example, if you are interested in becoming a park ranger, there's an independent site, rangercareers.com, that has preset search criteria with USAJOBS.gov and will generate the latest list of, you guessed it, ranger positions with the U.S. National Park Service.

Professional organizations, societies, and diversity organizations also have websites, newsletters, or classified boards. While these can often be flooded with private- and nonprofit-sector opportunities, agencies continue to use these to reach specific skill areas and interests. If you are a member of a group based on your professional trade or any demographic group (such as the National Black MBA Association, the Society for Human Resources Management, or the American Association of Retired People [AARP]), there might be a few similar federal jobs more closely aligned with your interests all in one spot.

Pros to special interest sites: You use specific searches and transparent networking channels.

Cons to special interest sites: They still require additional search and application efforts.

The Least You Need to Know

- USAJOBS.gov is the best place to find most available government jobs.
- When applying for a job, read the announcement very carefully for key words to make sure you are qualified. Don't waste your time on jobs you know you won't get!

- If you know where you want to work, concentrate your efforts first on looking at the employment or careers section on that agency's website.
- You can still find jobs offline, especially in newspapers and at career fairs.

Chapter 6

Networking for Government Jobs

In This Chapter

- How to network for the public sector
- How to do your own background investigation
- What questions you should ask
- Networking online

Networking, put simply, is a way of building professional and personal contacts to help you get a job. While this is really more art than science, you won't be a starving (and jobless) artist for long if you take the time to build and use your own network properly.

If you feel intimidated by the amount of time and skill that networking requires—or if you are worried that you don't know how to transfer your private-sector networking skills to the public sector—don't worry: we will walk you through the steps of successfully networking to get your government job.

Crafting Your Networking Strategy

You already have most of the ingredients for building your network. Whichever sector (public, private, nonprofit) you want to work in, your goal is the same: to have every interaction get you one step closer to landing the job you want.

The difference between networking for the public sector rather than for the private sector is that you will want to focus your contact building, research, and time on people who either work in government or who know someone who does.

In the private sector, you might be fortunate enough to meet someone through your network who is impressed enough to offer you a job directly. In the federal government, however, civil service laws require that the hiring be done through a competitive process and, in fact, hiring managers have a legal requirement to avoid any possibility that nepotism, partisan politics, favoritism, or other non-merit factors are involved. In addition, government agencies are required to give military veterans special consideration in recognition of their military service to the country, and procedures have to be followed to ensure that happens. So, while networking can still be very valuable in seeking a federal job, the reason behind networking is a little different. The bottom line is that networking in the federal government is more about gaining useful information and less about finding the person who will offer you a job.

So, in networking in the public sector, what you want to gather is information about such things as:

- What jobs are going to be opening up in the near future, so that you can be sure you look for them and don't miss the opportunity to apply
- What sort of skills or competencies are being sought, so that you can tailor your application accordingly
- Any special hiring flexibilities that are being considered that apply to you (for example, there are some special hiring authorities that allow managers to shortcut the normal hiring process for veterans, people with disabilities, returning Peace Corps volunteers, and so on)
- Who the selecting official or hiring manager will be for the job that you are interested in, so that, if you make it to the interview stage, you already know a little more about that individual

Here is a good action list for preparing for and building a network that will work for you:

1. Do your homework on agencies and the job(s) you want.
2. Create your network by putting together a list of people you know who might be able to help you, complete with their contact information.
3. Set up meetings (in person is best) with the people on your networking list.
4. Make a list of questions before you meet with each person in your network.
5. Think of other creative ways to network, such as setting up informational interviews and using social networking sites.
6. Follow up with thank you notes (handwritten if possible).

In this chapter, we'll walk you through these steps one by one.

Do Your Homework

By doing some research on the front end of your job search, you can demonstrate to the people you're networking with that you're serious about your government job search and your professional future. Learning targeted information now will build your confidence for discussing your interest in government work. This includes:

- Agency acronyms
- Agency missions
- Current agency leaders and decision makers
- News stories or current issues facing the agency

Obviously, you don't need to learn every acronym, mission, and person in a position of leadership for every agency. Given that there are more than 200 agencies, this would likely take more time and energy than is necessary at this stage in your job search. Instead, stick to the agencies where you might like to work.

Create Your Network

A network is a valuable thing to have when job searching, so plan well and take the development of a good network seriously. Even if you don't know any influential federal employees, you may have more connections than you think.

Start with Who You Know

Whether it's in a spreadsheet, rolodex, or notebook, get yourself organized from the beginning by brainstorming who you already know and then tracking your network—how you know them, when you've reached out to them, and how you did it.

> **Top Secret**
>
> When networking with your friends, family, and contacts, remember: it's not just those you know in government, but who *they* know in government.

Think about your inner circle by brainstorming family (next-of-kin as well as great-second cousins once removed) who are or were in public service. Sometimes even family with military service may have ideas or relationships with people who have stayed in the military or moved to civilian positions over time. Your parents or spouses' friends or professional interactions with government would be a good spot to branch out to next.

When building the base for your network, keep your communication simple and focused on your interest in government service. You want your network to spread the best word about your motivation, because they are your core sales team (and you are the product). They are also the ones usually most willing to take risks for you and take interest in your professional development.

Now you can start getting more adventurous in your networking conversations. The people in this second tier don't need to be government employees. Consider how often certain jobs require working with people in government and who you know who works with or has worked with government employees or agencies. For example, a private-sector attorney might have started his career in military law with other military lawyers who are still working for the government. A social worker that you are friends with might be working on a government-funded grant right now or may have relationships with Health and Human Services staff.

Alumni Associations

Most schools have lists of alumni who can provide advice and leads on job opportunities. Here's how to take advantage of that:

- Call or e-mail the alumni relations staff at your alma mater to see who else they know in your area or desired professional field.
- Call your campus career services office and see whether they have any federal agency connections.
- Search through your online alumni database (if your college has one).

Professional Associations

Members of *professional associations* can be great for networking, because they are linked into the occupational area where you'd like to work.

In addition to job fairs (see Chapter 5), professional associations can provide many other options for networking. Start by checking professional association calendars for local chapter meetings or upcoming conferences in your area. Often getting a membership (even if it costs a little bit) is worth it if the association's events are focused around your career interests as well.

> **def•i•ni•tion**
>
> **Professional associations** are nonprofit organizations that aim to serve the interests of the people in a particular professional occupation.

Come to events prepared to subtly self-promote. Have a resumé or two on hand just in case. The same goes for one-on-one meetings.

Direct Networking with Government Hiring Personnel

One way to build your network is to seek out contact directly with hiring managers and human resources personnel—in other words, go straight to the source: decision makers. This is a great piece of a larger networking strategy of talking to many people, but before you get started with direct networking, you should know a few things.

If people you are networking with work in government and currently have a job opening that you are interested in, they'll want you to learn more and apply, but they probably can't be as actively helpful to you as they might be in the private sector. As previously mentioned, this is due to a set of rules they are legally required to follow when hiring that are in place to prevent hiring managers from giving you (or anyone) an unfair advantage.

These laws and guidelines have shaped the way hiring and assessments are done in government. We will refrain from boring you with all the details, but keep these key themes in mind and know that they'll probably be on the minds of hiring managers:

- Government hiring personnel have to recruit qualified people from appropriate sources (meaning no nepotism or favoritism).
- Our government makes a concerted effort to build a workforce from all segments of society through open and fair competition. In other words, the government wants the very best person for the job.
- All job applicants should receive fair and equal treatment in all aspects.

Additionally, here are some "prohibited personnel practices" that hiring managers have to avoid (by law):

- Discrimination of any job applicant on the basis of race, color, religion, sex, or national origin, age, disability, marital status, or political affiliation
- Solicitation or consideration of any written or oral recommendation
- Giving an unauthorized leg-up to an applicant by writing the job description in a way that would increase that person's chances of being chosen for the job

Set Up Meetings

When President Obama told the nation that the best way to avoid getting the flu is to wash your hands, many people balked. Who needs to be told to do something as simple as washing their hands? But the truth is, sometimes we need to be reminded that the simplest things are often the most effective.

With the multitude of technologies available, it's easy to fall into a pattern of relying on virtual contact with others. After all, e-mails take a few minutes (and can be done in your pajamas), while in-person meetings require planning time, travel, and looking your best.

But we're here to tell you: in-person meetings can make the difference. Not only are they a chance for your personality to shine—which can't be done on a resumé or over e-mail—but your network is more likely to get personally invested in helping you when they see how committed and enthusiastic you are about your job search.

When setting up in-person meetings, make sure you have your talking points down. Feel free to use the following as starting points:

- Thank your contact for his or her time.
- Let your contact know you have done your homework and come to the meeting prepared. This will show that you are committed and worthy of helping out.
- Let your contact know what your goal is for your job search ("I think the Department of Energy would be the perfect place for me and I'm looking to find a position there"). Use this opportunity to express your excitement for the mission of the agency or agencies where you want to work.
- Let your contact know where you are in your job search. Have you submitted resumés? Where? Are you just starting out and looking for advice?

- Ask for help on specific items. ("I would be very grateful if you could give me some advice as to how to proceed with my job search" or "Do you have any contacts at the Department of Energy?")
- Listen. You are there to learn what your next steps should be.
- Ask your contact who else you should speak with about your job search. This is a great way to grow a network of people who can help you get closer to your government job.
- Send a thank you note. E-mail is acceptable, although handwritten is still preferred. This is not just the nice thing to do, it will remind your contact that he or she should be thinking of ways to help you get your job.

Plan Your Questions

When networking, it's important to plan your questions and craft them to make the people you're networking with feel comfortable and not put on the spot. You don't want anyone you're speaking with to feel that the only thing you want to know is whether or not he or she can get you a job. In fact, if you look at all networking opportunities as information-gathering sessions, then you will want to hear all of your interviewee's advice and suggestions, not just whether or not he or she can land you a job.

Questions should also match the formality of your networking setting. Read your surroundings (or better yet, try to control them by finding a place where you're comfortable and that is also convenient for the person you're meeting).

Here are some guidelines for what to say—and what not to say:

- **Ask questions.** You didn't go to the trouble of seeking out a new person for your network to have them just listen to your stories; you need to respect his or her time by using it efficiently and gathering information that will actually help you.
- **Stay grounded.** While it's important to know who's who, there's no need to name drop just for name dropping's sake.
- **Stay positive.** While you could have a personal connection with your interviewee, don't dive into messy pasts, terrible old bosses, or other gripes that could detract from the matter at hand—your job search.

- **Always ask the person you are talking to, "Who else should I speak with?"** Take notes and add these new people to your rolodex. Don't be intimidated if they have impressive titles and, conversely, don't be put off if they don't seem impressive enough to spend your time with (sometimes people with more junior titles or jobs know a lot about organizational structures and who else would be valuable to speak with higher up in the ranks).

Set Up Informational Interviews

Informational interviews are great ways to build your network. While it's not a good idea to flat out ask for a job during informational interviews (its purpose is, by definition, information gathering), many employees throughout government will be willing to give you a little bit of their time and some free advice.

Federal Facts

The federal government does not have any formal system for informational interviews, but that shouldn't stop you from setting them up on your own through your network.

It's always best to do informational interviews in person, so be willing to go the extra mile for these conversations—literally.

You should treat these conversations like actual interviews in the way you prepare for the conversation and, of course, in your follow-up afterward (send a thank you card or e-mail at the very least). Even if such consideration doesn't get you the job, it's simply good manners and good practice.

You should always come to an interview—informational or otherwise—with questions prepared. Here are some that you may want to consider asking (some are clearly geared toward people who currently have a government job):

- What does your job entail? What does a typical day look like?
- How did you end up where you are today?
- What's the story of your rise to this position and level of responsibility?
- How long have you been in your job and what brought you here? Education? Experiences?
- Are there senior people in your profession or agency who have been helpful in assimilating you into the culture of your organization?

- Are there things you know your agency or organization looks for specifically in your new hires for job *X*?
- Is there anyone else at your agency that I should talk with to get a better picture of what job *X* looks like on a day-to-day basis or to get more advice?
- Would you mind looking at my resumé and providing some feedback?

Use Social Networking Sites

In addition to the previously mentioned ways to build your network of friends, family, friends of friends, and government employees, you should consider using social networking sites (if you aren't already) to put your interest—and your resumé—out there.

You might be surprised to hear that some agencies are, indeed, using social networking applications to attract and inform applicants. In 2009, the General Services Administration (GSA) allowed employees to begin using popular sites such as YouTube and Facebook to conduct official business, such as recruiting new employees. Often these social networking sites serve much larger informational purposes for the agencies, but are great resources for you. For instance, the Department of State was one of the early leaders in savvy networking and recruiting to large audiences through Facebook, but additional unofficial pages connect co-workers and different offices to one another as well.

The Fine Print

Make sure your web presence (Facebook, MySpace, Twitter, and so on) is a representation of your *professional* self. Specifically, you should take down rants or questionable photos.

Make sure your latest resumé is the one available for public viewing. LinkedIn is a great professional networking site for posting your resumé because it makes your information easily accessible to those who might be interested in helping you get a job.

While nothing can replace a good old-fashioned face-to-face informational interview, you can certainly gather much more information from these pages and accounts than was previously possible. And you can get in touch with other tech-savvy professionals at some of the coolest agencies with a click of a button—just one more way to build your network and gather information.

Follow Up

Be sure to thank people for their time as you go. A simple e-mail will do, but handwritten thank yous are still appreciated. Just keep in mind that handwritten thank yous will take longer to get through the mail, due to the fact that all mail delivered to federal facilities is screened for safety reasons.

Also, keep your whole network in the loop once you have found a job—be sure to thank anyone who helped you throughout your search.

The Least You Need to Know

- A little research on the front end will build your confidence and help you determine where to focus your efforts.
- Build your network starting with the people you know and working out to people they know.
- Get organized by collecting contact information and keeping records of your interactions.
- To build your network and your chances of getting the government job you want, always ask who else you should talk with.
- Use informational interviews and social networking sites to increase your networking capacity.
- Following up with a thank you to everyone in your network is imperative.

Chapter 7

Understanding the Hiring Process

In This Chapter

- The journey of an application
- Average time from "submit" to start date
- Special hiring considerations
- What to do after you apply

The good news, as you already know, is that government is hiring a lot of people, in all fields, for interesting and well-paying jobs across the country and around the world. The bad news? The hiring process can be tricky and frustrating and might take longer than you expect.

Getting through the federal hiring process is like running a gauntlet in medieval times: it's easier to get to the end if you know what's coming at you. In this chapter, we'll walk you through the hiring process, explaining why it is the way it is and how you can navigate your way through it.

Note: This chapter deals with the general hiring process for government civil service jobs, which does not include political appointments, student programs, some special agencies, or overseas jobs. However, these are all covered in other chapters throughout this book.

How Is Hiring Done in Government?

Many people mistakenly think the government's hiring process is shrouded in mystery or impossible to understand. Though there is variation, the truth is that most agencies use the same general guidelines and procedures for hiring.

Unlike most of the private sector, the government has strict guidelines for selecting new employees. Yes, it can be cumbersome and time consuming, but for good reason: with so many people applying for government jobs, the selection process aims to ensure fairness and equal treatment for all applicants, and strives to make sure candidates are rated based on their merit and qualifications for the position.

It's important to understand that the federal government is not a single employer, but rather an umbrella organization under which there are literally hundreds of employers. Even within a single agency—for example, the Department of Homeland Security—there can be many divisions, such as the Transportation Security Administration, the U.S. Secret Service, U.S. Customs and Border Protection, and the U.S. Coast Guard. Each of these subcomponents conducts their own recruiting and hiring, so while the hiring processes are similar at each agency, you shouldn't expect a one-size-fits-all process.

Who Does the Hiring?

Okay, so the first question is, where does your application go after you hit the "submit" button on USAJOBS.gov and who looks at it? Here's a possible chain of events for applications that are submitted online:

1. When a position's "open period" ends and USAJOBS.gov stops accepting applications, someone from Human Resources (HR) logs in to USAJOBS.gov and determines whether the applications are complete.
2. The HR office cuts the applicants who don't meet the minimum requirements for the job.
3. The HR office then determines and shares the top applications with the *hiring manager.*

def•i•ni•tion

Hiring managers work with HR to have open positions filled at the department or office that they oversee. Hiring new employees isn't their sole function, but rather an added duty to their normal job, which could be anything from botanist to accountant. Frequently, the hiring manager will be the direct supervisor of the new employee.

4. The hiring manager reviews the applications, coordinates interviews for the top candidates, and checks references.
5. The hiring manager selects a new employee and sends that pick back to HR.
6. The HR office contacts the selected candidate to make the official job offer.
7. If the candidate accepts the position, he or she provides additional information to be used for a background investigation (more on this in Chapter 8).
8. HR negotiates a starting date with the applicant, who then begins his or her new federal job.

The Points System

For some jobs, the government uses a points system to rate each applicant. Think of it as being like your grade point average (GPA) in high school: the higher your score, the better. By understanding the points system, you can get a better idea of how you will be rated and what your chances are for getting the job you want.

As an applicant, you are given points for everything from your level of education to your writing skills. Then, according to government's "rule of three," the hiring manager may consider the three applicants with the highest scores and those candidates are typically invited for an interview.

The points system rating is used slightly differently for every agency and every job, but always gives each applicant a score between 70 and 100. If you don't meet the basic qualifications, it doesn't matter what your point system rating is—you won't get the job.

Category Rating

More and more, agencies are encouraged to use a selection process called *Category Rating*, which is considered to be a more progressive (read: better) way to hire new employees. Instead of being assigned a numerical score, your application is placed in a category such as "qualified," "well qualified," and "best qualified." Of course, if you aren't qualified, you are cut from consideration and not placed in any category.

How does your application get placed in one of these categories? Each agency sets the criteria for each category before the job announcement is posted. Here's an example of what that might look like:

- **Qualified.** Meets the bare minimum of the job listing, has a degree related to the job, has a minimum number of years of experience, and has decent writing skills.
- **Well qualified.** Meets the minimum qualifications and requirements. Plus, has an advanced degree related to the job, has three to five additional years of experience above the minimum requirement, and demonstrates above-average writing skills.
- **Best or highly qualified.** Meets minimum qualifications and requirements. Plus, has an advanced degree related to the job, has 6 to 10 (or more) additional years of experience above the minimum requirement, demonstrates exceptional writing ability, and has additional relevant experience.

def•i•ni•tion

The **Category Rating** system is one way that government organizations screen applicants by putting them into categories based on predetermined, job-related criteria.

Direct Hiring

In special cases, agencies are given the authority to make the process even easier through *direct hire*. The direct hire process is a lot simpler for everyone involved. You may still have to submit your resumé and whatever else is asked of you (which can include KSAs, which are discussed in Chapter 10, or questionnaires), but you generally avoid a long period of waiting.

def•i•ni•tion

Direct hire allows hiring managers to make job offers to applicants without having to go through the regular process, meaning no points system and no Category Rating. This is about the closest that government hiring comes to the private sector.

The circumstances under which agencies can use direct hire are:

- Critical hiring need, based on a new congressional initiative or an emergency such as a national disaster
- A severe shortage of candidates applying for a job or of employees filling an entire occupational area

Who Gets the Jobs?

Here's something a lot of people don't know: of all the people the government hires, 40 percent are new employees from outside government. The other 60 percent are comprised of candidates from within government, former federal workers who are returning to government, or others who qualify for unique status, which is discussed later in this chapter under "Are You Eligible for a Special Hiring Consideration?"

Of course, this might vary if, say, you're a nurse and there's a shortage of nurses in government. Then they might hire 90 percent of new nurses from outside the government.

Top Secret

On USAJOBS.gov, you can find out whether the job you want is being filled using direct hire in the "Overview" section of the job listing. Under "Who May Be Considered," it will read, "This position is being filled through the Direct Hire Authority for this occupation and is open to all U.S. Citizens."

How Long Does It Take?

The way government chooses new employees is vastly different from the private sector, where the process might go something like this: you apply by sending in your standard resumé, you get an interview, they like you, they offer you the job, you accept, you start.

Unfortunately, there's a lot more involved in the government hiring process, frequently causing the timeline from application to start date to be longer than in the private sector. But don't give up; there is a silver lining. Government managers are aware that the hiring process is less than ideal and they are working, slowly but surely, to make it more applicant-friendly. In 2009, the U.S. Office of Management and Budget laid out four steps to fix the government's broken hiring process: provide more feedback to applicants on the status of their application; condense job announcements; write job announcements in more plain language; and assess the hiring process from end to end.

For now, you should still expect that the process will generally take two to five months. Of course, some jobs will be filled faster (less than 30 days) or slower (nine months or more) than the average.

To give you a better idea of why it takes so long, here's a sample timeline, from start to finish, for a nearly year-long process:

February 15: You apply for a job on USAJOBS.gov.

March 7: Application deadline closes on USAJOBS.gov.

March 21: HR narrows down the candidates to those who meet the minimum qualification requirements.

April 7: All remaining applications are scored using the points system or rated using Category Rating.

April 14: HR sends the list of the candidates with the highest scores (or rating) to the hiring manager.

May 7: The hiring manager notifies you that you have scored (or rated) highly and the agency wants you to come in for a panel interview.

May 21: You have your panel interview.

June 21: You are notified that your panel interview went well and the agency wants you to come in for a one-on-one interview.

July 14: You have your one-on-one interview.

August 14: The agency informs you that you have been tentatively selected pending a background investigation for security clearance.

September 1: You turn in your security clearance forms.

December 1: You are granted security clearance and a start date is negotiated.

January 3: You start the job.

Are You Eligible for a Special Hiring Consideration?

Certain applicants for government jobs are given special consideration for employment because of personal or professional circumstances. This includes veterans of our armed forces, persons with disabilities, and other groups. The reasons for granting this status vary, but for the most part it is intended to honor those who serve and protect us, as well as to ensure that the government is making a concerted effort to have a capable and diverse workforce.

Veterans

If you have served in the U.S. military, you are entitled by law to "veterans' preference," which means that you will, in almost all scenarios, be hired over similarly qualified non-veterans. This is a way our government honors the service of our men and women in uniform.

By law, certain military veterans are automatically awarded 5 to 10 extra points in the points system or are put at the top of their category if HR is using Category Rating.

Federal Facts

Approximately one of every three new hires into government is a veteran. By law, agencies must submit Disabled Veterans Affirmative Action Program reports each year. The reports describe agency efforts to promote employment and job advancement opportunities for veterans in government. An annual report is then submitted to Congress.

To qualify for veteran's preference, you must have documentation that you received a general or honorable discharge from active-duty service and served for a minimum of 24 months or for however long you were ordered to active duty.

To earn the five-point preference, your service must *also* have been one of the following:

- During a war
- During the period of April 28, 1952, through July 1, 1955
- For more than 180 consecutive days, other than for training, at any time from September 11, 2001, to the end date of Operation Iraqi Freedom
- In a campaign that has been awarded a campaign medal or badge

Automatically qualifying for the 10-point preference are veterans who have done one of the following:

- Served at any time and have a service-related disability
- Received a Purple Heart

For more information about veterans' preference, see Appendix C.

Military and Civilian Spouse or Dependent Hiring

In the same way that our country honors veterans, there are certain spouses, widows, dependents, and mothers of deceased or disabled veterans who are also entitled to similar 5-point and 10-point score additions when they apply for government jobs.

As with any applicant for a government job, these spouses, widows, dependents, and mothers must first be qualified for the job in order to be eligible for special consideration (that is, to receive the extra points in the application process). Often, they must meet certain other qualifications as well.

Spouses and Widows

To help lessen the career-related burdens of moving for a loved-one-in-uniform's permanent change of station (pcs), the Military Spouse Preference Program is available to the husbands and wives of the armed forces, including the U.S. Coast Guard. This program gives spouses an advantage when applying to highly sought-after jobs pertaining to the Department of Defense. To be eligible for these positions, the spouse must register and complete training geared toward his or her new job.

In certain cases, the federal government goes even further, offering a special "noncompetitive" status, meaning that the candidate or spouse can bypass traditional hiring and simply be appointed to a position (again, only if the candidate is qualified). These cases include:

- Spouses of active-duty members of the military under orders to make a permanent move
- Spouses of individuals who are no longer on active duty in the military or those who are 100 percent disabled and/or retired
- Widows or widowers (who have not remarried) of service members killed on active duty

Dependents

Family Member Preference is available for other members of military personnel who are applying to certain positions at DOD. This program is applicable for spouses of active-duty service members and their children (though the children must be unmarried, dependent, and younger than 23).

Mothers

Also given strong (10-point) preference are military mothers whose child or children died in service or who are permanently and totally disabled.

If You Have a Disability

If you have a physical or mental disability, you may also be eligible for a special hiring consideration. This special hiring authority for those with disabilities is designed to remove barriers and increase employment opportunities for these individuals.

If you have a disability, once you have identified the agency where you want to apply, you need to have two pieces of information prepared:

- **Proof of disability.** This proof may be in the form of documentation obtained from licensed medical professionals, state or private vocational rehabilitation specialists, or any government agency that issues or provides disability benefits.
- **Certification of job readiness.** This determines that you are able to perform the necessary functions of the job.

After you have these together, your next step should be finding and contacting the person in charge of Selective Placement or the Disability Employment program at the agency where you'd like to work. You can find this by going to the agency's website or calling the agency's main phone number.

Contacting these individuals will help you, because they work with hiring officials and other people who have disabilities and who are already qualified for various positions within the agency. They also help to fit your skills and needs to the vacant jobs and provide you with reasonable workplace accommodations.

Monitoring Your Application

In 2008 alone, the Internal Revenue Service received nearly 300,000 applications for more than 16,000 positions. That's a lot to process! It's easy to think that your application, whether submitted online, faxed, or mailed, is lost in the ether. It's an especially easy assumption to make if, like many applicants, you don't hear back from anyone for a while—or ever.

Chances are that your application is not lost. The truth is that you've got a lot of competition out there. With hundreds—sometimes several hundreds—of applicants for every government job, it takes time to get through them all.

Once you've applied online, watching your application's status may be as simple as retaining your password to the online system and logging back in to check it. If you submitted a paper application or used an e-mail address, pick up the phone and call the hiring manager for that position. A good opening is, "Good morning, my name is Patricia Jackson and I applied for the environmental engineer position, which sounds like a perfect fit for me. I hope I am not bothering you, but I wanted to check on the status of my application."

Be aware that there are "prohibited practices" for federal hiring managers and HR staffing professionals, so they might not be as forthcoming with information in order not to be thought to show favoritism. Prohibited practices include discrimination on the basis of age, gender, race, color, disability, political persuasion, or marital status. Nepotism (favoring relatives or friends for a job) is also a prohibited practice, as is encouraging someone to withdraw his or her candidacy in order to improve or hurt someone else's chance to get the job.

Top Secret

It takes a *long* time for federal agencies to receive snail mail because all mail is X-rayed for safety. Consider sending an e-mail instead so that your message gets to the recipient while the agency is still making its decisions.

Be proactive while you wait:

- Follow up with a thank you note.
- Call the helpline for the online application system if you are worried that your application is lost.
- Attend agency outreach events or information sessions.
- Go to industry-specific career fairs.
- Apply to other federal jobs that are similar or of interest to you.

The Least You Need to Know

- Arming yourself with knowledge about the hiring process will help you set your expectations and help you create the best application possible.
- The hiring process can take three to six months or longer, so be prepared for a wait and don't get too discouraged if you don't hear back from anyone right away.

- If you are disabled or a veteran (or spouse, widow, dependent, or mother of a veteran) who meets certain qualifications, you can receive additional points on your application. But remember, you still have to be qualified for the job!
- Go after the job you want, even after you've applied. Be proactive by following up with a phone call and/or thank you note.

Chapter 8

Background Check and Security Clearance

In This Chapter

- Why the government does a background check on all potential employees
- Levels of clearance
- How much time it takes to get through the process
- Why you might be denied clearance—and a job

An essential part of determining whether a potential employee (you) is suitable for federal employment is the background check, which can take up to several months, depending on the job and the type of investigation the position requires.

Jobs that require greater trust in the employees due to the nature of the duties usually require a more in-depth investigation. This is particularly true of positions that may entail access to sensitive information or require a security clearance.

Setting Your Expectations

Knowing up front how long the process can take will help set your expectations and manage your time (many people find temporary employment or stay in their current jobs until they get the results of their background check). The good news is that many positions permit the new employee to begin working once the background check process has started, instead of waiting until the check has been completed. Even people whose positions require a high-level security clearance may be granted an "interim" clearance to begin working once some basic checks have been completed (with favorable results) and the more time-intensive checks are underway.

Although in recent years investigations for jobs that require security clearances were known to take a long time, this is no longer always the case. Recently, the Office of Personnel Management (OPM), which conducts 90 percent of the background investigations for the federal government, has eliminated the backlog, thereby drastically reducing investigation times.

In 2004, a security clearance investigation typically took six months (for a Secret clearance) to a year (for a Top Secret clearance). This was due to a tremendous backlog of clearance investigations and was often cited as one of the most common sources of frustration in the hiring process, not only because it took so long but also because applicants might not hear from the agency for months at a time.

In 2009, from April 1 through the end of June, OPM completed 90 percent of initial clearance investigations in less than 40 days. Although this does not include the time that an agency may take to evaluate the investigation and make a decision to grant a clearance (*adjudication*), many agencies are completing their evaluation process in less than 20 days. This means that even if you need a high-level security clearance, it is possible that your investigation could be finished in just a few months.

def•i•ni•tion

Adjudication is the decision process that produces a judgment for whether or not you are suitable for the security clearance required by your position.

Additionally, knowing what investigators are looking for will help you provide the information needed for the background check to proceed without delays.

Levels of Clearance

Government uses background checks to ensure that all employees are "reliable, trustworthy, of good conduct and character, and loyal to the United States." However, while every government employee goes through a background check, not everyone will need to receive a security clearance investigation, particularly if the job does not require the candidate to handle sensitive or classified information.

National Security Positions

If your job requires a security clearance investigation, it is usually because your position requires you to be eligible for access to Confidential, Secret, or Top Secret information. You will generally see high levels of clearance associated with positions in the intelligence community (including the CIA and FBI) as well as the State Department, the Agency for International Development (USAID), and the Department of Defense (DOD).

The levels of clearance are:

- **Top Secret.** Classified by the fact that misusing the information to which you have access could cause exceptionally *grave damage* to our country.
- **Secret.** Classified by the fact that misusing the information to which you have access could cause *serious damage* to our country.
- **Confidential.** Classified by the fact that misusing the information to which you have access could cause *damage* to our country.

You should know that just because you receive a particular clearance, it doesn't mean you can choose to see any and all information that is classified in that category. You will also have to be approved to see information on a "need to know" basis.

Examples of jobs that may require security clearances are federal air marshals (Top Secret), bomb appraisal officers (Secret), and foreign service officers (Top Secret).

Public Trust Positions

Investigations for Public Trust positions are required when a person in that position could potentially cause a moderate or high degree of damage to the efficiency or integrity of our government, even though the position is not a national security position. Public trust can apply to anything from debris policy specialists at the Federal Emergency Management Agency (FEMA) to educational aid on military bases overseas to landscape architects with the Forest Service.

Examples of jobs that could be positions of Public Trust are information technology (IT) specialists who protect government IT systems, finance officers, auditors, those whose jobs require the protection of sensitive but unclassified information (such as human resources officers who have access to employees' tax and retirement information), customer service representatives, and public liaisons.

Federal Facts

Investigations for non-sensitive, low-risk positions do not involve clearances because there is a low risk that a person in such a position could damage the efficiency or integrity of the government.

As you could probably guess, investigations for low-risk positions are the least in-depth checks. Much less information is collected and much of the investigation is done by mail.

High-Level Security Clearance

Jobs that include access to sensitive information generally require a more intensive background investigation that may include polygraph tests, in-depth interviews, and so on.

Examples of agencies that may require high levels of security clearance include:

- The U.S. State Department
- The intelligence community (e.g., the CIA and FBI)
- The U.S. Agency for International Development
- The Department of Defense
- The Department of Energy
- The Department of Homeland Security

What Is Involved in Getting a Security Clearance?

There are three main phases to receiving a security clearance. Understanding this process and the kinds of information that will be collected will help you navigate (and prepare for) the investigation and clear the security clearance hurdle:

1. **The application process.** This phase involves verification of U.S. citizenship, fingerprinting, and completion of the Questionnaire for National Security Positions. Be sure to answer all questions, even if they are already on your

resumé or answered elsewhere. Your application must have information that meets the three Cs: *correct*, *complete*, and *current*.

Make sure you also include the following information:

- ❑ Writing or typing that is legible and correct. Always double-check your application. This is an easy way to delay the handling of your investigation.
- ❑ Zip codes for everything, from places you have worked to where you have lived.
- ❑ The month and year for all your information; the agency will not accept any gaps in time.
- ❑ Your full name (be sure to include your middle name).

2. **The actual investigation of your background.** During this phase, friends, colleagues, and neighbors may be contacted and interviewed. Reports from all the investigators are collected into a single file, "The Report of Investigation." This report is sent to the federal agency that asked for the investigation, because officials there will make the final hiring or security clearance decision.

3. **The review of the results of the investigation by the hiring agency.** The scope of your background check will vary depending on the job you're applying for, but will likely include where you've worked, where you've gone to school, where you've lived, and whether you have a criminal history. For higher-level investigations, your credit may be reviewed, and investigators may talk to people who know you. This can include friends, relatives, neighbors, as well as past employers and co-workers.

The Fine Print

If you are working while waiting for your security clearance to come through, be prepared for investigators to call your current employer to verify certain information. Make sure you let your current employer know that he or she might be receiving a call—you don't want your employer to be caught off guard.

Do you have the right to refuse a background investigation used to provide a security clearance? Sure—if you don't want the job. Providing the information is voluntary, but if you choose not to provide it, you may not be eligible for employment.

How Long Does It Take?

The security clearance timeline varies for each position and depends on the level of clearance needed for the job and each individual's background. In the *fiscal year* 2009, the fastest 90 percent of initial security clearance investigations (not including adjudications) were conducted in an average of 33 to 64 days, depending on the level of security clearance.

def•i•ni•tion

The government operates on a **fiscal year**, which runs from October 1 through September 30 of the following year.

So why does it take so long? First, a lot of hours go into getting the facts on your history, interviewing people you know, and so on, especially for a high-level clearance. Second, many of the sources are obtained through voluntary cooperation. Third, many people simply don't take the time to fill out their applications properly, which causes more work on the part of the investigators and slows down the process for everyone.

Submitting Your Information Online

OPM understands that background investigations can be cumbersome for jobseekers. To lessen the burden, OPM created a one-stop website for submitting information for the investigation. Electronic Questionnaires for Investigations Processing (e-QIP) allows applicants to enter, update, and transmit their personal investigative data electronically over a secure Internet connection to their employing agency for review and approval.

Applicants can access and log out of e-QIP (www.opm.gov/e-qip), so they can update it as needed instead of having to complete it at one time.

What You Need to Know About Security Clearance

A background check is required for all federal jobs. It is completed after a conditional job offer has been made to evaluate the person's reliability, trustworthiness, conduct, and character. The agency will inform you of all forms that need to be completed.

The full security clearance process begins after the job offer is made for positions related to national security.

It may be possible to work for the agency in a non-sensitive position while you wait for the security clearance. While all jobs require a background check, not all actually require a full security clearance.

Honesty is the best policy. A basic background check includes a review of law enforcement records and verification of education, past employment, and citizenship. Being honest is more important than having a spotless record. Past mistakes will be considered on a case-by-case basis, but lying (including omission of important events) will generally disqualify you for a job. The length of time that has passed since the last incident and the applicant's level of involvement are taken into consideration.

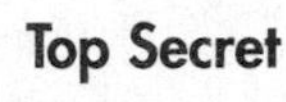

Top Secret

Don't worry too much if there is something in your past that you feel can hurt your chances at "passing" the investigation. You should get the chance to explain anything in the background investigation that could cause an agency not to accept you as an employee.

For example, let's say you're applying for a job requiring a low-level security clearance and you got in trouble in college for being drunk and disorderly. If you are honest about it (and you aren't *in* college), you may still be considered for that job. On the other hand, if you report that you never drink and someone tells an investigator that you did, in fact, get in trouble for drinking in college, then the fact that you were dishonest could damage your chances for being granted a clearance. Remember, your friends and associates are obligated to tell the truth, too.

The Investigations

So you want to know who's digging into your past? Some investigators are federal employees and some are contract investigators working on a government contract. They all do the same work and follow the same laws, regulations, and rules. For some investigations, an investigator may interview you to expand and clarify the information you put on the security questionnaire, but for others, the investigation may take place after you have filled out the questionnaire without further input from you.

What Are Investigators Really Looking For?

As a rule of thumb, the higher the level of security clearance required for the job, the further back in your past they will go. Your chances for getting a security clearance could be greatly damaged if at any point in time you were:

- Dishonest or fraudulent in the hiring process
- Seeking to overthrow the U.S. government or involved in terrorist acts

Depending on the level of investigation that you need, the government may need additional information about:

- **Dual citizenship or foreign birth.** This takes extra time, as the investigator must verify birth abroad and verify immigration records.
- **Family members who are from other countries.** Key considerations are whether or not family members have connections to a foreign person, group, government, or country that may create a potential conflict of interest.
- **Drug use or criminal record.** Students can still apply for federal jobs and should be honest about their experience. In making its decision, the agency will consider the individual's age, circumstances, and how long ago the event occurred. Agencies look at these instances differently based upon their unique duties and missions, so an applicant may be hired at one agency but not another. For more information on this, go to www.hirenetwork.org/fed_occ_restrictions.html.
- **High or delinquent debt.** For example, at the Transportation Safety Administration (TSA), if an applicant has bad debt of over $5,000 (outside of student loans) and the issue cannot be mitigated, there is a possibility that he or she will not be found suitable for employment. Having delinquent federal debt could also affect whether you are found suitable for employment or for a security clearance.
- **Mental health conditions.** Mental health counseling in and of itself is not a reason to revoke or deny a clearance. Because mental health disorders can affect how one deals with stress, work, and life, the government takes these conditions—including emotional, mental, and personality disorders—into consideration. However, the primary interest in this information is whether or not it is going to significantly impact your ability to do your job or whether it might cause you to be a security risk.

Providing Incomplete or Inaccurate Information

In order to pass your investigation, you should avoid the following common mistakes:

- **Withholding relevant information.** If it's discovered that you withheld relevant information, you may be reinvestigated later on.
- **Not telling the truth.** Give the facts accurately and don't lie about anything.
- **Failing to register with the selective service.** Selective service registration is required for all males born after December 31, 1959. If you fall under this requirement, failing to register could be an impediment to employment.

Once you have a security clearance, and the need for it continues, you might undergo a reinvestigation every 5 years (Top Secret), 10 years (Secret), or 15 years (Confidential).

Checklist: Getting Your Security Clearance

Be prepared. Begin collecting needed information as soon as possible. The types of information required include:

- ❑ Past home addresses
- ❑ Past jobs
- ❑ Contacts who knew you from all locations (home and work—even school for graduating college students)
- ❑ All foreign travel dates and foreign contacts

Typically, positions with Top Secret security clearance require information about your background going back 10 years, whereas Secret and Confidential jobs require information going back 7 years. However, some of the questions on the security questionnaire pertain to your whole life. These questions will use the word "ever" (as in "Have you ever …" or "Did you ever …").

The Fine Print

Students can prepare in advance for their background investigation, but they can't initiate it themselves (it can only be initiated by their prospective employer). Students usually have to provide approximately 7 to 10 years of their employment/life history.

Follow up with the security office or human resources office after a reasonable interval (roughly a month) if you have not heard back. Contact your security officer to advise that officer of any changes you need to make on the form after you submit it.

The Least You Need to Know

- Everyone has to go through a background check so that our government can see if candidates are suitable for employment. However, not all jobs require security clearance.
- There are several levels of security clearance, depending on the position and the sensitivity of the information associated with that position.
- Be honest! A common reason people get turned down for clearance is because they lied about something or omitted relevant information during their investigation.
- The process of passing your background check and getting security clearance can take anywhere from under a month to more than a year, so be prepared for a wait.
- Gathering your information ahead of time will help the process go smoother and more quickly.

Chapter 9

Creating Your Government Resumé

In This Chapter

- The importance of writing a good federal resumé
- Using USAJOBS.gov to create a federal resumé
- Insider tips on resumé writing
- Finding your government GS-level equivalent
- How to make your resumé stand out
- Applying for jobs offline

Writing a good resumé is an important part of applying for any job—it's the way you market yourself to a potential employer. What is different, however, is the way you put together a resumé that will get you an interview with a federal agency. Say goodbye to the rules you once learned about resumé writing. Federal resumés are different than you're probably used to, but with a few tips and some attention to detail, you'll be steps ahead of many other applicants.

In this chapter, we will walk you through the process of writing a winning government resumé, helping you navigate the USAJOBS.gov resumé process and offering inside tips that will bring you one step closer to getting your government job.

Forget What You Know About Resumé Writing

Not all resumés are created equal. While you may find yourself summarizing your work history in a one-page document for a private-sector job, your federal resumé should usually be more detailed and therefore longer. A federal resumé builds off the information in a typical resumé and goes into more depth about your skills, duties, and accomplishments.

While it may seem like drafting a multipage resumé is just another tedious task, there are actually some great benefits to including as much information as possible:

> **Top Secret**
>
> If you are applying for an entry-level job, your resumé should be two-to-five pages; more experienced workers' resumés will be even longer.

- **Creating opportunities to highlight your accomplishments.** Entry-level and experienced workers alike are forced to cut information about previous jobs down to only a few bullets in a private-sector resumé. A federal resumé allows you to talk in depth about the duties of your former jobs, your accomplishments in the workplace, and the relevant skills that you bring to the table.
- **Making the process fair to all applicants.** The federal government has tried hard to make the process of creating a federal resumé as fair and easy as possible for everyone. With USAJOBS.gov, you do not have to worry about formatting, fonts, and other parts of making a resumé look "pretty." A resumé template is automatically generated for you with a standard format and font, putting you on an equal footing with all other applicants—at least in the formatting sense.
- **Assessing your fit.** Just because you like the sound of a certain job, that doesn't mean you are qualified for it. Creating a federal resumé will give you an idea of whether you are a good fit for a position because you will create a list of the skills and experiences you can bring to an employer and can determine whether those meet the needs of the agency.
- **Preparing for the interview.** A detailed resumé helps you to prepare for upcoming interviews by getting your brain thinking more in depth about the accomplishments and skills you have to offer.

Creating Your Federal Resumé

To apply for most federal jobs, you must use USAJOBS.gov to write a federal resumé. Click on My USAJOBS, create a username and password, visit the Resumes page, and you're ready to get started (see Chapter 5 for more details).

Creating a federal resumé on USAJOBS.gov is a four-step process of entering information on the website. The following sections review each step in more detail.

Getting Started

Confidentiality: Federal agencies have the ability to view your contact information, current employer, and references through a search of USAJOBS.gov. While it is unlikely that an agency would use this information for anything if you have not applied for a position, some people just prefer to keep this information private. If you do not want to allow agencies to see this information, you must mark "confidential" in this section.

> **The Fine Print**
>
> Some agencies have their own website for applicants, so don't be alarmed when you click "apply online" for a job on the USAJOBS.gov site and are automatically redirected to that agency's website to complete the application process.

Candidate Information: This section provides basic information about you, including your full name, contact information, citizenship, and whether you qualify for veterans' preference. Your Social Security number is also a required part of your federal resumé, so be sure to fill it in.

Highest Career Level Achieved: This drop-down box categorizes your work history from "Student" to "Senior Executive." Click on whichever category is most appropriate for your current situation. The rest of your resumé will show your actual job experience in more detail.

Federal Employee Information: If you are or have been a federal employee, click Yes in this section. You will then be asked to provide information about your former series, pay grade, and dates of employment within the federal government.

Experience

Work Experience: In this section, you can list all the jobs you have held during your career. You must include information about employers, titles, dates, hours worked per week, and duties and accomplishments on the job. While you can add as many jobs as you'd like, be sure to provide more detail about your relevant work experience. More experienced workers should also consider listing only jobs held within the last 10 years.

Education: This section allows you to list your education history. You are required to include the name and contact information of the schools you have attended as well as your degree. You may also include the dates you attended, your major and minor, grade point average, credits earned, honors, and any relevant coursework, licensures, and certifications earned while at the school. Adding your relevant coursework is a great way for an agency to see your knowledge and experience.

Job-Related Training: If you have completed training courses that are relevant to the position you are applying for, include that information in this section. Some examples of job-related training are courses on project management, budgeting, or computers. Be sure to include the dates of the training classes you took.

Related Information

References: Including references is an important—and required—part of your federal resumé. Adding references before you apply for a job will help to speed up the process if you receive an offer. Include the names and contact information of either personal or professional references who can speak to your ability to complete the job.

The Fine Print

Ask potential references in advance if it's okay to include them on your resumé. This will give them time to prepare and will also signal to them in advance that you are looking for alternative employment opportunities. It might come across as unprofessional to have your supervisor find out that you're looking for another job by receiving a phone call from your interviewer. Avoid this awkward situation by giving your references a heads-up that you've applied for another position.

Additional Language Skills: The federal government may strongly desire knowledge of one or more foreign languages, depending on the job. Include the language as well as your ability to speak, read, or write it.

Affiliations: If you are involved in professional organizations, you may include the name of the group and your role in this section of the resumé. Some examples of affiliations are the Project Management Institute, Society for Human Resource Management, United Professional Sales Association, or National Society of Professional Engineers.

Professional Publications: USAJOBS.gov allows you to include information about any professional publications you have contributed to in the past. Include the title of the publication, name of the article, the issue date, and the names of other authors (if applicable).

Additional Information: In this section, you may include any awards or honors, leadership activities, or additional skills that may be relevant to the position and may provide some more background about your abilities and accomplishments. You may also provide an explanation for obvious gaps in your employment history in the "Additional Information" section. For example, you might note if you were doing independent study or traveling during a period of unemployment.

Availability: This feature allows you to choose your type of work as well as your desired work schedule. In the "type of work" section, you can select permanent, temporary, internships, and seasonal and intermittent positions. Seasonal jobs are for specific times each year where there is peak need (for example, summer in a national park) and an intermittent position is for working irregular intervals (for example, to cover for other employees on extended leave). Some announcements may also list "detail" opportunities, but those typically pertain to a current federal employee who is willing to move to a different job for a specific period of time and then return to his or her original job afterward. Your desired work schedule could include full-time, part-time, shift intermittent, and job share (splitting one full-time job with one or more other employees) opportunities and may also involve different times of the day, such as a night shift at a VA hospital.

Specific Work Environment: Based on your work experience and personality, you also have the option to select a specific environment that works well for you.

Desired Locations: If you would be interested in jobs in certain parts of the country or the world, specify that information in this section. Greater flexibility in your desired locations will provide more job and promotion opportunities for you in government.

Finishing Up

Make Searchable: Federal agencies have the ability to search resumés in the USAJOBS.gov system. This section allows you to "activate your resumé," making it searchable and accessible to agencies across government. You may also save your resumé and finish it later.

While USAJOBS.gov allows you to add quite a bit of information, not all of the fields listed in the preceding section are required. Federal resumés must include the following information (marked with a red asterisk in USAJOBS.gov):

- Candidate Information
- Federal Employee Information (simply check "No" if you have never worked for the federal government)
- Work Experience
- Education
- References
- Affiliations

Another important piece of information to remember is that the USAJOBS.gov system allows users to create up to five federal resumés. This enables you to create resumés for specific jobs and save them all for future applications. The relevant experience, keywords and phrases, and employment history you give can be tailored to different jobs.

Insider Tips for Writing a Winning Federal Resumé

The best advice we can give you is to build your resumé off the posting for the job you are applying for. Creating a general resumé may help you to gather your thoughts on paper, but it is less likely to get you an interview than if you create a resumé tailored to the job you want.

Tie your relevant skills and experiences into a federal resumé that fits the job you want. One way to do this is to find keywords in the "Duties" section of the vacancy announcement and *use those exact words* throughout your resumé. For example, some keywords in an executive assistant position might be "direct administrative processes," "distribute phone calls and manage visitors," and "monitor correspondence." For an electrical engineer opening, you may find keywords like "use computer models," "conduct reliability studies," and "monitor the performance of systems."

The Fine Print

Don't write about *everything* you've ever done—include only what is relevant to the job for which you are applying. Use the majority of your resumé to feature your relevant skills and experience. If you have had additional work experience that you'd like to include, do so very briefly.

Here are some additional tips:

- **Use the "Duties and Accomplishments" section of your federal resumé to highlight your metrics.** Numbers impress hiring managers. Numbers, percentages, and data can be a great way to describe the specific impact you had in a particular job.
- **Check your spelling and grammar.** One of the biggest complaints from federal agencies is that applicants frequently do not edit their work and often have spelling and/or grammatical errors in their federal resumés. Use a word processor or ask a peer or professional to check your spelling and grammar. Doing so may help you avoid being overlooked when it comes time for an agency to select candidates for an interview.
- **Sell yourself and your achievements.** Don't be shy about showing your knowledge, skills, and accomplishments in your federal resumé. Give the agency representative a reason to make you one of his or her top candidates.
- **Keep your private-sector resumé saved on your computer.** Some agencies use third-party application systems that are not USAJOBS.gov and may require a different kind of resumé. If you have any questions about what documents to send, contact the agency's human resources representative for clarification.

What's Your Government GS-Level Equivalent?

One major source of confusion for people transferring from the private sector to the federal government is where they fall on the General Schedule (GS; see Chapter 5). The best way to determine your *GS-level* equivalent is simply to look at the duties of the job you are considering. If you have completed the outlined duties in the past or are confident that you could do so in the future and can show that you are qualified in your federal resumé, apply for the level stated in the job announcement. If you are unable to perform the duties outlined, consider looking at positions in a lower grade.

def•i•ni•tion

GS level (General Schedule Level) is the pay grade, which goes from levels 1 through 15 (15 being the highest). Your GS level will depend on a number of factors, from your education to your experience to the job itself.

You can add your targeted GS-level equivalent on your resumé to show the agency that you've thought about how your skills match the position's requirements. When writing out your list of accomplishments, include a line that states your equivalent level of experience at your previous jobs. Your resumé must demonstrate that you have a certain number of years of specialized experience performing the duties of the job to allow you to qualify at a certain GS level.

For example, an entry-level applicant with a Bachelor's degree may qualify for a GS-5 administrative position. A mid-level jobseeker also looking for an administrative job may apply for a GS-11 position that will require three to four years of additional related experience. By including your proposed GS-level equivalent on your federal resumé, you can present your argument to the agency regarding your appropriate salary range.

Relevant education may also guide you in the right direction when determining your GS-level equivalent. If you have recently graduated with a Bachelor's degree, look at GS-5 jobs. If you recently earned a Bachelor's degree with outstanding academic achievement (grade point average of at least 3.0 out of 4.0), apply for GS-7 positions. Graduates with a Master's degree will enter at a GS-9 (sometimes higher), and those holding a doctorate are eligible for GS-11 (or higher) positions.

Put Your Best Foot Forward

Now it's time to put into practice all the tips we've discussed in this chapter. Take a look at the following sample job posting, then compare the "before" and "after" resumés. The following numbered lists key you in to the main strengths or weaknesses on each resumé.

1. Don't use an unprofessional-sounding e-mail address. "Party animal" is totally inappropriate for any resumé!
2. Don't lie about your GPA. If it's a 3.6, list a 3.6—don't round up to a 4.0. The easiest way to get dismissed from the applicant pool is to lie.
3. Add specific dates of employment—or as specific as possible. Be sure to list your most recent experience first.
4. List the specifics of how many people John oversaw, recruited and so on.
5. Provide more details: Materials for what? How were they used?
6. Watch out for acronym overload! Spell out all acronyms and make sure all information is relevant to an audience who may not be familiar with these acronyms.
7. Researched and wrote for whom? How many briefs? On what topic? Think about what you can highlight that directly relates to the job posting.

8. If you worked with others, provide details about the capacity in which you worked with them.
9. Go ahead and provide your references. Don't make hiring officials ask for more information on their own. Make it easy for them.

International Development Program Specialist

JOB SUMMARY:

The U. S. Agency for International Development (USAID) is seeking an International Development Program Specialist to serve in Paraguay. Candidates must agree not only to serve at any of the overseas posts, but also in Washington, D.C.

MAJOR DUTIES:

Top ▲

DUTIES: *(The duties described reflect the full performance level of this position)*

Will be responsible for researching, writing, and articulating economic challenges in Paraguay. Support small team of development professionals and interact regularly with local citizens, businesses, and NGOs. Prepare briefs and other written materials to support the U.S. mission in Paraguay. Frequent travel to rural areas may be required. Will need to communicate fluently in Spanish. Will particularly utilize economic and business terminology in Spanish. Plan, direct, and execute outreach to financial institutions. Will also support the media relations team in dealing with local media. Analyze and evaluate the administrative aspects of mission-oriented programs. Recommend program plans, goals, objectives, and milestones, which serve as the basis for changes in the organization and administration of programs affecting USAID's grant recipients. Will need to exercise knowledge of the grant process. Support the hiring of outside contractors for grant implementation. Assist with the budget reporting.

A fictitious job posting for an international development program specialist.

Now take a look at the improved "after" resumé. You'll notice it's much more detailed and longer than the "before" version. It's a great example of how you can translate a private-sector resumé into one that will get you noticed in the federal government.

John D. Applicant
1111 Pleasant Drive, Washington, D.C. 20005
202-555-1234
① partyanimal@jobsearch.com

Education
University of Virginia, Charlottesville, Virginia
May 2005
B.A. in Foreign Affairs and Italian Language
② GPA: 4.0

Relevant Experience
Virginia Community Service Organization, Fairfax, Virginia
Program Coordinator
③ 2008

④ -Oversee mentoring programs in limited resource communities
-Recruit, train, and manage mentors and youth
⑤ -Develop marketing and training materials
⑥ -Utilized the FMP and GHPRD for CQ at HQ

IDO
Title: Political and Economic Section Assistant
2007

⑦ -Researched and wrote briefs
⑧ -Worked with Peruvian professionals

International Development Organization
Title: Public Affairs Assistant
2005 – 2006

-Wrote articles in bureau newsletter & press releases
-Drafted memoranda for the director
-Supervised contractors on communications project
⑨ References furnished upon request.

Sample "before" resumé.

John D. Applicant
1111 Pleasant Drive, Washington, D.C. 20005
Phone: 202-555-1234
① E-mail: jdapplicant@jobsearch.com
Country of Citizenship: United States of America
Veterans' Preference: No
② Highest Grade: GS-09 equivalent
Contact Current Employer: Yes

AVAILABILITY

Job Type:

Permanent
Temporary or Term Appointment
Federal Career Intern

Work Schedule: Full Time

DESIRED LOCATIONS

③ U.S.-D.C.-Washington/Metro
Paraguay

WORK EXPERIENCE

9/2007 - 6/2008
Virginia Community Service Organization
Salary: $50,000 per year
Fairfax, Virginia
Hours per week: 40

Title: Program Coordinator

④ -Oversee three mentoring programs in limited resource communities
⑤ -Recruit, train, and manage 25 adult mentors and 30 youth
⑥ -Develop marketing and training materials for use in programs and other county mentoring initiatives
⑦ -Write and manage program grants, hire outside contractors for grant implementation
⑧ -Communicate in Spanish with 50 program participants and their families
- Coordinate written and oral communication at a level equivalent to GS-09

⑨ (Contact Supervisor: Yes, Supervisor's Name: Clyde Jackson, Supervisor's Phone: 703-555-1212)

01/2007 - 08/2007
IDO (International Development Organization)
Lima, Peru
Grade Level: GS-07 equivalent
Hours per week: 45

Title: Political and Economic Section Assistant

-Researched and wrote 10 regional economic and political briefs for regional director
(10) -Worked with South American professionals in regional chambers of 55 commerce, banks, NGOs, and government offices to compile briefs
-Utilized Spanish language skills and political and cultural knowledge in a variety of settings

(Contact Supervisor: Yes, Supervisor's Name: Lisa Miller, Supervisor's Phone: 202-555-2323)

12/2005 - 12/2006
IDO (International Development Organization)
Grade Level: GS-05 equivalent
Washington, D.C. U.S.
Hours per week: 20

Title: Public Affairs Assistant

-Wrote 30 articles in bureau newsletter and press releases
-Drafted weekly memoranda for the communications director
-Supervised 20 contractors on communications project
-Contacted and pitched media for program publicity
-Assembled financial and budget information for use in IDO material
(Contact Supervisor: Yes, Supervisor's Name: Nina Bishop, Supervisor's Phone: 202-555-4545)

EDUCATION

University of Virginia
Charlottesville, Virginia
Bachelor's Degree - 5/2005
(11) 130 Semester Hours
Major: Foreign Affairs, Spanish Language (double major)
GPA: 3.50 out of 4.0

LANGUAGES

Spanish: Spoken: Fluent, Written: Advanced, Read: Advanced
Italian: Spoken: Good, Written: Good, Read: Good

AFFILIATIONS

National Italian Club Member; American Foundation Member

REFERENCES

Joe Reference, Professor of Italian Language and Literature
Phone Number: 202-555-3333
(12) E-Mail Address: jreference@profs.edu
Reference Type: Academic

Additional Skills:

-Strong written and oral communication skills
-Strong analytical and problem solving capabilities. Utilized SPSS, statistical analysis software
-Grant writing experience (awarded "Dream Catchers" Program Grant by Community and Recreation Services, Fairfax County Government, December 2006)
-Regional expertise in Balkan, Post-Soviet, and Western European political issues (including extensive regional travel and language capabilities)
-Proficient in Microsoft Office programs (Word, Outlook, Excel, Project, PowerPoint, Access)

Leadership and Service Roles:

Kaleidoscope Center for Cultural Fluency Social Diversity Program, Director, September 2004 - May 2005
-Developed forums for dialogue between diverse student groups
-Built partnerships between student groups through cultural programming

Italian Club: President, September 2004 - May 2005
-Recruited executive committee members, planned meetings, managed a membership base of 40+ students
-Organized club involvement in national Italian-American collegiate workshops and events
-Created community events with local Italian businesses and restaurants

(13) **Other Roles at the University of Virginia:**

-Council of the College of Arts & Sciences: Italian Department Representative, September 2004 - May 2005
(14) -International Residence College: Academic Affairs, Committee Chair, September 2003 - May 2004
-Jefferson Literary and Debating Society: Elected Member, January 2005 - May 2005
-European Society: Culture Chair, January 2004 - January 2005

Sample "after" resumé.

1. Use a general and professional e-mail address—nothing too cute or personal.
2. HR officials need to see which level you have reached outside of government service and how that directly translates to a GS level.
3. This shows that you are open to working in various locations, which widens your pool of opportunities when agencies have multiple locations.
4. It's always good to show that you know how to do a lot on a small budget and with limited resources.
5. Listing actual measures will go a long way with hiring officials.
6. Show how you have used your skills for tangible product development.
7. Show how you have used your skill successfully.
8. Show that you understand the GS level at which you are performing. This makes it easier for the hiring manager to understand why you are a good fit for this GS level.
9. List the name of your supervisor and contact information so that hiring officials don't have to come back to you later. In short, you want to make their lives as easy as possible. Make sure you have talked to your current supervisor. Note that if you say, "No, do not contact my current supervisor," this can actually hurt your chances of being chosen for that job. At the very least, provide an alternative contact.
10. Show your ability to communicate and collaborate across organizations.
11. If available, semester hours show the hiring officials that you have completed your coursework if there are hour requirements for that particular job.
12. Academic references are good if you are a recent graduate. Otherwise, use only professional references. Stay away from personal references if possible.
13. These are general and tailored skills that you are listing related specifically to the job posting. Brag a little bit! Write out specific programs and details to show how you acquired them and/or how you have used them.
14. Including this information shows that this person has sought culturally diverse living experiences in the past, making him or her a good candidate for other cultural opportunities.

Applying Offline

USAJOBS.gov has become a great tool for applicants to search for jobs, create a federal resumé, and apply for the position they want. Still, some applicants prefer submitting an application by mailing it in to an agency. However, unless the vacancy announcement stipulates that the agency will accept only paper applications, you should submit your application on USAJOBS.gov. Otherwise, your application could get lost in the shuffle—or receipt of your application could be significantly delayed due to the fact that all snail mail is irradiated for security purposes.

Job postings on USAJOBS.gov will often tell you whether the agency will accept paper applications via mail. If the announcement states that the agency does not accept applications via mail, don't waste your time sending one in. You can also contact the human resources office at the agency to find out whether you are able to submit a paper application for the position, but really, this is the electronic age and demonstrating your computer competence is likely to be a plus.

The Least You Need to Know

- Unlike in the private sector, where a one- to two-page resumé is standard, federal resumés are generally three to five pages or more.
- Focus your resumé on your skills and experience that is relevant to the job for which you are applying.
- Tailor your resumé to include keywords and phrases from the job announcement.
- Provide as much detail as possible while keeping it relevant to the job posting.
- If necessary, and if the agency permits, you may apply by mail, fax, or in person. Simply contact that agency to see if this is acceptable and what their process is for receiving offline resumés.

Chapter 10

Completing Your Application Package

In This Chapter

- KSAs made easy
- Writing winning KSA essays
- Tips on answering government questionnaires
- A sample application questionnaire

Your federal resumé is an important part of the application process, but it's not the only step toward getting a federal job. The government uses at least two other ways to determine whether you're the right fit for a position: Knowledge, Skills, and Abilities (KSAs) and questionnaires.

KSAs require the applicant to write several short-answer responses (essays) that range from assessing soft skills, such as "Ability to communicate in writing," to hard technical skills, such as "Knowledge of the Microsoft Office suite."

While KSAs are popular among some agencies, others require you to answer application questionnaires, which use multiple-choice and short essay responses. Other assessment tools might also be used, such as the

Foreign Service Exam at the State Department. The good news is that each federal agency is required to provide information about how it will rate or assess its applicants, so you will know up front what is expected of you and how you will be judged.

In addition to responding to KSAs and questionnaires, you may be asked for additional pieces of information, such as your college transcripts. If you miss any piece that is asked of you, your application will likely be disqualified—so read carefully and follow through!

In this chapter, we will demystify the process of answering KSAs and questionnaires. We will give you insider tips to help you write the best essays possible, ensure that your chosen agency notices your application, and get you started on the road to a great government job.

The ABCs of KSAs

For many agencies, a resumé does not provide enough information about the way an applicant has addressed challenges or made an impact in his or her previous professional positions. Therefore, they rely heavily on the information you provide in your KSA responses. Unfortunately, for many people KSAs are often the most confusing and difficult part of the application process.

Federal Facts

KSAs replaced the civil service exam many years ago as a way for agencies to assess candidates beyond their resumé and to rank candidates for consideration. However, since each agency has the authority to develop its own assessment process, a job applicant may well encounter some unique requirements, including written tests.

You should view KSAs as an opportunity to expand upon the information in your federal resumé (see Chapter 9), taking great thought, care, and attention to detail to craft them. They are a way for you to market yourself and your experiences, prove your worth, and give agencies a better view of what you can offer them. If you have compelling examples of your work in your federal resumé, discuss them in as much depth as possible in your KSA responses.

Subpar KSAs will likely not get you an interview with an agency. KSAs vary based upon the job you are applying for, so the essays that are required for an engineer are vastly different than those needed for a nurse, secretary, or program manager.

To give you a better idea of what agencies need to see in your KSAs, let's define what they are looking for:

- **Knowledge.** The understanding of facts and information needed to perform a certain task—for example, knowledge of engineering principles and concepts.
- **Skills.** The proficiency to perform a certain task based on knowledge or experience—for example, skill in directing and supervising staff to meet organizational objectives.
- **Abilities.** The capability to do something well as the result of knowledge or practice—for example, ability to establish and meet goals.

One of the biggest challenges that applicants face is decoding the KSA *prompts*, or statements that an agency requires you to provide a written response for. For example, a KSA prompt that states "Ability making presentations in front of a group" is similar to an interviewer asking you to describe a time when you had to make a persuasive argument or presentation for a large audience and the tools and techniques you used. A KSA that prompts you to write about your "Ability to gather facts and communicate findings clearly, both orally and in writing," is similar to an interviewer asking about a project you worked on in a previous job during which you had to write a report and present the findings to an audience.

def•i•ni•tion

A **prompt** is a phrase that will tell you what to write about in your KSA. Think of it as being like an interview question.

Depending on the job you are applying for, an agency will ask you to respond to a wide variety of KSA prompts. Here are some sample KSA prompts by job title.

Administrative Officer:

- Skill in oral communications and problem solving
- Ability to project intermediate and long-range planning
- Ability to prepare reports and briefings

Pharmacy Technician:

- Ability to solve problems and make recommendations
- Knowledge of, and ability to follow, written instructions for compounding

- Knowledge of policies and procedures for inventory management
- Knowledge of the computerized prescription process

Program Analyst:

- Ability to gather, compile, and analyze data in order to determine facts, draw conclusions, and recommend corrective action
- Ability to communicate, both orally and in writing, the results of complex analyses
- Ability to perform successfully on an individual basis and as part of a team of professional staff

Insider Tips for Writing KSAs

If KSAs still seem overwhelming, don't panic. We recommend using the simple CCAR (Context, Challenge, Action, and Result) method to respond to KSAs. Agencies recommend CCAR to organize your thoughts and create a coherent answer. Using the CCAR method, let's walk through a KSA prompt that asks the applicant to demonstrate the ability to communicate orally:

- **Context.** Set the scene for the rest of the essay. The context section provides an overview of the situation you were in when you took action to resolve a problem. *Example:* "As a new teacher in a struggling school district, I was in charge of teaching students from a variety of backgrounds."
- **Challenge.** State the problem that you faced in the example you provide. *Example:* "Many of the students had trouble understanding English, as it was not the primary language spoken in their home."
- **Action.** Talk about the steps you took to solve the problem. *Example:* "I used my oral communication skills to increase in-class interaction with the students and provide information in a more understandable manner through games and presentations. I also created a buddy system that matched high-achieving students with those with language barriers."
- **Result.** Share the outcomes of your actions. If possible, use numbers to highlight your accomplishment. *Example:* "Of the 10 students who started the year with failing grades, 90 percent passed my class with a C or higher. The high-achieving students also increased their test scores and rated the class highly because of the opportunity they had to help their classmates."

The CCAR method allows you to organize your thoughts and experiences in a way that is easily transferable to a narrative paragraph.

Some more insider tips for writing KSAs are:

- **Use examples that show off your accomplishments, not someone else's.** If you plan to use an example that involves a team, focus your essay only on your role and not that of other people. An agency wants to see the actions that you—and you alone—took to resolve a challenge.
- **Tell a story.** A KSA should be a narrative in the first person. After providing a catchy context and challenge section, you can use bullets to describe the actions you took and results you achieved. Be sure to use complete sentences.
- **Make your KSA readable.** Many people fall into the trap of using acronyms or jargon that the person reading the application may not understand. Use plain, understandable language for a wide audience. Ask a friend or colleague to read your essays to be sure they make sense.

The Fine Print

If you come across a KSA that is incredibly specific or it seems that you could answer it only if you were a current federal employee, then you may want to reconsider applying for this job. It's most likely targeted to a specific audience: current federal employees with experience in a specific area.

- **Remember that spelling and grammar count.** Agencies notice spelling and grammatical errors, and you don't want to give them such an obvious reason to disqualify you from consideration when competition among applicants is intense. Save potential embarrassment and ask a friend or colleague to read your responses to ensure they are spelled and written correctly.
- **Use keywords from the job announcement in your KSA essays.** For example, in Chapter 9, we mentioned keywords in an executive assistant job description ("direct administrative processes," "distribute phone calls and manage visitors," and "monitor correspondence"). If you have experience fulfilling the duties of the job for which you are applying, use those examples and include the announcement's keywords in your KSA response.

  You may want to include language similar to this: "In my previous position as an assistant at Bettis Industries, I oversaw a variety of existing administrative processes (including payroll submissions, service requests, accounts receivable) and implemented new administrative processes as identified by me or by management. In addition, I answered and distributed phone calls and voicemails and greeted all levels of visitors to our offices. I also monitored all incoming and outgoing correspondence to our CEO's office, delivery of mail, tasking of responses, distribution of voicemails, and response to public inquiries received via e-mail."

- **Use numbers to demonstrate your impact.** Just like your federal resumé, KSAs are a prime place to provide empirical evidence of your accomplishments. If you are able to use numbers (including quantities and percentages) to show your impact, do so.
- **Cite more than one example.** For each KSA prompt (for example, "ability to communicate in writing"), you should provide three to five narrative examples. This can mean quite a bit of writing, so take time to think of the best examples to highlight in your application.
- **Keep an eye on length.** The total length of each KSA response should be one half page to one page. This should include three to five paragraphs for each prompt. Each paragraph should include one example. So if you're asked to explain your ability to communicate in writing, your answer should be three to five paragraphs long, using one paragraph per example. Don't make the mistake of providing too little or too much detail.
- **Take your time.** KSAs should take you at least 15 minutes to write. Think of the best examples you can provide and take the time to turn those into a compelling story.
- **Remember that USAJOBS.gov provides all the prompts that you can expect.** If you think of KSAs as a test, one of the great parts of USAJOBS.gov is that it basically gives you all the questions that will be on the test. Just look under the "Qualifications and Evaluations" tab on USAJOBS.gov and see the actual prompts that the agency wants you to respond to in your application. You can then take the time to write outstanding KSA essays before you have to submit your entire application package.
- **Where appropriate, reuse KSAs.** If you are applying to a specific job series, many of the KSA prompts will likely be the same. You should

Top Secret

Many applicants make the mistake of simply giving up on their KSAs by leaving them blank or halfheartedly completing them. This means that if you take the time to complete your KSAs—and write them thoughtfully—then you are already ahead of the competition.

copy and save KSA responses on your computer (perhaps in a Microsoft Word document) and reuse them later as appropriate.

The End of KSAs?

With a goal of making the federal hiring process both more efficient and applicant-friendly, the Office of Personnel Management (OPM) and Congress are both considering paths that might get rid of KSA essays. However, the process that emerges from these efforts may still have an essay component or something similar..

Sample KSAs

We wouldn't let you wade into the KSA waters without an idea of what to expect and how to respond. Here's a common prompt:

Ability to communicate in writing

A bad response might look like this:

"Over the course of my career, I have produced many reports for a large audience. My colleagues have often commended me for my ability to write compelling arguments."

Here's what a good response might look like:

"In my current position as donor relations manager, I produce written materials for a wide external audience. Last year, I was asked to create an information-sharing campaign for our donors. This was a significant challenge as our contact with donors had traditionally been ad hoc and lacked a unified message. In response, I created a monthly newsletter for our donor community that identified major initiatives within the organization and invited them to upcoming events. The newsletter reaches 500 individuals each month, and I have received positive feedback in the form of phone calls and e-mails from more than 300 members of our donor community. Additionally, 35 percent of donors provided additional funding to the organization this year, citing greater familiarity with our initiatives as the main reason for their increase in giving.

"In addition, while I was a student I developed my strong written communication skills in a variety of capacities:

- During my junior year, I spent a semester as a congressional intern, a position that allowed me to draft correspondence and news releases. My congressman commended my ability to produce clear, concise written products.

- Throughout high school and college, I was a staff writer for the school's weekly newspaper. I wrote in-depth feature stories on a variety of topics and was selected for a regional writing award during my sophomore year in college.
- As chapter president of my sorority during my senior year of college, I wrote weekly reports on our sorority's volunteer activities that were sent to my organization's senior leadership."

So what's the difference between the two? The second response gives much more detail with specific examples of how you developed and used writing communication skills successfully.

Answering Application Questionnaires

Although KSAs have been for some time now a popular way for many agencies to screen candidates, agencies also use application questionnaires to do basically the same thing.

Application questionnaires vary in length, but may have 50 to 100 questions, as well as a combination of multiple-choice and short-essay questions. The format of the multiple-choice questions may be yes/no or true/false. There may also be statements that require you to summarize your experience or expertise in performing certain tasks using a scale that ranges from "no experience" to "expert." If you find yourself answering "no experience" or "little experience" to several of these questions, you are likely not qualified for that particular position.

An important question that will likely show up on an application questionnaire is one that requires you to identify your appropriate GS level. In most cases, you will have the option to choose a GS level based on questions asked in the questionnaire that identify your knowledge, skills, and abilities to perform the essential tasks of the job. For example, when applying for a position that allows you to be hired as a GS-12 or GS-13, you can answer the questions associated with both GS levels and determine which level is most appropriate given your level of experience.

Of course, unless you already work for the federal government, you probably don't know what type of experience equates to a certain grade level. Carefully reading the description of duties and responsibilities in the job announcement should help you get a better idea of where you fit in.

The Fine Print

Honesty is the best policy when filling out any job application, and answering a questionnaire is no different. Your resumé and experiences should match your questionnaire responses. If you claim to be an expert in every question asked in the multiple-choice section but your resumé doesn't match your answers, the agency may suspect that you are being dishonest. Provide honest answers to the questions you are being asked and avoid a potentially embarrassing situation in the future.

Sample Questionnaire

Following is a sample application questionnaire for a program analyst position.

For the GS-12: One year of experience at the GS-11 level in the federal service, or equivalent, which has equipped the applicant with the particular knowledge, skills, and abilities to successfully perform the duties of the position.

1. Do you meet the specialized experience described above?

    A. Yes

    B. No

2. Please give 1–2 examples of your experience that relates to the specialized experience above.

    (Maximum length of 8,000 characters)

3. Choose the type(s) of written products you have produced as a regular part of a job.

    A. Issue/position papers or summary reports on organizational data that included analysis and recommendations.

    B. Communication plans.

    C. Guidelines or procedural instructions for implementing new initiatives.

    D. Recommendations for solutions to policy or reporting problems.

    E. Correspondence that consolidates input from a number of different sources (including contradictory viewpoints).

    F. Reports, presentations, or briefing materials.

    G. Organizational assessments.

    H. None of the above.

4. Indicate your experience gathering and evaluating information and data.

   A. I have applied analytical and evaluating methods, theories, and techniques to provide recommendations on administrative, management, or technical issues (e.g., conducting studies; researching and analyzing official documents; compiling and charting statistical data; gathering, summarizing, and analyzing information for incorporation into final reports).

   B. I have tracked and monitored completion of office assignments and prepared reports that evaluate results and document any trends.

   C. I have obtained accurate and sufficient information on congressional, industry, or public inquiries and recommended responses based on evaluation of the information.

   D. I have conducted analysis, reviews, and studies of operational and administrative programs and processes in order to recommend solutions and improvements for the efficiency of the office.

   E. I have not performed any of the above tasks.

5. Which of the following have you done as a routine part of your professional work experience?

   A. Established priorities among multiple assignments

   B. Established timelines for multiple assignments

   C. Closed out assignments

   D. Started up and managed assignments through completion

   E. Established and monitored assignment progress

   F. Met deadlines

   G. Anticipated and resolved problems

   H. None of the above

6. Which of the following best reflect your ability to perform quantitative analysis and evaluation?

   A. I have no education, training, or experience in this area.

   B. I have had formal undergraduate level education/training in this area. However, I have not yet applied this ability in work situations.

C. I have had formal education/training in this area, and work experience in performing quantitative and qualitative analysis and evaluation.

D. I have performed this task on the job under close supervision by a supervisor, manager, or senior employee to ensure compliance with correct procedures.

E. I have performed this task as a regular part of a job, independently and usually without review by a supervisor, manager, or senior employee.

F. This task has been a central or major part of my work; I have performed it routinely.

7. In which of the following events have you communicated verbally or made oral presentations?

A. Speeches

B. Conferences

C. Meetings

D. One-on-one discussions

E. Telephone inquiries

F. Training

G. Technical assistance

H. Interviews

I. None of the above

The Least You Need to Know

- KSAs and questionnaires are essentially interviews on paper.
- Completing your KSAs—and doing so thoughtfully—is half the battle for completing your application.
- When writing KSAs, use the CCAR method: Context, Challenge, Action, and Results.
- Agencies are looking for keywords directly from the job description in your KSAs.

Chapter 11

The Interviewing Process

In This Chapter

- Different types of interviews
- Preparing for an interview
- Getting ready for interview success
- How to sell yourself
- Following up after the interview

It may be tempting, after making it through the online application process and being scheduled for an interview, to think your government job is close to being in the bag. Sure, take a moment to celebrate making it through the first round (it's a feat worthy of celebration), but keep your eye on the ball; interviews are exceedingly important for closing the deal. Consider it the last stage of the assessment process.

While government interviews vary in length and format, we'll cover all the ins and outs (and do's and don'ts) to help you be as prepared and confident as possible.

Types of Government Interviews

If you've been called in for an interview, it likely means you are one of a *very* short list of people who are being seriously considered for that position. However, this is not a guarantee. You can be included among a dozen or so folks who are vying for one position, and the final selection will be based on the results of several rounds of interviews.

There are many ways agencies might test your skills, strengths, and general professional abilities through the interview format, but the two main ways are through your standard one-on-one interview and a popular federal version of a panel interview.

One-on-One

As the name implies, this is an interview between one jobseeker (you) and the hiring manager or another decision maker. However, you may have one-on-one interviews with numerous people in that agency or department before a job offer is made. Whatever the case, keep this information in mind:

- One-on-one interviews are to find out more about you as a person (How will you interact with your colleagues?) and as a professional (Have your prior experiences prepared you for this job? For example, how much do you really know?).
- Although it is called a one-on-one, you may be observed by others during the interview.
- Each one-on-one interview is a new interview, so you should treat it as such. Even though you will say the same thing multiple times, keep in mind the information is new and important to each interviewer.
- Hiring managers are making increased use of a "structured interview" format during which they ask each applicant being interviewed the same series of questions intended to draw out relevant job-related information about each applicant. Don't worry if the interview seems rather formal; it may simply mean this is a structured interview and the interviewer is not wasting time talking about sports or the weather.

Federal Facts

Some agencies take advantage of the opportunity to interview at career fairs or other public events to find employees (typically for jobs that the agencies have permission to fill outside the usual competitive process). These are generally one-on-one interviews and should be treated with as much professionalism as any other interview.

Panel

Panel interviews are a favorite approach in some agencies. Not only are multiple team members able to grill the candidate, but it also turns out to be a rather efficient approach to making an informed decision about candidates, because a number of people have the chance to provide their perspective and opinion. Of course, for the interviewee (you), it can be intimidating to sit in front of a panel of people who are there solely to judge you. (No pressure.)

Here are a few elements that make panel interviews a unique experience:

- You will have questions coming at you from all angles (figuratively and literally).
- You will have the opportunity to ask a number of people questions about the job and the organization so that if you are offered the job, you can better decide whether it's the right job for you.
- You will have to be good at remembering names during and after this interview. Generally all the panelists will already know each other. Thank them or address them by name—you'll win points for holding your own.

Phone Interviews

To be honest, phone interviews are a mixed bag. Many agencies use a phone call as an initial screen to save time and/or money and learn some basic information: Can this person answer our questions? Do we want to take the time to speak with this candidate in person?

Phone interview pros:

- Phone interviews can help you stay in the running if you aren't able to come in to interview right when the agency is scrambling to start meeting candidates.
- You can take notes while talking and generally control your environment so that the situation is less stressful for you.

Phone interview cons:

- Phone interviews are generally difficult because you will need to pay special attention to people's voices and listen carefully. You will not have the advantage of observing body language or other visual cues to guide your responses. Phone interviews are still real interviews, and hiring managers or HR professionals will make a decision about you without actually seeing you.

Federal Facts

Agencies sometimes pay for candidates to travel to the interview location (assuming you are out of town) if their budgets allow or if the interview is for a high-level position. In government speak, this is referred to as "invitational travel."

- There is always a chance that your tone of voice can come across the wrong way on the phone.

In addition to being well prepared for your phone interview (you should be just as prepared as if it were an in-person interview), make sure you have good phone reception or are using a land line in a quiet place to reduce the risk of static, background noise, interruptions, or other distractions.

Video Interviews

Agencies that have the technological capability may choose to conduct interviews via live video-conference instead of flying candidates in. You will typically be asked to come to a federal office building in your area to be a part of it. This is a great way for the agency to save money while widening the pool of potential employees. A popular video interview format is panel interviewing so that multiple decision makers can "see" the interviewee. Treat this as an in-person interview in both your preparation and your professional dress.

Awaiting the Call for Your Interview

After you have submitted your application for consideration, you never know when a call could come from an agency. Some agencies send e-mails to kick off the interview initiation process (for example, "You have been selected to interview for position x; please call this number or respond to this e-mail to arrange a time for your first conversation with our agency"). Others will give you a congratulatory call to announce you've made it to the interview part of their process.

If you receive a call for an interview, you still have work to do. Be sure to write down the following information before the caller hangs up:

- The name of the caller
- The agency that caller represents
- The return phone number
- Confirmation of the job title (if you applied for multiple jobs)

- Time and date of the interview (or at least tentative dates/availability)
- Location (this is in case some error occurs and you don't receive additional location information for a promised follow-up or if the follow-up information requires you to do some additional research)
- Any other items you need to bring (such as writing samples)
- Additional assessments you may need to go through while you're there (for example, a writing test)

You should also attempt to gather the following information either over the phone or via e-mail from the person arranging your interview:

- The name(s) of interviewer(s)
- The interview format
- Security/access requirements and the time required for getting on site (it often takes 15 to 20 minutes to get through a federal building's security process—sometimes longer)
- Parking or transportation instructions
- How long the interview session is expected to last

Prepping for Your Interview

It takes diligence, persistence, and a lot of preparation time to put your best foot forward during interviews, but it is well worth the effort. Hiring managers and other interviewers want to be impressed and want to spend their time in good conversation with people whom they'd be comfortable working with and who can do the job.

Do Your Homework

You can find out nearly everything you need to know by doing an Internet search on your government agency; you may also be able to find info on the people who will interview you. Look to see how the organization is ranked on www.bestplacestowork.org. Get to know the mission and the challenges of the organization. Prepare thoughtful questions to ask your interviewers.

Mock Interview Prep

The level of confidence you project is almost as important to your interview style as the answers you give. If you're a nervous wreck when it comes to interviews, don't worry. A little practice goes a long way.

In addition to being prepared by learning the background of your agency and the people who will be interviewing you, mock interviewing is a great way to build up your confidence. Try having a friend who is in HR or who normally conducts interviews (in any sector) do a mock interview with you a few days in advance. Prepare standard answers to questions like the following:

- Why do you want to work with this particular agency? Answer this by being honest and informed about the agency mission and the skills, interests, and objectives you have that can be put to good use at the agency.
- What makes you a good candidate for this position? Answer this by reviewing the requirements for the position as listed in the job announcement or collected through informational interviews or online searching.
- Can you walk me through your resumé and employment history? Answer this by picking up on themes from your past and drawing parallels to what you know about the position for which you are interviewing. Again, review the job announcement!

Top Secret

Have your mock interviewer ask you a few unexpected questions to keep your mind sharp. No interview will ever be scripted out for you, and you want to be prepared for whatever curveballs may come your way.

Before You Go

The worst thing that can happen is to get this far in the process and then have something go wrong that you could have prevented. Here are some tips to make sure you are completely prepared for your interview:

- Identify the actual place you need to be on interview day as best you can (but know that sometimes security access or timing of receipt of information can often derail this type of prep).
- Do a dry-run commute to the interview location (as much as it's logistically possible). Federal agencies often have offices in multiple buildings close together.

- If you can't get to the location in advance, at least use a reliable Internet map tool or estimate your public transit time needs so you have a realistic commuting schedule in mind in advance.
- Give yourself more time than you think you'll need to arrive at the interview. It's always better to be early than just in time or, even worse, late.
- Lay everything out the night before: government-issued ID (for example, your driver's license), directions, extra copies of the resumé you used to apply to this job, attire (see the following section), a list of names of the interviewers (if provided in advance), and any other notes you've made.
- Review your answers to standard questions and practice with a friend or family member.

What to Wear

As with any job interview, you will want to plan your interview wardrobe carefully. If anything, you will want to be more conservatively dressed for a government interview than for other sectors, just to be on the safe side.

For both men and women, you will want to go easy on the perfume or cologne and leave the facial piercings and distracting jewelry at home.

Here are a few more recommendations for those of you who are lost when it comes to interview attire:

Men:

- ❏ Dark or neutral suit
- ❏ Professional closed-toe shoes
- ❏ Long-sleeved, button-down shirt (ironed)
- ❏ Tie
- ❏ Portfolio or briefcase

Women:

- ❏ Dark or neutral skirt suit or pantsuit
- ❏ Professional pumps or flats (closed or peep toe)
- ❏ High-necked shirt or shell
- ❏ Hosiery
- ❏ Purse and/or portfolio and/or briefcase

Again, these suggestions might seem conservative to you, but they still reflect the standard in government unless you are specifically instructed otherwise.

The Fine Print

There's no reason to bring a lot of stuff to your interview. If you bring a purse, briefcase, or portfolio, travel as light as possible and leave anything that's not essential at home. Remember, you'll need to go through a security checkpoint.

During Your Interview

Your government interview is not limited to the formal sit-down. You should go out of your way to be professional and courteous, whether you are greeting the receptionist or security desk professional or shaking the administrator or chief's hand. Extend this behavior even when visiting the restroom or talking casually after the official interview with a staff member who could potentially be a peer or a boss. Assume that you are being evaluated from the time you enter the building to the time you leave.

Keep these do's and don'ts in mind:

- Do make eye contact during the interview.
- Don't fidget or play with your hair.
- Do sit up straight. Good posture conveys professionalism and confidence.
- Don't try to answer a question if you don't know the answer. As always, be honest!

For more tips, check out *The Complete Idiot's Guide to the Perfect Job Interview, Third Edition*, by Marc Dorio (Alpha Books, 2009).

Prepare to Sell Yourself

Interviews are the time to sell yourself and set yourself apart. It can't be stressed enough: hiring managers want to see that you're committed to the agency's public service mission and will come ready to work if you're offered the job.

You should prepare a short speech tailored to the job. The speech should include why you believe in the agency's mission, why you would be perfect for the job based on your specific skills and experiences that relate to the position, and, of course, how grateful you are for the agency's consideration. Some people call this the "elevator pitch" or the "30-second sound bite." Regardless of what you call it, you will likely need to summarize yourself in 30 seconds or so at some point during the interview. It's your concise answer to the question, "Why should I hire you?"

Top Secret

Additional conversations regarding salary, benefits, and other HR matters should be primarily conducted between yourself and the HR professional or recruiter.

Post-Interview Etiquette

Follow up in a way that shows you respect the interviewers' time and the overall hiring process. Thank you notes (handwritten or via e-mail) are a must. If you've met with multiple people during the interview, it's particularly helpful to send a short thank you to everyone who met with you—not just the hiring manager.

If you have been asked to schedule a test or provide any additional information (such as additional references or an official transcript), make sure to do so as soon as possible after the interview unless instructed otherwise. If for some reason your transcripts or anything else is delayed, be sure to contact the persons who interviewed you and let them know.

As we've said, the federal hiring process can be lengthy, so don't be discouraged if you don't hear back right away after the interview. You might even ask during the interview when the hiring manager expects a decision to be made. Two or three weeks after the interview—or after the date you were told that a decision would be made—it is acceptable to call and ask someone in the HR office for an update.

The Least You Need to Know

- There are several ways that government does interviews. Be ready for a one-on-one or panel interview.
- Preparation is key. If you make it all the way to an interview, don't miss out on a job offer simply because you haven't taken the time to do your homework about the job or the organization.
- Interviews are as much about screening people out as they are about finding the right person. Avoid standing out in a negative way; for example, dressing inappropriately, showing up late, or simply being unprepared will leave an impression, but not one that will be helpful to you.

- Follow up with a thank you note (an e-mail message is quick and perfectly acceptable).
- Don't be discouraged if you don't hear back for a couple of weeks; it's normal. It's also fine to follow up with a phone call after two or three weeks have passed.

Part 3

Government Jobs at All Levels

A common fear among jobseekers is that they aren't the right person for a government job: "I'm too young." "I'm too old." "I've worked my whole career in the private sector." Not to worry! We're talking about a workforce of roughly 2 million people in dozens of occupational areas. One of the great things about government work is that there are truly jobs for all ages, backgrounds, and levels of experience.

This part will tell you what opportunities there are for student, entry-level, mid-career, and encore-career jobseekers. This section knows no age limits.

Chapter 12

Student Opportunities in Government

In This Chapter

- Internships as a way into a permanent federal job
- Where to find student opportunities
- Tips for standing out
- Examples of individual internships and programs
- Internship opportunities for students with disabilities
- Learning a specialized skill or trade through an apprenticeship

Calling all students! Student internships (sometimes called student programs) are a great way to get your foot in the door for a future government job. Available for high school, college, and graduate school students, these opportunities give you the chance to learn about the public sector while allowing the government to audition talented individuals (you!) for future jobs.

Tens of thousands of students work for our government each year through internships or temporary employment, and you can, too. It's just a matter of finding those opportunities and contacting the right people at the right time. In this chapter, we'll outline what opportunities exist, how to find them, and how to apply for them.

Getting Your Foot in the Door

There are opportunities for students in virtually every agency and occupational area. Considering there are roughly 2 million federal employees (not counting the military or the Postal Service), the hunt for new employees never ends, and student programs are one way that agencies can find new talent to fill positions. Translation: After you have successfully gotten and completed your internship, you may have an advantage in obtaining a full-time government job. Even if you aren't interested in a permanent government job, student internships are still great experience that you can add to your resumé while serving the American people.

Federal Facts

For most internships, students can simply submit a regular resumé—no KSA essays or other time-consuming applications are required.

Student internships in government are not filled through the same process as other civil service jobs. This doesn't mean that you won't have to compete with other applicants to get in. Rather, it means that agencies don't have to jump through all the hoops and cut through all the red tape that they do to fill full-time, permanent positions. Additionally, most internships do not require an extensive background check, though some positions with a high level of security clearance may (for example, an internship with the Secret Service is definitely going to require a background check). See Chapter 8 for more about background checks and security clearance.

There are essentially two avenues to finding a federal student internship. The first is the Washington, D.C., route. Students apply for internships in the nation's capital and live there for a period of time (summer, fall, spring, a year, and so on).

The second route is finding federal employment close to home or school. This may seem antiquated (read: old school), but a good place to go is the blue pages in your phone book. These are the government pages, and contained in them are the names and contacts of agencies in your area. Don't hesitate to use the contact information to call or e-mail the agency directly to ask whether it is accepting students for internships or short-term employment. Just be sure that when you call you know the agency's mission and reason that you are interested in working there. Also, have your resumé ready to send at a moment's notice. It is often a matter of inquiring at the right place at the right time—and if the time is indeed right, you will want to submit your resumé then and there.

Where to Find Student Internships

The Studentjobs.gov and students.gov websites are online resources to help students find internship and temporary employment opportunities. Agencies post student jobs on Studentjobs.gov just as they post regular jobs on USAJOBS.gov, but the focus is instead on entry-level jobs, temporary jobs, and student internships.

It's a good idea to open an account if you don't already have one. You can follow the MYSTUDENTJOBS link and use the resumé builder to create your online federal resumé. Agencies can then view your resumé and contact information from the site, and you can submit as many applications as you please. You can browse through the job and internship announcements or sign up to have announcements that match your needs e-mailed to you weekly.

Students.gov is full of helpful information on finding internship opportunities, applying for financial aid, and exploring careers.

However, none of these websites serve as a comprehensive database of government student internships. Your best bet is to determine up front which agency (or agencies) you are interested in and go directly to their websites to search for student opportunities (see Appendix A for a list of federal agencies). With a few clicks, you can go to an agency's career page, where you can view current opportunities for both student jobs and internships.

You can also try a multifaceted approach of online research, calling, and e-mailing. For example, let's say you're interested in the Department of Health and Human Services and want to find out what programs are open to students. You can visit hhs.gov and search under "student" or "internship," search on Studentjobs.gov, or call or e-mail the agency's human resources department directly to express your interest and request information.

Another option is to pay a visit to your campus career center. Set up a meeting with a career services representative and express your interest in interning with the federal government. He or she may be able to offer you advice, resources, or even federal contacts. Also speak with targeted faculty and ask whether they have any resources or advice.

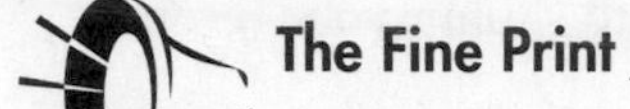

The Fine Print

Internships in D.C. are more competitive than in other locations, and summer D.C. internships are the most competitive.

If you have friends who have participated in a federal internship, ask them about their experience and if they can help you make contacts in government. Be sure to attend career fairs at your university or local community, as these are a couple of places where federal agencies often recruit.

For more advice on utilizing your contacts to get an internship, see Chapter 6.

When to Apply for Internships

If you're looking for a summer internship, you should start searching between November and January to give yourself ample time to complete the application process—and to meet the often early deadlines. This is extremely important because these internships fill up fast. If you wait until spring to apply for a summer internship, it's likely you will miss the boat.

Internships run throughout the year, so if you are applying for the fall, winter, or spring term, always start the application process at least six months in advance of when you want to start your internship. Internships are most competitive in the summer months, since students are typically out of class and searching for work experience. So if you can do a fall, winter, or spring internship, your chances of getting the one you want go up significantly.

Additionally, unpaid internships are typically easier to find and get—at any time of the year. The good news is that the majority of internships in the executive branch of government are paid.

How to Stand Out in the Application Process

Number one, write an excellent resumé (Chapter 9 shows you how). Hiring managers may view hundreds of resumés for a single internship, and yours needs to stand out. Translate your experience, whether it's waitressing or volunteering for a homeless shelter, and turn it into concrete knowledge, skills, and abilities.

You must be able to sell yourself and communicate your experience effectively. List your experiences (extracurricular activities, volunteering, clubs) as actual jobs. Don't exclude these experiences simply because you weren't paid to do them. Employers won't expect you to have a huge amount of work experience, but they do want to see how you have spent your time and what leadership skills you have developed as a student.

Furthermore, they don't just want to see that you flipped burgers and worked as a cashier. Rather, they want to see that you developed leadership, customer service, interpersonal, and business management skills through that job. Highlight the fact that you learned to deal effectively with others, responsibly handled money, followed direction well, and displayed a positive attitude. Just make sure that your references can back this up.

When prepping your resumé and considering how your various experiences relate to the internship you want, ask yourself questions such as:

- What leadership skills have I developed as student body president (or editor of the school newspaper, etc.)?
- How will the skills I acquired on my sports team or club be used at this internship?
- What classes have I taken that have provided me with knowledge that would make me an asset to this particular internship?
- What skills did I gain during my experience volunteering at my local animal shelter (or soup kitchen, women's shelter, etc.)?

Second, having an excellent resumé means *no typos or grammatical errors!* The number-one complaint from HR personnel (read: the people who are most involved in filling these internship positions) is that student applications are chock-full of typos and poor grammar. This shows them that the student is either (a) not detail-oriented, (b) not well-educated, or (c) lazy. Not good things. In short, typos are the quickest way to get your resumé tossed from the pile of eligible applicants for an internship. On the flip side, to avoid typos and poor grammar, follow this time-tested formula:

1. Pay careful attention to every detail as you go.
2. Read over your resumé and application at least twice.
3. Have at least one other person look over your resumé and application, preferably someone who is a whiz with grammar, such as your English-major roommate.

Another way to stand out in the application process is to highlight relevant school coursework and provide a transcript. This will show you have knowledge that will directly impact your ability to do good work for them.

For example, if you are applying for an engineering internship at the Nuclear Regulatory Commission, add a section on your resumé showing that you have taken physics, engineering, computer science, or courses related to the agency and the work you will be performing there. It's also a good idea to list any and all software programs that you have experience with: SPSS, AutoCAD, Dreamweaver—even Facebook.

Often, agencies will see this experience (especially newer software and social networking sites) and feel they can learn from you. This experience will bring value to the agency.

Federal internships are competitive, so prepare for a wait. If you haven't heard back from the agency within a few weeks, be proactive and contact the agency by phone or e-mail to check the status of your application. Polite follow-up allows you to show persistence, and perhaps even impress the person doing the hiring even before an interview.

Student Educational Employment Program

This program makes it possible for students to pursue federal employment while they continue their studies. The program has two subcomponents: the Student Career Experience Program (SCEP) and the Student Temporary Employment Program (STEP).

Be careful when you're searching for these opportunities; they aren't always titled STEP and SCEP in the online postings. Your best bet is to check with an agency (call them or visit their website) to see what type of SCEP, STEP, and other internship opportunities they have available.

Student Career Experience Program (SCEP)

The SCEP is for students who want to gain focused career experience that can help them reach eligibility for non-competitive, permanent employment after the completion of the program—meaning that they are eligible to apply and be hired for a job without having to go through the full application process.

Each year, more than 15,000 students are typically hired under this program, which requires a written agreement between you, your school, and the agency. Your school needs to confirm that you are taking a full-time load and that the program relates to your major. After you have successfully completed the program (640 hours), the hiring agency may decide to hire you as a permanent employee. Out of the 640 hours required for the SCEP, up to 320 can be waived for superior performance—yet another reason to put your best foot forward if you get into this program.

A SCEP may entail a psychology student working at the Department of Education, analyzing the effectiveness of K-12 programs nationwide, or an engineering student working on utilizing AutoCad and developing plans for a new green building project. As long as the experience supplements what a student is learning in his or her academic studies, it is considered "directly related."

Most positions in the SCEP are paid, but whether or not the student will receive pay varies by hiring agency. Students are also eligible to receive full benefits, including health and life insurance (bonus!)

Top Secret

You should go after a SCEP opportunity if at all possible. SCEP is the most effective way for students to get into government service in that it offers a direct route to future federal employment.

Student Temporary Employment Program (STEP)

STEP is somewhat more flexible than SCEP in that employment does not have to be related to your field of study in school. This program is essentially a paid federal internship. Opportunities are available throughout the year, part- or full-time.

In any given year, well over 40,000 students are given jobs under STEP, which allows hiring managers to employ students without a formal agreement with their school, and without having to provide a specific type of work experience. To be clear, STEP experience can be directly related to the student's major, but it does not have to be.

Students in the STEP are not eligible for non-competitive hire upon completion of the program and must go through the regular hiring process (this is why we recommend you try for SCEP if you are interested in a full-time job with government after graduation). However, up to 320 hours of STEP experience can be converted to SCEP hours if the experience is related to the student's major. There is no guarantee that the hiring agency will convert hours, but if the student (you!) makes a great impression and does an exceptional job, it is a possibility.

Agencies are not required to post STEP openings on USAJOBS.gov, so check with the agency in which you want to work to see whether it participates in the program.

Eligibility

The STEP is open to students at all levels, but they must be enrolled at least half-time in classes during the program. The SCEP is open only to undergraduate and graduate students of at least 16 years of age. Current U.S. citizenship is required for both programs. Interested students must contact their school's career center, guidance office, faculty members, or federal agency of interest.

Check with your school to ask about its minimum GPA requirements, because these requirements tend to vary from school to school. Based on the agency of application, students may also have to pass a background test. The Office of Personnel Management has additional information on the STEP and SCEP programs on its website, opm.gov.

Other Examples of Student Opportunities

Each agency has its own way of incorporating student programs and internships into its work. In the following sections we give you a few examples, but your best bet will be to contact your chosen agency or agencies and ask where you can find more information on student programs.

Central Intelligence Agency (CIA) Intern Program

The CIA has many student opportunities—part-time programs, undergraduate and graduate internships, and scholarship programs. Students' assignments are designed to be meaningful and challenging. The CIA gives students the opportunity to develop themselves professionally while preparing for permanent federal employment. Eligibility requirements vary based on the program, but all applicants must be a U.S. citizen and have at least a 3.0 GPA. Applicants who have lived or worked abroad, speak multiple languages, or have previous military experience are preferred. Applicants must have exemplary writing and interpersonal skills and have a strong interest in foreign affairs. Successful completion of a background investigation is required. All CIA student opportunities are located in the D.C. area. To view a complete list of student opportunities and apply, visit cia.gov and follow the "careers" link to "student opportunities."

Top Secret

It's true: you can get your foot in the door to a full-time job through your government internship, but there is no guarantee that you will get a job offer at the end of your internship. During your internship, focus on impressing your supervisor and colleagues with your good work, great attitude, and unfailing work ethic.

Washington Internships for Native Students (WINS)

This program is an eight-week summer internship for American Indian, Alaska Native, and Native Hawaiian students. The federal agency will cover the intern's transportation, housing, and tuition costs, and will even provide a $200 weekly stipend for his or her personal expenses. The application process has several steps, and students must submit their application form, essay, transcripts, letter of recommendation, recent photograph, and letter of support from their tribal council. Interns will take the Washington Leadership Seminar in Tribal Issues and Native Studies and will receive six credit hours. As a part of the program itself, the intern must write and submit a funding proposal for a project he or she plans to carry out within the candidate's respective community. To learn more and apply, visit www1.american.edu/wins.

Minority Leaders Fellowship Program

This program enables students to live and work in Washington, D.C., over the summer, spring, or fall terms. Students, who must be African American, Asian American, Hispanic American, Native American, or Pacific Islander, will receive funding for housing and a $125 weekly stipend. Minority students must be U.S. citizens currently pursuing their Associate's, or Bachelor's degree to be eligible. Ideal candidates will have a demonstrated commitment to campus and community leadership. The application process includes the official application, which must be signed by the president of the applicant's university; two letters of recommendation; three personal statements; and a transcript. This program requires that the student receive academic credit for the internship, which must be approved by the applicant's college or university. Interested applicants should visit the Washington Center website at twc.edu to fill out the application form and view additional information.

Secret Service Volunteer Program

The Secret Service Volunteer Program offers academic credit and is designed for current high school or undergraduate students with at least a 2.5 GPA. Because the majority of assignments are clerical in nature, including tasks such as filing, scanning, record keeping, and running errands, the Secret Service does not require previous work experience. Students must work at least 12 hours a week for at least one semester and can work in Washington, D.C., or in a Secret Service field office in various locations across the United States.

This program allows students to explore the Secret Service as a career option, receive academic credit, and gain work experience that will be useful for their future careers. Because of the Secret Service's high security level, volunteers must pass a Top Secret clearance background examination. To apply, you will need to submit your resumé and an application form. Visit secretservice.gov and follow the "employment" tab to "student volunteer service." From there, you can access the application form posted on the Office of Personnel Management's website. If you are outside of Washington, D.C., submit your resumé and application form to the Secret Service location nearest you.

National Endowment for the Arts (NEA)

NEA offers volunteer internship opportunities for undergraduate and graduate students throughout the year. Students will gain experience with the federal grant process and oversee arts activities nationwide. NEA also offers interns many networking opportunities and the chance to prepare for a career in public service.

Interested applicants must submit a cover letter and, if they desire, a transcript, letter of recommendation, and list of references to the NEA no later than one month before they would like to begin volunteering. For more information, visit arts.endow.gov/about/Jobs/Internships.html.

Federal Bureau of Investigation (FBI)

The FBI offers summer volunteer internships in dozens of locations across the United States, including New York, Boston, Houston, Los Angeles, and Seattle. The internship program at the FBI headquarters in Washington, D.C., offers high school, undergraduate, and graduate students a chance to work with experienced FBI agents. Interns are given increasing responsibilities during their 10-week program and experience what it feels like to be a part of the bureau. Students from any degree program are welcome to apply.

Interested applicants must have at least a 3.0 GPA, be a current student, and pass a background check. The application includes a resumé, transcript, two letters of recommendation, an essay, a photograph, and the completion of several FBI forms. To download the forms and submit your application, visit fbijobs.gov and follow the link to "internship programs."

Department of Justice (DOJ)

The DOJ offers first-, second- and third-year law students the opportunity to take part in various substantive internship opportunities throughout the year. Students can focus on civil rights, criminal justice, the environment, drug enforcement, and more. The application requirements and process vary depending on the program. Visit the usdoj.gov website and search under "volunteer legal intern" for more information and to apply.

Internships for Students with Disabilities

The Workforce Recruitment Program (WRP) is a resource for government agencies and private businesses to recruit exceptional undergraduate, graduate, and law students with disabilities into temporary and permanent employment. Eligible students must be currently enrolled full-time, have a disability, and be a U.S. citizen.

The way the program works is this: Interested students contact their college or university's disability or career services representative and ask them to contact a WRP representative. A WRP representative will schedule a visit to the student's campus and conduct an interview. From this interview, the representative will compile the student's information (and any comments the representative would like to make) and post it on the WRP database for the use of federal and private employers. Employers can then use this information to contact the student through their university to offer internship and job opportunities based on the student's area of study, work experience, geographic location, and interests. It's up to the employer to initiate contact or offer employment. Pay, position, and duration will vary based on the hiring agency or business.

The WRP does not accept calls or questions from individual students, so if you are interested and eligible, you must go through a university representative to establish a connection. For more information, visit wrp.gov.

Other Avenues to Government Internships

In addition to direct application opportunities for student internships, there are at least two programs that aim to match up student interns with federal agencies. These programs are *not* run by the government, but do seek to give outstanding students the opportunity to work in government.

Hispanic Association of Colleges and Universities (HACU)

HACU consists of hundreds of colleges and universities that actively promote the success of Hispanic students in higher education. The Hispanic population has become our nation's largest and fastest-growing minority group, with two thirds of Hispanic students pursuing higher education in the United States. HACU provides Hispanic students with internship, study abroad, and career development opportunities.

A HACU representative matches the student's degree with a specific agency, but students are not able to choose the agency in which they would like to work. However, the HACU representative works with the school to ensure that the student's interests are matched and that the experience is beneficial to that student.

Applications are reviewed and finalists are notified that they have been chosen for an interview. Interns can work in Washington, D.C., or various locations throughout the nation. Visit hacu.net for a complete list of programs and participating colleges and universities. Scholarships are available to students in need. Interested applicants must apply online.

The Washington Center for Internships and Academic Affairs

The Washington Center is an independent, nonprofit organization that partners with colleges and universities to match outstanding students with Washington, D.C., internships. These internships provide students with extraordinary work experience that may assist them in their future career or academic endeavors. Students work full-time and earn college credit. Students are placed year-round in federal agencies, embassies, international, or nonprofit organizations—even in congressional offices and the White House.

The Washington Center provides the full package: program placement, housing arrangements, academic credit, an academic course, lecture series, tours, and more.

Students from all majors and backgrounds are eligible. Interested students must be pursuing their undergraduate or graduate degree and have at least a 2.75 GPA. Before beginning the application process, students need to gain approval from their Washington Center campus liaison ensuring that the student will receive academic credit. If you are unsure if your university has a designated liaison, you can contact the Washington Center at info@twc.edu, or call (800) 486-8921. If your school does not have a liaison, you are still eligible to apply, but you must find a faculty sponsor who can confirm that you will receive college credit.

The Fine Print

There are fees associated with the Washington Center for Internships and Academic Affairs. These fees help cover, among other expenses, housing. Spring 2010 fees were roughly $11,000. If this sounds out of your league, don't fret; financial aid is available.

Post-Internship Program

The Federal Service Student Ambassadors program gives students the opportunity to lead outreach efforts on their college campus *after* the completion of a federal internship. This is a great opportunity for students who want to gain professional experience and use that experience to lead outreach efforts to their peers, informing them of federal internship and job opportunities.

Students will take part in a Washington, D.C., training session; have regular updates with faculty and D.C. staff; and receive a stipend for their service. Students are responsible for planning and implementing events on their college campuses, writing and submitting pieces for their college newspaper or alumni magazine, working roughly seven hours per week, and completing other relational and outreach efforts.

Students with leadership experience and a demonstrated commitment to public service will stand out in the application process. To be eligible, students must be accepted into a federal internship and currently pursuing their degree. To fill out an application form, visit makingthedifference.org and follow the link to "student opportunities."

Apprenticeships

The Registered Apprenticeship program is headquartered in Washington, D.C., but is implemented nationwide. Apprenticeships allow students to learn a specialized skill or trade in preparation for a full-time career. The average apprenticeship program is four years long but can range anywhere from one to six years.

Some of the roughly 1,000 occupations offering apprenticeships include carpenter, chef, dental assistant, electrician, and truck driver. Apprenticeships come with a pool of bonuses, including career training, a full-time career (upon completion of the program), college credit, certification, and a paycheck.

If you're interested in the field of health care, for example, a registered apprenticeship will match you with a mentor who will guide you through a planned technical program. The program content and length will vary based on the occupation you choose. In the field of health care alone, you can become a certified nursing assistant, medical laboratory technician, optician, paramedic, or pharmacy assistant through a registered apprenticeship.

Eligible students must be at least 16 years old, and for some apprenticeships you will need to be 18 years old. Depending on the program or employer, application materials may include proof of age, level of education, assessment of physical capability, interviews, transcripts, and a record of previous work experience. Visit the Office of Apprenticeship website for a complete list of occupations offering apprenticeship programs, as well as an analysis of occupational trends in the industry.

Interested applicants should visit the Department of Labor's career site at careervoyages.gov and follow the "apprenticeship" link. This will allow you to enter your state and zip code and search for apprenticeship representatives in your area. You can call or e-mail your representative to find out what current opportunities are available and how you can apply.

The Least You Need to Know

- Getting a full-time federal job is not easy. Interning with a government agency is a great way to get your foot in the door.
- Since there is no central database for all student opportunities, you will want to go through several channels, including Studentjobs.gov, students.gov, individual agency websites, and your phone book's blue pages. You will also want to call your chosen agency's human resources department.
- A lot of young people don't take the time to make their resumés, applications, and other materials perfect. Get ahead of the competition simply by being detail-oriented.
- There are internships for all interests. Do your homework and go after what you want!

- Impress your employer with your dedication, resourcefulness, and ability to do an excellent job. This is one sure way to increase the odds that you will be asked back or even be offered a permanent job.
- Apprenticeships, which are generally for blue-collar positions, are a great way for young people to learn a specialized skill or trade.

Chapter 13

Entry-Level Jobs: Getting In

In This Chapter

- Entry-level jobs in government
- Who might hire you
- How your college major can work for you
- What programs are designed to help you get in
- How to make your experience count

It's often said that the hardest part of getting a government job is getting your foot in the door. However, with tens of thousands of federal employees retiring or leaving government over the next few years, there is a great need for replacements. To fill this gap, many people will move up within government and new people will be brought in from outside government. In particular, there is and will continue to be a great need for entry-level hires in all areas of government.

Whether you are fresh out of school or thinking about a career change, the federal government may have a great entry-level job for you. As is the case with most government jobs, competition for entry-level positions can be fierce. In this chapter, we will explain which entry-level jobs are available in government, how well they pay, where they are, and how to get them.

Defining Entry-Level

Entry-level typically refers to jobs that do not require a great amount of experience. Some entry-level positions are considered "trainee" jobs in which new hires learn the details of the job from more experienced colleagues or supervisors or through classroom or job training.

As you learned in Chapter 4, you are eligible for many of the lower GS levels if you have at least a high school diploma. Most jobs from the GS-1 to GS-4 levels are clerical and administrative support positions.

To qualify at the GS-5 level, you must have completed four years of undergraduate education at an accredited college or university or possess a combination of education and relevant experience, depending on the job. A Bachelor's degree does not have to be fully completed as long as you have four years of higher education. As a rule of thumb, applicants with a Bachelor's degree will qualify for many jobs at the GS-5 level and a combination of education and experience can be substituted for a Bachelor's degree. Also, both paid jobs and volunteer work can substitute for the experience needed.

Remember that education alone may not be enough to qualify for some positions. General and specialized experiences are required in differing amounts based on the job. Specialized experience pertains directly to the job that you are seeking. The good news is that for many entry-level jobs, education alone may qualify you. Of course, if you have both education and relevant experience, that can give you an advantage over the competition.

There are several ways to start at the GS-7 level. One is to have completed at least one year of graduate education. Another way is to meet the requirements for Superior Academic Achievement (graduating in the upper third of your class, maintaining a 3.0 overall GPA and a 3.5 GPA in your major, or sustaining membership in an approved national scholastic honor society). The third way to start at the GS-7 level is with a combination of education and experience. One year of specialized experience can make you eligible for consideration at the GS-7 level, as long as this experience relates directly to the job you want.

Federal Facts

Promotions and raises in the government are generally more rapid than in the private sector, especially during the first three to five years.

Who Wants to Hire You?

Federal agencies are hiring entry-level employees all the time, from Cabinet-level agencies such as the Department of Energy (which has more than 15,000 employees) to small independent agencies such as the National Council on Disability (which has 10 employees) to the Department of Army (which has over 300,000 civilian positions). Who wants to hire you is a matter of where the jobs are, what the agency's mission is, and how your skills and experience fit into fulfilling that mission.

Region

Location and concentration of agencies play important roles in the number of entry-level jobs available to you. States and districts with more federal agencies and employees—California, Texas, the District of Columbia, Virginia, and New York—will naturally have the most jobs.

Agency Size

The Department of Defense (DOD) and the Department of Veterans Affairs (VA) currently employ the largest number of entry-level employees, followed by the Department of Homeland Security and the Department of the Treasury. It is no coincidence that the DOD and VA are also the largest federal agencies. Based on size alone, they will have the most entry-level job openings at any given time.

Occupational Areas

It's also easier to land an entry-level job at an agency where your skills are in demand. *Mission-critical jobs* must be filled in order for the agency's overall mission to be met. These jobs differ, though, and one agency's mission-critical job may not be critical to the next.

For example, pharmacologists at the Food and Drug Administration are critical to reaching the agency's mission of ensuring the safety and efficacy of drugs and medical supplies. Conversely, pharmacology would not be a mission-critical job at the Federal Trade Commission.

def•i•ni•tion

Mission-critical jobs are positions that must be filled for the agency to meet its obligations to the American people. These positions vary based on the agency's mission and workforce needs at any given time.

The best way to get a sense of where you can find mission-critical jobs is by examining the missions of different government agencies to see what skills are needed to meet each mission. The Partnership for Public Service also periodically publishes a *Where the Jobs Are* report (www.wherethejobsare.org) that shares the projected hiring needs of the largest federal departments and agencies. For example, the report released in September 2009 calculated more than 270,000 mission critical jobs that agencies will need to fill over a three-year period.

For example, the CIA needs information technology (IT) specialists to operate and protect computer networks, and the Department of Agriculture needs food safety workers to ensure consumer well-being. An occupational shortage of these skills would prevent these agency missions from being met. If your background or major doesn't fit directly into an agency's mission, don't fret; your skills are likely needed elsewhere in government.

Government Jobs by College Major

Regardless of what you study in college, you can find your niche in government, which has a job related to every major from economics to English literature to international relations. To gain a better idea of how your major translates to specific positions within the federal government, USAJOBS.gov has compiled a list of federal jobs by college major.

For example, a business degree is good preparation for work as a budget analyst, internal revenue officer, trade and contract specialist, and more. A major in chemistry prepares a jobseeker for the work performed by chemical engineers, consumer safety officers, and toxicologists—all jobs within the federal government. A major in journalism prepares a jobseeker for the work performed by public affairs specialists, market reporters, and technical writers.

If you are straight out of school, you may find yourself unfamiliar with many job titles and descriptions that are common to those already in the job market; this list will give you a sense of what kind of job you should go for based on your specific educational background.

Not all jobs in the federal government require a specific major and many jobs are open to all majors, as long as you have the right skills and experience for the job. Environmental protection specialists, civil rights analysts, and general investigators are just a few of the many positions that are open to all majors.

Top Secret

The Making the Difference website lists agencies that are hiring the most employees from your major or background. Check out www.makingthedifference.org/federalcareers/.

Many recent graduates don't realize that a college major is not always a clear-cut path to a specific career. Graduates with a biology degree may end up working in human resources, and those with a psychology degree may become contract specialists. Many people start their first job in a position or field unrelated to their college degree. After several years in government, you may decide to stay in that field and pursue a career within it or you may change your career path after working in a position related to your degree.

As a rule of thumb, don't limit yourself to one type of position within government based on your college major. Try to explore a range of jobs based on your skills and interests. This will open you up to building a new skill set and increase your options and job prospects.

Backgrounds and Majors That Are Most in Demand

The hiring needs of the federal government change over time. As communication becomes increasingly computer based, it's crucial that the federal government recruit workers that are proficient in computer technology. As the nation shifts to meet its post-9/11 security requirements, the Department of Homeland Security has a great demand for law enforcement workers and such.

Information technology, mathematics, science, health, and education positions can be challenging to fill, as many individuals holding these degrees opt for careers in the private sector. Health care and computer-related occupations are among the fastest growing, and workers in these fields will find their skills in increasingly high demand.

Entry-Level Programs

In an effort to attract a new generation of talented entry-level employees—and meet the growing needs of our nation and our world—the government has developed several programs for those seeking federal government employment for the first time. Note that these programs are in addition to all of the individual entry-level jobs offered across the board at government agencies.

Top Secret

Getting an initial job in the federal government is much more difficult than switching jobs or moving into different agencies once you are in government.

Presidential Management Fellowship (PMF)

The PMF program is designed to build the next generation of government leaders. The program consists of roughly 80 agencies that recruit outstanding students pursuing their graduate, doctorate, or law degree in any academic discipline. Of the thousands of PMF applicants, only about 400 are accepted each year.

This challenging fellowship lasts for two years, and most of the fellows are then converted to permanent jobs. Fellows typically receive 160 hours of official classroom-oriented training and may be able to rotate every few months to gain experience in a variety of work environments. Public administration, foreign policy, health care, and criminal justice are among the national and international assignments given to PMFs.

To be considered for this program, you must be nominated by your school's dean, chairperson, or academic program director (otherwise known as the nomination official). Check with your dean's office or career center to find the name of the designated nomination official and your university's nomination deadline date. The official will review your accomplishments, capacity for leadership, demonstrated commitment to policy, and ability to lead and manage projects.

As a PMF, you will be on the GS-9 level and gain eligibility throughout the program for promotion to a higher level. After the first year, you will be eligible for a move up to the GS-11 level, and after the second year, the GS-12 level. There is also the potential for accelerated promotions.

To begin the application process, create a USAJOBS account and build your online resumé (see Chapter 9), print the PMF Nomination Form (which can be downloaded from the Office of Personnel Management [OPM] website, www.opm.gov), complete the online questionnaire, and submit any supporting documentation that is asked of you.

Federal Facts

More than 90 percent of all PMFs are offered permanent positions after completing the PMF program.

Federal Career Intern Program (FCIP)

Don't let the word "intern" fool you. The FCIP program essentially provides a chance for federal managers to do targeted recruiting for permanent jobs.

The Federal Career Intern Program recruits outstanding entry-level candidates for an initial two-year appointment. At the end of two years, federal agencies have the opportunity to offer permanent jobs to successful participants. In 2007, for example, more than 17,000 individuals were hired under this program. People hired under the FCIP generally start out at the GS-7 or GS-9 level and become eligible for promotion to the GS-12 level after two years.

FCIP opportunities are available everywhere from the General Services Administration in Kansas City to the Department of Veterans Affairs in Seattle. Agencies also routinely recruit on college campuses and at career fairs, so check with your university's career services office for information about current opportunities.

Here are some examples of FCIP opportunities:

- **Department of Veterans Affairs.** Called the Technical Career Field (TCF) program, this two-year opportunity allows entry-level employees to advance their technical skills in positions such as biomedical engineer, contract specialist, human resources manager, and supply processing specialist. This program is much like an apprenticeship and is heavily focused on providing the individual with technical rather than general career experience. Interns will learn from experienced specialists (known as preceptors), especially during the second year of training.

  If you are interested in viewing a full list of career fields and applying for this program, you must contact your local Veteran's Affairs Human Resources Department. Placement is filled locally, and you can locate contact information on the website, www.va.gov, or in the blue pages of your phone book. If you are required to relocate for your final placement within the agency, the Department of Veterans Affairs will cover your moving costs.

- **Department of Energy.** The Department of Energy's Corporate Career Intern Program is designed to recruit entry-level professionals to a range of career fields, including engineering, business administration, computer science, physical and social sciences, and public policy. Interns will create their own Individual Development Plan and take part in various tasks and responsibilities through the two-year program in preparation for non-competitive, permanent placement within the agency.

  The Department of Energy utilizes USAJOBS.gov and Studentjobs.gov to post job announcements. You can create or log on to your account, submit a resumé, and complete the questionnaire required for your application. You can apply in advance for this program and monitor the status of your application on USAJOBS.gov or Studentjobs.gov.

The Fine Print

The FCIP is being reviewed by the government and may change, so before diving into the application process, read up on any changes that may have been made since the publication of this book.

- **General Services Administration (GSA).** GSA's Federal Career Internship Program is used to fill many GS-5 though GS-9 positions for two to three years. There are positions available in information systems, finance, public building service, and more. Once again, interns work with the agency to develop their own Individual Development Plan, so the overall experience varies from intern to intern. Rotation to other positions or offices is encouraged, and the goal is to provide the intern with a wide range of career experiences.

To learn about current FCIP opportunities, call or e-mail the human resources department at GSA or find state and local contact information on the GSA website (see Appendix B). You can also search the GSA jobs page at gsa.gov.

AmeriCorps VISTA

Run by the Corporation for National and Community Service, AmeriCorps provides a platform for thousands of Americans to affect change in communities across the country. The programs aim to meet vital community needs in education, public safety, health, and the environment.

There are four different AmeriCorps programs: AmeriCorps VISTA, State, National, and National Civilian Community Corps. Out of these four programs, only participants in AmeriCorps VISTA are given special hiring status, meaning that they are eligible for non-competitive hiring. This gives them a leg up in the application process.

AmeriCorps VISTA volunteers are paid a nominal stipend and serve low-income communities with the ultimate goal of reducing poverty. The program, which lasts one year, is a great way to gain leadership and professional skills for Americans who have either (a) graduated college or (b) have a few years of work experience. According to the AmeriCorps website (www.americorps.gov), this might be a good fit for you if you are patient, an organizer, and a self-starter.

On USAJOBS.gov, AmeriCorps VISTA volunteer alumni can apply for additional jobs that are not available to the general public, although you should know that AmeriCorps VISTA participants are not *guaranteed* federal employment after their service.

Peace Corps

Many former Peace Corps volunteers have gone on to prestigious positions in government, nonprofits, and the private sector. This program is a great opportunity for entry-level jobseekers who would like to travel, give back to the community, and build leadership skills. Volunteers serve a two-year term, at the end of which they have one year of non-competitive eligibility for federal employment. Once again, this makes it possible to be hired without having to compete with other job applicants for the same position. See further information about Peace Corps in Chapter 3.

Peace Corps and AmeriCorps VISTA service also counts as retirement credit for federal employees. In a nutshell, these programs are a great opportunity to develop professionally, receive eligibility for non-competitive hiring, and invest in your career future.

Public vs. Private Sector

Finding and applying for entry-level federal jobs requires a higher level of personal effort than in the public sector. Blame it on a lack of centralized information and active recruitment, but if you want the job, you are going to have to dig a little deeper to put in additional time and effort.

Entry-level jobs in the private sector are much more visible; you have no doubt seen tons of private-sector job postings or perhaps seen recruiters from various companies on your campus. On the other hand, federal agencies may not have been on your radar, since many agencies have somewhat limited resources for launching mass recruiting campaigns.

Not Just for Recent Grads

Not fresh off a college campus? No problem. Age is not a factor in the filling of government positions, whether entry or higher level. In fact, experience trumps a recent graduation date or significant university prestige. So take heart if you have the experience but lack the twenty-something status. Those who have been laid off or are changing careers are valuable to the federal workforce. In this case, highlighting relevant experience is the key to landing the job. In fact, you will be one step ahead of your younger counterparts just by having experience.

The bigger question is: if you are coming from the private sector and have several years of experience, are you willing to take the pay and lower-level status associated with entry-level positions? If the answer is yes, then definitely apply. Once you get in, you have an open door to advancement within the federal government. Competitive benefits, leadership opportunities, and secure prospects for future earnings are also in store.

You also will have an option to move to a different job within your agency or even across agencies. As you continue to work within the federal government, you can build your salary, vacation days, seniority, and retirement savings. To sum it up, the federal government is a reliable source of entry-level jobs for enthusiastic and hard-working people of all ages and backgrounds.

The Least You Need to Know

- Entry-level talent is needed in all occupations across government.
- All majors and backgrounds are useful in the federal government.
- As a rule of thumb, larger agencies have more positions to fill.
- Entry-level jobs are for every age. In other words, the government does not discriminate.

Chapter 14

Mid-Career Moves and Encore Careers in Government

In This Chapter

- Deciding whether to change careers or return to the workforce
- Mid-career moves into government
- Revising your resumé to become more "federal-friendly"
- Considerations for Senior Executive Service (SES) positions
- A career after a career
- Finding the right fit for your experience

You might be asking, "What if I'm interested in government, but I already have years of experience in another sector, or perhaps a lifetime of valuable experience?" If you are one of these workers and are inspired to make a difference with a switch to government, we've got good news: Whatever your skill set, whatever your age, and whatever your motivation, the government wants and needs you.

A move to government work is often considered a move toward stability, improved work/life balance, and challenging professional opportunities—all at the same time. Whether you seek out the same position in the federal government that you held in another sector (e.g., accountant, biologist, executive assistant) or you seek to chart a totally new direction, there are exciting opportunities available.

Making a transition to federal government during the middle of your career can seem scary for some people. Many worry that they will actually be discriminated against because of their age. For others, the enormity of government may seem a bit daunting. We're here to quell your fears and let you know the lay of the land.

Your big questions will probably be the following: "Where can I work? What kind of work will I be doing? How do I get in?" In this chapter, we provide specific guidance if you're a seasoned professional in the private sector who is seeking interesting and challenging work using your transferable skills or if you are a retiree who wants to return to the workforce. You've come to the right place!

Getting Started

You might have heard this before, but it can't be said enough: Start your government job search as early as possible. You should know from reading earlier chapters in this book that it generally takes longer to transition into government than to, say, a private-sector job.

If actually applying for a federal job is still off in the distant future for you, make sure you plan accordingly. You don't want to have an unnecessary gap in your work experience or income stream or get avoidably bogged down in a security clearance process if, for example, you have lots of international contacts or a longer history to be investigated.

> **The Fine Print**
>
> Be prepared for a wait after you apply for government jobs. Although some people get hired into government in a relatively short amount of time, for other applicants it could take more than a year.

Deciding on Your Next Career Move

Changing careers or returning to the workforce after you have retired or left a job for other reasons is a big decision. Part of getting a federal job is getting mentally prepared for some potentially significant changes in your status.

You might have to consider changing locations; learning the ropes from someone with less experience than you but who's already been a federal worker for a while; or even taking a pay cut. The key word here is "might," because these types of changes aren't givens. You also might take on new challenges or work directly on exciting projects, get a pay increase, or gain amazing new employee benefits for you and your family. The key is to keep an open mind and be willing to ask lots of people questions so you can be as informed as possible about this personal change.

Research (in all its many forms) is very important for you so that your move is as personally rewarding as possible. This includes networking, web research, and, in particular, understanding career paths of government professions by contacting a human resources representative at the agency or agencies in which you have an interest in working (see Appendix A).

Looking for Mid-Career Opportunities

The term *mid-career* actually covers many different types of jobs at all grade levels. For many people, mid-career government positions will be those listed as GS-12 to GS-15 (see Chapter 4 for more information on the GS pay scale). However, if you are switching career fields or have spent 20 years in a lower-level job, you may only qualify for a GS-5 or GS-7 (or lower) grade level.

Depending on where the position is located in the country and what type of occupation you're seeking, these GS levels will fluctuate, so be sure to read the individual job descriptions to get a feel for the duties and required skills.

Top Secret

Some experienced candidates are willing to start at lower grade levels to get in the door or because they are willing to switch career fields. So you may want to take a look at all possibilities before you decide where to apply. There are typically more openings at the lower grade levels. At the higher grade levels, however, fewer applicants qualify and the competition may be a little less intense.

Remember, mid-level positions listed as "status" are only open to current or former federal employees. If you find the job of your dreams but it is listed as "status," the trick is to find a similar job posting on USAJOBS.gov that is open to "all sources" or "the public." Often the positions are listed multiple times, especially at the mid-range levels.

Also, keep an eye out for job postings that indicate the agency is using any type of special hiring authority that might allow hiring of experienced professionals outside of the usual competitive process.

Resources you will want to check out include *Where the Jobs Are* (www.wherethejobsare.org) for location and skills research, as well as agency websites.

Keeping Your Current Career Trajectory in Government

If you are looking to continue following a career path within government similar to your current or prior experience in another sector, your marketability in government will be enhanced.

Interesting positions might be listed at GS levels below what you feel you are qualified for given your expertise. When this is the case, keep an eye out for *career ladder positions* that might be advertised at multiple levels (for example, a GS-12, GS-13, or GS-14 position) and you might end up being considered for higher GS levels within that career ladder.

> **def•i•ni•tion**
>
> **Career ladder positions** are those that let you come into the government at one GS level and then move up to higher GS levels while staying in the same position (with no additional competition required for a promotion).

As a reminder, make sure you spend time researching and considering the pros and cons of a lateral move. It may be a way to get your foot in the door and then prove yourself as you work to make a difference on behalf of the American people.

How to Translate Your Resumé

You might ask whether your corporate resumé (after 35 years with, say, IBM) is ready for prime time with the federal application process. In two words: probably not. A resumé is an important component of the job application process, but you will need to translate your corporate experience into language relevant for federal jobs you are seeking. Federal human resource office staff and hiring managers must be able to readily compare your prior work experience to the qualifications required for their federal jobs. In other words, you will need to revamp your resumé to become more "federal-friendly."

For starters, get rid of acronyms and "corporate-speak" terms that won't be understood by federal officials (more on this a bit later in the chapter). Next, don't assume that "shorter is better" in terms of explaining your work experience and the roles and responsibilities listed in your resumé. For example, if your last position was as a corporate "Global Development Manager," think about how that experience could be described in terms more often used by federal agencies. Did you, for example, determine technology investments? Did you manage supplier or contractor performance? Did you determine strategies that impacted key business strategies in areas such as marketing of services or communications with customers?

This expanded approach gives you an extra chance to draw attention to your strengths and address the specific skills the agency is seeking. Be sure to describe not just your roles and responsibilities, but the result or outcome that was achieved.

Take a look at some examples:

- Instead of saying, "managed key procurements," elaborate by saying, "put in place contract performance criteria and evaluation measures, monitored contract performance to ensure that terms and conditions were met, and took actions to ensure timely delivery of products and services."
- Instead of saying, "I implemented IT security measures," elaborate by saying, "I developed operating systems featuring information technology network security compliance, certification, accreditation, and risk management components, as well as procedures for ensuring overall effective security governance and regulatory compliance."
- Instead of saying, "I am an accomplished project manager," elaborate by saying, "I utilized the full range of my project management skills, including scheduling, forecasting, determining program objectives, developing project performance measures, managing resources, and setting specific work goals and time frames for subordinate employees and operating units."

Top Secret

Unlike most corporate practices, there is no need to strive for a *minimum* number of pages for your resumé. Take all the space needed (within reason) to fully describe your experience through words that will make sense to the federal reviewer, who may be unfamiliar with the corporate world or private sector practices.

Don't forget to focus on accomplishments and emphasize the audience or beneficiaries of your work. For example, don't just say that you "provided regular reporting using a Microsoft Access database at the Jones Company." Instead, provide specifics: "provided weekly dashboard updates to senior management using reports pulled from a customized Access database on project elements, including earned value, schedule and monetary risks, that led to preemptive detection of risks which allowed project completion three weeks ahead of schedule and overall cost savings of 15 percent under the original estimate."

How Do My Skills Transfer?

You might be surprised to find that your current profession or skills will translate directly to a federal agency. The best tip we can give you is to think of your experience in terms of how relevant it is to the job you are applying for in the federal government.

You will need to decode both your current non-federal resumé and the federal speak in the job announcement. You can do this by summarizing how common skills and experiences link to the specific type of federal job in the announcement.

Lost in Translation: No Acronyms

Avoid the use of acronyms (unless they are federal acronyms) since federal reviewers will likely have no clue about the program, duties, or results you are describing if you are coming from a specific corporate culture or non-government background.

Even if an acronym would be commonplace to a potential hiring manager, remember that the first line of review for your resumé is generally a human resources professional who does not have deep knowledge about your specific line of work. If it is absolutely imperative to include an acronym, you *must* spell it out the first time—no exceptions. Don't let your hard-earned experience outside of government get lost in translation as you communicate with hiring managers. For example:

- Instead of using the acronym P&L, spell out "profit and loss."
- Instead of using the acronym CHQ, spell out "corporate headquarters."

Networking and Your Industry

You don't have to make the full resumé translation just using your own vocabulary. Use your networking channels (see Chapter 6) and additional web searches to find ways to say the same things that will be familiar to federal officials reviewing your application. Look closely at the job announcement for the position you are applying for and specifically use relevant phrasing or terminology as you build your resumé.

More experience means you will likely have a larger network to start with when you begin your job search. Dust off those business cards from past meetings, and remember what we said in Chapter 6: it's not necessarily who you know, but who *they* know. Here are a few other networking tips to consider:

- Network with as many seasoned contractors and/or government employees as you can to find out about jobs in your field.
- Identify key officials within agencies where you are interested in working and ask them if they would be willing to grant you an "informational interview" so you can find out more about the job outlook and key needs of their organizations.

The Senior Executive Service (SES)

In federal government, higher-level managerial jobs are in the Senior Executive Service (SES). This special group of leaders was established by Congress in 1978. Around 10 percent of the approximately 7,000 SES positions are politically appointed, but the rest are not. We'll focus on the ones that aren't for political appointees. As might be expected, the competition for these jobs is very high, but if you have been a successful executive in the private sector, one of these jobs might be just right for you.

So, what are these jobs and how are they different? Most of the SES jobs are in general management and are responsible for leading major components of an agency. They may be located in Washington, D.C., or in regional offices across the country. In addition to SES positions, some agencies have other high-level jobs listed as Senior Level (SL) or Senior Scientific and Professional (ST).

Federal Facts

Private-sector equivalents of SES jobs include positions such as chief financial officers, human resource directors, or directors of research or policy.

The SES Application Process

The SES selection process is different from that of the GS or other government hiring. While applicants can find the vacancy announcements on USAJOBS.gov, application packages will need to address both the candidate's technical and professional qualifications for the specific job as well as a standard set of leadership competencies or Executive Core Qualifications (ECQs) as defined by the U.S. Office of Personnel Management (OPM). ECQs are generally more encompassing than your average

KSAs, and applicants are expected to present articulate and comprehensive statements addressing these competency areas:

- Leading change
- Leading people
- Driving results
- Business acumen
- Building coalitions/communications

A Few Other Notes on SES

Landing an SES, SL, or ST job is pretty difficult for someone applying from outside government since many federal agencies tend to grow their own leaders. At the same time, this is not impossible. Some private-sector employees have successfully made the move and enjoyed transitioning into a position of government leadership. The key is to be realistic about your capabilities and not to waste time applying for jobs that you are not fully qualified for. Further, you may have a better chance applying for a GS-14 or GS-15 managerial job and, after serving a year or two at these levels, then applying for an SES job.

Encore Careers

Unlike past generations, people are now working longer (well into their 60s and 70s) and looking for more meaningful opportunities to give back to their community, to a specific cause, or to their country.

Encore careers can come in all shapes and sizes. From a Fortune 500 company senior manager taking a new position as a GS-15 in the Department of the Treasury to a private-sector technology guru who became a part of the exciting work done using technology to enhance Department of Agriculture economic development services—the sky is the limit.

def•i•ni•tion

An **encore career** is one that a retiree begins when he or she rejoins the workforce or when someone with a full career in one field or sector moves to another job in another field or sector. Such employees often begin encore careers to find meaning through continuing work, to get or maintain benefits, to make a difference and give back, or all of the above.

Government might be a great option for an encore career if you're yearning to work with your hands or be outdoors after years in a cubicle or craving a measure of workplace flexibilities you could have only dreamed about when you were initially building your career. An encore career with government also could be a way to give back to your country if you're willing to start at the bottom of the ladder again. You could contribute greatly by being a mentor or inspiring newer professionals and helping them in their development.

Whether you're a retiree who has been out of the workforce for the last five years or you're just now planning your retirement after a long career, your experience will likely be highly valued in government. Experienced workers 55 years of age or older now represent more than 11 percent of the new hires to the federal government. This will likely increase, since only five years ago they represented less than 8.5 percent.

Not only is our government open to hiring retired workers, but this is a great way to give back after a fulfilling career in another sector or profession.

Even if you don't see yourself staying in federal service for the rest of your life, it's a great place to keep learning and stay current. Agencies often have professional development stipends or are willing to provide tuition repayment if their budgets allow. They may also let you work part-time. In fact, 24 percent of the new federal hires 55 years or older are part-time workers. With flexible work schedules, you could work hard for the government and still have time to enjoy the "life" part of the work/life balance.

Marketing Your Experience

Think about what skills an agency might not have developed "in house," but would be wanting from a new employee. Did you work on a grant or at an institution that was federally funded? Do you have experience at a private-sector organization that sells to the government? Do you know a foreign language that's in demand? Have you taken specialized training courses or gained certifications over the years that could be added to your resumé? Don't hold back—agencies want to see all your experience.

Many job applicants from other sectors forget to beef up their federal resumés to include items that might have been commonplace or assumed in their long-term career. For instance, if you are a certified public accountant (CPA) and you list that title with your name at the top of your resumé, take the time to list this credential and other details in the body of your resumé as well. The same thing goes for any business classes or courses. If everyone with your title at a particular company was Six Sigma or

Total Quality Management (TQM) trained, then make sure you specifically name each of these knowledge areas on a list of courses or certifications.

Consider these items as they relate to you and write them out on your resumé:

- Language skills, including foreign languages, American sign language, and translation and interpretation certifications
- Technology, such as social networking sites, Microsoft Office (Excel, Word, Project, Outlook), Adobe products (Photoshop, Acrobat, Contribute), HR/ payroll systems
- Technical tools, including programming languages, data analysis, and statistical programs
- Professional certifications that you gained through a job, such as Project Management Professional (PMP)
- Company-specific training classes, explained in your resumé so someone from outside that company culture can understand the content of those classes
- Community and civic involvement, where you can describe the results of your participation or leadership

Where Government Needs Your Experience

We can't say it enough: government needs your experience. However, it's up to you to find the job that will utilize you to your full potential.

Federal Facts

According to the Partnership for Public Service 2008 report *A Golden Opportunity*, "Federal agency managers cited several reasons why they consider older workers to be good hires. The most common were their strong commitment to the agency mission, a hunger to do good work, and talent developed through different work and life experiences."

Key Agencies Recruiting Experienced Workers

While workers over 50 are hired into all types of positions across government, there are some agencies that have hired a larger percentage of new staff from the older worker population.

For example, the Department of State is seeking to diversify its foreign service officer cadre with experienced workers. The Federal Aviation Administration is hoping to bring in a variety of experienced program and project managers for its NextGen aviation modernization project. And Department of Defense organizations continue to build out of their non-military workforce and would welcome experienced workers. These, and a growing number of other agencies, are excited to accept experienced talent as their own experienced talent retires or needs to be infused with passionate encore careerists with a new perspective.

Agencies that have recently hired candidates over the age of 50 into over 20 percent of their job openings include:

- The Small Business Administration
- The National Science Foundation
- The Agency for International Development
- The Office of Personnel Management
- The Nuclear Regulatory Commission
- The Government Printing Office
- The Department of Energy
- The Department of Commerce
- The Broadcasting Board of Governors
- The Department of Veterans Affairs
- The Department of the Treasury

Some agencies even make a specific effort to recruit experienced workers. You might see agencies advertising job openings at www.retirementjobs.com, AARP, or other boomer-specific websites. The National Institutes of Health (NIH) has been named as one of AARP's Best Places to Work for those over 50 and the Internal Revenue Service has conducted specific outreach efforts through a variety of media and its own website to reach experienced talent. Additional agencies seek AARP's and retirementjobs.com's age-friendly certifications, so check for new additions to these lists.

Skills in Demand for Experienced Workers

According to the Partnership for Public Service's *A Golden Opportunity* report, hiring managers and HR staff reported that older workers are in demand for occupations "that typically require experience to master," which include scientists, engineers, IT staff, procurement professionals, lawyers, and accountants, as well as "entry-level positions that involved direct contact with the general public."

In short, technical skills and maturity in handling customer service situations are most in demand.

Breaking New Ground

Even as an experienced worker from another field, you will want to demonstrate your dedication to the new career. This can include performing volunteer work, seeking out educational opportunities, and more.

For example, if your experience is in an office setting but you want to become an animal technician, consider volunteering at a local pet rescue shelter to gain credibility. If you're not sure how to start a new volunteering endeavor, consider working with a civic organization, place of worship, or local nonprofit organization; you might expand existing services or partner with someone you already know and shadow that volunteer to support his or her work.

You can also seek out educational opportunities to build new sets of skills that could be applied in a government job. Community colleges, continuing education programs, and even executive education programs might be worth considering if your skills have gotten stale or you've taken some time out of the workforce for personal reasons.

Retraining during both the research phase of your job search (try a class to see if you might like a new career field) or as you try to break into a new field can be valuable, encouraging, and necessary to land the government job you want.

Workplace Flexibilities

As we noted in Chapter 4, federal agencies often offer workplace flexibilities to attract and retain employees. Compressed work schedules, the ability to job share (two people splitting the hours for one job), or working from home could all potentially be offered by an agency. Specific offerings will vary by agency, so read the benefits information in the vacancy announcement and make sure to visit the website for the agency.

Managing Your Expectations

Remember, as someone making a mid-career sector change or seeking out an encore career, you may need to exercise more patience and diligence than you've ever had to do in previous job searches. Do not lose heart; there are success stories and lots of new and happy federal employees who, just like you, have a lot to offer—not the least of which is seasoned talent, dedication, and an external perspective.

In addition, you may need to practice patience and perseverance once you show up for the job (and every day afterward). Be prepared for a new way of decision making, dealing with the congressional budget cycle and delayed gratification. But don't abandon what you've learned through all your previous experience, because that's exactly what will make you a valuable employee.

The Least You Need to Know

- The government is in need of experienced workers as baby boomers retire en masse. You can take advantage of this opportunity by considering the government for your encore career or mid-career switch.
- Take the time to translate your resumé into government-friendly terms. It will be well worth the effort.
- Our government is definitely not ageist when it comes to hiring employees. In fact, experience is highly valued.
- You can return to the workforce after you retire by joining the federal government. It's a great way to give back while continuing to earn a living.

Part 4
Other Ways to Work in Government

The majority of this book focuses on the roughly 2 million jobs in the federal civil service. However, we recognize that many people dream of working on policy in a congressional office or becoming a federal judge. Some people are interested in working for their state's law enforcement or helping nonprofits find grant money.

In this part, we explore the many opportunities to work in or with government outside of the federal civil service. We'll look at opportunities in the legislative and judicial branches as well as state government jobs. We'll give you the inside scoop on political appointments, grantees, contracting jobs, and temporary jobs. You didn't think there was just one way to work in government, did you?

Chapter 15

Working on Capitol Hill

In This Chapter

- The makeup of the legislative branch
- Job opportunities in the many arms of Congress
- It's all about networking
- How to get connected
- What to know when applying for a Hill job

In the heart of our nation's capital, thousands of jobseekers flock to Capitol Hill (aka the Hill) to take part in the making of legislative history. Work on the Hill is exciting, challenging, and inspiring. It's also highly competitive.

In this chapter, we will give you a clear sense of what jobs are available on the Hill—from chief of staff in a Senate office to press assistant for your hometown representative—and how you can qualify for those jobs.

What Is the Legislative Branch?

The *legislative* branch contains the United States Congress, which is made up of the Senate, the House of Representatives, and a handful of supporting agencies. Congress has the responsibility to establish laws and make

def•i•ni•tion

To **legislate** is to create, consider, and enact laws.

amendments to current laws. The Senate has the responsibility of "advice and consent" on high-ranking presidential appointments. Senators, members of the House of Representatives, staff, and various supporting employees work on the Hill.

The House and Senate perform their own set of duties, but work together to achieve the overall mission of Congress. The House of Representatives has 435 members, each of whom is elected for a two-year term by constituents in the representative's home district. The Senate has 100 members—two senators from each state—who are elected for a six-year term in office.

Members of Congress have the duty to represent and enact legislation on behalf of the American people. Their priorities may vary significantly based on issues that arise during their term in office, the needs of their constituents, and the activities of the committee or committees on which they serve.

What Kind of Jobs Are Available on the Hill?

Within each member's personal office are administrative and policy jobs, and the number of staffers in each office varies widely. For House members, there are generally around 10 staff positions in the Washington, D.C., office and 3 to 5 staffers back home in their congressional district. Although it's hard to pin down an exact figure, Senate offices generally have between 15 and 35 employees in Washington, D.C. The number of staffers back home depends on the size and population of the senator's state.

Unlike the work that occurs in the personal offices of representatives and senators, which is heavily focused on each member's state or district, committees are where most of the serious policy work occurs and where bills take shape. As with other congressional offices, staff sizes vary widely across committees but average around 40 staffers.

Legislative positions within committee offices are generally more specialized than those found within personal offices and often require prior policy experience. Where a legislative staffer in a personal office may handle a wide array of issues (for example, one personal office legislative assistant might be assigned responsibility for issues related to alcohol, tobacco, and firearms; banking; budget; business and economics; elections and campaign finance; government affairs; gun control; pensions; small business; Social Security; taxes; telecommunications; and trade), the legislative staff on committees focus on narrow sets of policy issues and tend to specialize in particular areas. Because of their policy expertise, committee staff members often remain in their positions despite changes in committee chairmanship or party control; in a member's personal office, job security depends almost entirely on the political fortunes of the member.

The House of Representatives currently has 20 standing committees. Standing committees are permanently established within the House and Senate. The Senate has 20 standing committees, 68 subcommittees, and 4 joint committees. Joint committees employ members from both chambers of Congress and generally contribute to the policy debate in both chambers. Subcommittees handle a more specialized set of duties that support the work of standing committees.

Most competitive applicants for Hill jobs have at least a Bachelor's degree; a strong interest in government or politics; prior experience on the Hill (although this is not a prerequisite); and the ability to thrive in a fast-paced, ever-changing environment. For all positions, it pays to have some policy experience. At the very least, you must have a strong desire to learn and work on public policy.

Top Secret

You don't have to be a political science major to work on the Hill. All majors can be valuable depending on the job the office is looking to fill. Also, writing and critical-thinking skills are highly valued, so English majors are also well received.

Positions and eligibility requirements may vary slightly from office to office, but generally include administrative, legislative, district-focused, committee, agency, and internship positions. Most Hill staffers start off as interns or entry-level employees and work their way up.

Congressional Office: Administrative

Who: **Chief of Staff**

What: The chief of staff oversees the entire office, both in D.C. and the home district. He represents the member if he or she is not present, hires employees, and serves as project coordinator. The chief of staff often serves as a member's political advisor and personal office liaison to the campaign.

Eligibility: The candidate must be well seasoned in administration, management, and the political dynamics of both Congress and the member's state or district. He must be a master multitasker and work well under pressure. Prior Capitol Hill and public relations experience is highly preferred.

Who: **Office Manager**

What: The office manager supports the work of the chief of staff; helps supervise employees; and oversees the human resources, IT, financial, and administrative needs and responsibilities of the office.

Eligibility: Previous administrative and managerial experience is required and knowledge of computers and database management is preferred. The ideal candidate will have at least a Bachelor's degree and demonstrate superior interpersonal skills, attention to detail, and the ability to motivate others.

Who: **Director of Communications**

What: The director of communications handles media relationships and oversees the communications team. She makes sure that the member and the staff are projecting the right image and that the member's accomplishments are communicated to constituents back home.

Eligibility: A degree in communications or a related field and previous journalism, public relations, or marketing communications experience are required. The candidate must have exemplary writing and oral communication skills. Previous experience on the Hill and knowledge of the legislative process are preferred.

Who: **Press Secretary**

What: The press secretary is in charge of communications with media outlets. Writing speeches, member articles, and news releases are among the press secretary's assigned tasks. The press secretary must keep up relations between the senator or representative and his constituency, as well as the general public and media.

Eligibility: A degree in communications or public relations is preferred. The candidate must display impeccable writing and oral communications skills. Journalism and Hill experience are highly preferred.

Who: **Assistant Press Secretary**

What: More prevalent in the Senate (because senators have larger staffs), this person supports the work of the press secretary.

Eligibility: Much like the press secretary, this employee must have extensive writing experience and is preferred to have previous experience on the Hill.

Who: **Systems Administrator**

What: The systems administrator is in charge of everything technology-related. She usually maintains the office database and must provide technical support.

Eligibility: The candidate must have experience with a broad range of computer software. Consulting or business management experience is a plus. The systems administrator must also display keen interpersonal and communication skills.

Who: **Scheduler**

What: The scheduler oversees the member's schedule, setting meetings and making reservations and travel arrangements, both in D.C. and in the home district.

Eligibility: This is one of the most important and demanding positions in a congressional office. A competitive applicant will have prior administrative experience, preferably on the Hill. Outstanding attention to detail, ability to work in a fast-paced environment, and grace under pressure are crucial for this position.

Who: **Receptionist**

What: The receptionist is an important team player, and serves as the office gatekeeper. This person greets visitors, answers the phone, responds to constituent inquiries, and arranges congressional tours. Often, the position is filled by an entry-level applicant from the member's home district.

Eligibility: An ideal candidate will display a deep interest in government and have exemplary interpersonal, oral communication, and writing skills. As the first person visitors see when entering the office and the first voice they hear over the phone, the receptionist must show enthusiasm and a positive attitude.

Top Secret

On Capitol Hill, everyone starts at the bottom and works their way up. How do you get to the top? Demonstrate your commitment by getting in early and staying late—people on the Hill hate clock watchers. Also, show a willingness to take on additional tasks and help whenever and wherever needed. Doing these things with a positive attitude can make the difference between remaining in a low-level position and moving up the office ladder at lightning speed.

Congressional Office: Legislative

Who: **Legislative Director (LD)**

What: This person is in charge of the legislative agenda of the office, which includes advising the member on legislation and overseeing the legislative assistant(s). The LD ensures that the member is briefed on the committee and floor schedules (that is, which bills will be voted on and when) and able to cast an informed vote. LDs may draft bills or amendments for the member and stay connected to a range of constituents from the member's home district and other Hill offices.

Eligibility: Prior legislative experience is important (preferably on the Hill), in addition to analytical, research, and writing experience. Strong attention to detail and the ability to manage others and meet tight deadlines are required.

Who: **Legislative Assistant (LA)**

What: Most congressional offices employ multiple legislative assistants, each assigned a particular portfolio of issues. Their portfolio is determined by the member's legislative interests, committee assignments, and state or district priorities. LAs are responsible for advising the member on the policy issues in his or portfolio.

Eligibility: Like the LD, an LA will benefit from prior legislative experience and possess excellent writing and oral communication skills. An LA must be prepared to meet with constituents, interest groups, and lobbyists and conduct legal research in order to provide sound policy advice to the member.

Who: **Legislative Correspondent (LC)**

What: An LC is responsible for constituent correspondence (including letters, e-mails, and phone calls). This person must also be in close contact with interest groups and may conduct legal research and provide support to the LAs and LD. An LC sometimes oversees the interns.

Eligibility: Strong attention to detail and impeccable writing and oral communications skills are required. Although not a prerequisite, LCs should enjoy meeting with constituents and be familiar with the member's state or district.

Congressional District or State Offices

District offices deal more closely with constituents and citizens from the member's home state or district. Constituents can voice their concerns directly to the district office, get assistance with federal agencies and federal grants, and request tours of the U.S. Capitol building.

Every member has a district office; most House members and all senators have more than one (depending on the district's geographic size). The district office averages about three to five staff members, including those listed in the following subsections. Staffers are generally from the member's state or district or a nearby district; many have previously worked on the member's campaign.

Who: **District Director**

What: The district director oversees the district office and employees and represents the representative at various functions in her absence.

Eligibility: Significant administrative and managerial experience is required to perform this job function. District directors must be well tuned to the political dynamics at work in the state or district and able to provide strategic direction to the representative's activities in the state or district. Excellent project management, interpersonal, and multitasking skills are essential.

Who: **Caseworker**

What: For many constituents, the most significant interaction with a member's office is with a caseworker. These staffers have direct contact with individual constituents in the representative's home district and respond to inquiries, requests, and complaints. Caseworkers often intervene on behalf of constituents who have encountered a problem with a federal agency

Eligibility: This employee must have excellent listening and communication skills, a customer-service mindset, and the ability to solve problems and multitask. A degree in social work or law is preferred, and in many districts bilingualism is valuable.

Who: **Office Manager**

What: The office manager supports the work of the chief of staff, helps supervise employees, and oversees the human resources, IT, financial, and administrative needs and responsibilities of the office.

Eligibility: Previous administrative and managerial experience is often required and knowledge of computers and database management is preferred. The ideal candidate will have at least a Bachelor's degree and demonstrate superior interpersonal skills, attention to detail, and the ability to motivate others.

In short, the positions just listed are generally the same across the board—you won't find too much deviation from district to district.

Committee Office

Congressional committees are subcomponents of the House and Senate and are intended to make the work of Congress more manageable. There are committees to handle major issues such as agriculture, education and labor, foreign affairs, natural resources, and taxation, to name a few. Most committees have subcommittees, which are even more specialized. Every member of Congress is assigned to serve on at least one committee.

Committees and subcommittees are an important part of the legislative process, and they require staff to support the committee members. Committee staff members are typically hired by the committee chair or by a subcommittee chair. The number of staff positions depends on each committee's priorities, budget, and scope of responsibility.

Professional staff members are assigned a portfolio of issues for which they are the primary point of contact, so applicants for these positions should know the legislative process well. Staff members often meet with constituents, interest groups, and lobbyists; draft legislation; schedule and manage legislative and oversight hearings; and advise the committee chair, committee members, and their staffs. Many professional staff members have extensive experience and expertise in one or more issues.

Committees range in size from 10 to 70 members. Staff sizes vary dramatically, but the average committee employs about 40 people. Committee budgets and staffs are much larger than those of members' personal offices, so they are a rich source of job opportunities and a good way to use and develop one's policy expertise. Salaries vary based on a range of factors, but committee positions are generally well compensated. Committees employ both administrative and legislative employees, and many committees also maintain an investigative staff to perform needed oversight of federal agencies and programs.

Top Secret

Call the committee office and check the status of your application after a week or two. Persistence pays off.

Committee staff members do a large amount of writing, so impeccable writing skills are crucial. Committee work is a good fit for someone who wants to work on a specific issue and already has expertise on that issue. Committees are also the place to be for individuals who wish to pursue investigative and oversight work.

Committee staff positions are highly desirable, and the competition can be fierce. Having previous experience or contacts on the Hill is the best way to hear about current openings. Occasionally, committees will post job openings on their websites; more often, especially for senior positions, candidates learn of openings by word of mouth. Visiting committee and subcommittee offices in person to drop off a resumé is a good way to make a personal connection and inquire about current or future openings.

Legislative Branch Support Agencies

Committees and personal offices could not function without the support of several support agencies. These agencies employ professional, nonpolitical staff without regard to election outcomes or party control. They are a good choice for individuals who value job security over political affiliation.

- The **Library of Congress** is the research arm of Congress. It serves many important functions, such as maintaining thorough and accurate historical records and providing research tools and materials for the use of Congress and the public. Within the Library of Congress is the Congressional Research Service (CRS), which provides integral, nonpartisan legal and policy research for members and staff. With more than 700 employees—attorneys, procedural experts, policy analysts, and more—the CRS is on call to assist Congress with its work. Employees research issues such as homeland security, health care, environment, science and technology, and every other issue that comes before Congress. To learn more, go to www.loc.gov.
- The **Government Accountability Office (GAO)** was designed to serve as the investigative arm of Congress and assist Congress in fulfilling its oversight responsibilities. The work performed at GAO directly and continuously serves to inform Congress regarding the management of the programs and agencies of the federal government. GAO's work is wide ranging: it can investigate a specific program at the request of a congressional committee, conduct a broad assessment of the long-term fiscal outlook of the nation, and do everything in between. GAO employs specialists in many different disciplines; some of the more common ones include accountants, statisticians, IT specialists, program analysts, and criminal investigators. To learn more, go to www.gao.gov.
- The **Congressional Budget Office (CBO)** supports the work of Congress as it relates to federal spending and revenue. Congress could not move forward if it were not for the continuous work of the CBO. Before a bill can be presented and passed, the federal budget implications must be considered—and this is where the CBO comes in. The reports prepared by the CBO are highly influential and enable Congress to make more informed decisions. For employment at the CBO, candidates should have a graduate degree in economics, public finance, industrial organization, public policy analysis, or a related field. Internships are available throughout the year, and ideal candidates should be pursuing a graduate degree in a related field. To learn more, go to www.cbo.gov.

- The **Government Printing Office (GPO)** works to make government information available and accessible to all, and provides assistance with printing and publishing the vast array of documents and public records produced by the federal government each year. Careers in administration, finance, human resources, sales and marketing, printing procurement, operations support, library services, and acquisitions are available. Positions include printing services specialists, program coordinators, human resources managers, and web and graphic designers. These positions and more are needed for the GPO to carry out its mission. Visit the GPO website (www.gpo.gov) or USAJOBS.gov for current openings.
- The **Architect of the Capitol** is responsible for maintaining and preserving congressional buildings on Capitol Hill, including the U.S. Capitol building, the Supreme Court, congressional office buildings, the Library of Congress, the U.S. Botanic Gardens, and more. The office has architectural, engineering, and administrative hiring needs. Check the website (www.aoc.gov) or USAJOBS.gov for current vacancy announcements and to apply for jobs.

Other agencies that support Congress include the Copyright office, the Medicare Payment Advisory Commission, the Open World Leadership Center, the Stennis Center for Public Service, and the U.S. Capitol Visitor Center.

Where Can You Find Capitol Hill Jobs?

The main sources for job postings for Hill jobs can be found online at rcjobs.com (published by *Roll Call*), TheHill.com/employment, dyn.Politico.com, and BradTraverse.com. HillZoo.com is a great website set up specifically for Hill internships.

Congressional Staff Jobs

Before going to any of these websites, do some research to figure out which members of Congress or committees best match your personal interests and expertise. Who are the members who share your policy inclinations or party affiliation? Which committees most impact the things you care about? Knowing something about the different members and committees will allow you to narrow your job search and increase the chance that the job you land will be the right fit for you.

In addition to looking at the websites we just mentioned, you should directly contact your hometown and/or home state representatives and senators. Their information is easily found online through the Library of Congress (http://thomas.loc.gov/ or www.congress.gov) or in the *Congressional Staff Directory*, a reference book that lists each House and Senate member, committee, and staff member. It also includes additional biographical information about members in leadership positions.

Contact House and Senate offices through e-mail, by phone, or in person to inquire about current job openings both in the personal and state or district offices. Most inquiries should be directed to the chief of staff. Keep in mind that House offices from your home state, or a state where you have spent a significant amount of time, will be most inclined to respond positively. In your cover letter and when contacting the office, point out the connection you share with the representative.

Top Secret

Jobs on the Hill are not subject to the same rigid application procedures as executive branch jobs discussed in most of this book. Hiring personnel can often hire at will, much like in the public sector.

On the Hill, nothing beats the power of networking for opening doors. If you have family or friends on the Hill or if you know someone who knows someone, use it to your benefit. If you are on a college campus, let your faculty and career counselors know that you are interested in working on the Hill—they may have friends or alumni contacts who can help with job leads or informational interviews.

No matter who you know (or don't know), take the time to do some research online. Most members' websites have a link for those interested in becoming an intern and explain how you can apply. If you are interested in a specific committee, visit its website or call to get more information on jobs.

Both the House and the Senate have placement offices that can be found on their websites. These offices post numerous opportunities, but those postings are by no means a complete list of job openings on the Hill.

Most openings on the Hill are advertised through interoffice e-mails and word of mouth, and are filled very quickly. This is a prime example of why it is so important to make and retain contacts on the Hill—it is often the only way you will hear of openings. Don't forget that you can always physically walk from office to office and drop off your resumé with the staff assistant manning the front office. This low-tech approach has worked for years and remains a great way to make a personal connection.

Committee Jobs

To apply for work on a congressional committee, you can contact the majority or minority staff director, who functions as the committee chief of staff for his or her respective party. The staff director will be able to direct you to current information and openings. Also, if you visit the committee website, you can access contact information and direct your inquiries there.

Legislative Branch Support Agencies

Most job openings will be posted on the agencies' individual websites or on USAJOBS.gov. Some agencies allow applicants to submit resumés for current openings or as a general application for future consideration.

Other Ways to Find Hill Jobs

Working and volunteering on campaigns are great ways to get your foot in the door for a Hill job (if the person you are working/volunteering for wins, of course). You can also build your resumé early on by joining the student government in high school and college and building the skills needed for the job you want. More than anything, though, you need to network, network, network. Because turnover is high on the Hill, you have to stay on top of your job search and your contacts. Persistence and patience pay off when it comes to finding jobs on the Hill.

Internships

Interns serve in nearly every office on the Hill. They provide assistance wherever it's needed, often drafting constituent letters, conducting research, and helping manage the front office. Internships on the Hill are available year-round.

Internships are a terrific way to get your foot in the door; they can also be challenging to find and land. The House and Senate post some internship openings on house.gov and senate.gov, but your best bet is to visit your target representative or senator's website. To check for openings (in addition to your networking and research efforts), you can also do an online search for "congressional fellowship." This will yield a slew of congressional programs with organizations such as the American Political Science Association, the American Psychological Association, the Brookings Institute, and the American Association for the Advancement of Science.

In the Internet age, it may seem foreign to make a phone call or visit the office of your representative or senator in person, but remember: on Capitol Hill, the most important advantage you have is the ability to make a personal connection.

You can also send your resumé, cover letter, and writing sample to the office's internship coordinator. Be sure to follow up with a phone call after a week or so to check the status of your application, and don't be afraid to resend it if you do not receive a response.

> **Top Secret**
>
> You don't have to work for a representative or senator from your home district or state. If you find a member of Congress who has a voting record or political leaning akin to yours, it's a good idea to reach out to that representative or senator.

To say that Capitol Hill internships are highly competitive would be an understatement—they are beyond competitive. Openings are not well advertised because there is no shortage of eager and well-qualified applicants. It takes persistence and drive to locate opportunities and get yourself in the door, but if you are seriously interested and want to intern on the Hill, don't let a little competition discourage you from searching and applying. Get out there and pound the pavement!

Staffers are interested in students and graduates who are passionate about government, specific issues, or the state or district that the member represents. Experience in student government or on a political or advocacy campaign is also highly attractive, as are demonstrated leadership skills and a commitment to academics and community service.

The Library of Congress, Congressional Research Service, Government Accountability Office, and Congressional Budget Office all provide internship programs. Information for these internships can be found on their individual websites. You can also search for internships on Studentjobs.gov.

The Page Program

Administered through the Office of the Clerk, the Page Program has given young people an opportunity to learn about the legislative process up close for almost 200 years. Pages attend the Page School for a full academic year (fall and spring semester), live in the Page Residence Hall, and work in Congress.

The school day starts early for Pages (first classes begin at 6:45 A.M.). They study general subjects such as English, math, science, and social studies. Their duties in

Congress include mostly administrative tasks such as delivering mail and packages, answering phones, and taking messages.

> **The Fine Print**
>
> Pages are allowed to go home only on the weekends and when Congress is in recess. They are not allowed to go home during the week unless it is an emergency. They are also required to wear their hair "conservatively."

Interested students must contact their representative and seek sponsorship from a current member of Congress. Students typically must submit a resumé, writing sample, high school transcript, and letters of recommendation. Only high school juniors with at least a 3.0 GPA are eligible to apply.

In 2009, pages were paid a yearly salary of more than $21,000, minus taxes and fees for the residence hall, which is furnished and implements a 10:00 P.M. curfew on the weekdays and a midnight curfew on the weekends.

Congressional Fellowship Program

The Congressional Fellowship Program allows political scientists, federal executives, journalists, international scholars, and students with complete or near-complete Ph.D.s to get involved in the legislative process for a nine-month period.

The main objective of this program is to spread knowledge of Congress and the legislative process. Therefore, candidates must have a strong interest in public policy. They must apply online by submitting a resumé, personal statement, list of references, and a writing sample to the American Political Science Association. The best candidates will be invited to travel to Washington, D.C., for a panel interview and await acceptance into the program.

Things to Consider When Applying for Hill Jobs

Anyone who works on the Hill will tell you that the downsides to their job are the long hours, stressful working conditions, and modest pay. Sure, there are sacrifices to make when working on the Hill, but there is also a huge payoff. Hill staffers gain invaluable work experience and priceless networking and career opportunities.

Here are some other things to think about when applying for a Hill job:

- **Set your expectations.** You may have to hear a dozen "no's" before you even get considered for a job or internship, but once you get that first "yes," you are in the club.

- **Consider the difference between House and Senate.** The culture of the two chambers could not be more different. The House runs by majority rule (the Senate by two-thirds majority). The House often runs at a quicker pace than the more deliberative Senate, where individual senators wield the power to slow down pieces of legislation. Senate staffs are generally larger than House staffs and may allow for more specialization in one area.
- **Earn your stripes.** Only a select few start on the Hill in the highest-level jobs. Most Hill staffers start at the bottom and work their way up. The good news is that a majority of Hill offices promote from within or value external candidates with Hill experience, so it does not take long for a high-performing employee to move up the ladder. Many people find full-time jobs after earning their stripes as an intern, which can help you gain contacts and put you in the right place at the right time when a permanent position surfaces. An internship is a fantastic way to learn the culture and language that you'll need to know as a full-time employee.

The Least You Need to Know

- The legislative branch is comprised of the House of Representatives, the Senate, and supporting organizations.
- To get a job on Capitol Hill, search online, work on a campaign, get involved in student government, but above all, be persistent!
- Turnover on the Hill is high and positions open up regularly, but competition for jobs is fierce.
- Internships are a great way to get your foot in the door on the Hill.
- Be willing to put in your time to move up on the Hill. It doesn't happen overnight, but hard work and persistence will pay off.

Chapter 16

Judicial Jobs

In This Chapter

- The scope of the judicial branch
- Jobs available in this branch
- How to find and apply for judicial jobs
- Supreme Court fellows and student internships

In addition to considering jobs in the executive and legislative branches of government, you may want to think about applying for a job in the judicial branch. The judicial branch is much smaller than the executive branch, employing roughly 32,000 people, and therefore has a more limited set of job opportunities.

In this chapter, we will cover what the judicial branch does, what kinds of jobs are available, and where to find judicial jobs.

What Is the Judicial Branch?

As you probably remember from your high school government class, the judicial branch interprets the law and is a coequal branch of government.

Federal Facts

The judicial branch cannot make or amend laws. This can only be done by Congress.

Also known as the judiciary, this branch is in charge of interpreting the Constitution, administering constitutional law, and deciding cases.

The judiciary is comprised of the U.S. court system, which includes the Supreme Court, the courts of appeals, and the district and bankruptcy courts.

What Types of Jobs Are Available?

There are many different jobs and occupations within the judicial branch. There are nearly 1,800 judges across our country employed by the judicial branch. But if you think the court system is only made up of judges, lawyers, and court reporters, think again. The court system needs employees in areas such as human resources, accounting, information technology, and law enforcement, in every region of our nation.

Aside from the Supreme Court, there are many places to work in the judiciary. The Administrative Office of the U.S. Courts, Federal Judicial Center, U.S. Sentencing Commission, and the U.S. Probation and Pretrial Services System employ thousands of people.

The Administrative Office (AO) of the U.S. Courts

The AO is the support arm of the judicial branch. It implements judicial procedures, promotes accountability, and offers assistance. The AO is also in charge of maintaining communication with Congress and the legislative and executive branches.

The AO provides administrative, technical, legal, financial, and management services to the judiciary, all of which require a diverse mix of occupations and positions to be filled. Among these are attorneys, statisticians, engineers, analysts, human resources specialists, and public administrators.

The Federal Judicial Center (FJC)

This is the education and research arm of the judicial branch. It conducts research on the policies and practices of the court system and provides continuing education for federal judges and court employees. The FJC offers a range of education, information technology, law, and history positions.

U.S. Sentencing Commission

The U.S. Sentencing Commission works with data, develops sentencing policies, distributes information, and advises executive and legislative branch employees. The commission needs various employees in areas of research, public affairs, administration, counsel, and education.

U.S. Probation and Pretrial Services System

Officers in the U.S. Probation and Pretrial Services System serve the critical role of overseeing defendants and offenders, ensuring the safety of communities, conducting investigations, and preparing reports that the courts use to determine sentencing and release.

Probation and pretrial services officers generally receive excellent pay and benefits and a high level of job stability.

The Fine Print

Due to the level of physical and mental stress that officers in the Probation and Pretrial Services System work under, they are forced to retire by age 57.

Interested in applying? You must have your Bachelor's degree from an accredited college or university and be physically healthy and under the age of 37 (again, due to the level of mental and physical stress). You must also pass drug and background tests.

Public Defenders

Federal public defenders are responsible for providing legal counsel to those who cannot afford an attorney. They are hired by district federal defender offices and are government employees. Federal public defenders may not participate in the private practice of law.

Public defenders must have their J.D. (a.k.a. law) degree and be a member of the bar of the state where they plan to work. Candidates must also have several years of experience as a professional trial attorney to be eligible for work as a public defender.

The Office of Defender Services (ODS) has an official website, fd.org, that posts information and employment announcements. Follow the "employment" link to a list of current job announcements throughout the nation.

Examples of Jobs in the Judiciary

There are thousands of jobs available in the judiciary for jobseekers of varied backgrounds, including educational backgrounds. Here we have included some examples of jobs, salary ranges, and job descriptions.

Human Resources Specialist

U.S. Bankruptcy Court—Charlotte, NC

Salary: $37,279–$46,625 (2009)

The HR specialist will be responsible for personnel recruitment, training, and assistance in addition to administrative and project management tasks. He or she must have a Bachelor's degree and at least two years of experience working in human resources. Excellent project management skills, attention to detail, and demonstrated leadership abilities are required.

Information Technology Security Manager

U.S. Court of Appeals, Second Circuit—New York

Salary: $72,271–$85,083 (2009)

This employee will be responsible for advising and training employees on IT security, assisting with the design and execution of security standards, and assisting with all matters related to IT security. The ideal candidate will have at least three years of technology experience and extensive knowledge of computer programs. Excellent communication skills, adaptability, and the ability to travel are required.

Legal Secretary

Office of the Federal Defender—Sacramento, CA

Salary: $36,611–$45,057 (2009)

The legal secretary will provide executive-level administrative and clerical support to the federal defender and district attorneys. Duties will include implementing secretarial policies and procedures, conducting phone calls, proofreading, filing, and performing other tasks as assigned. Qualified candidates will have at least their high school diploma and at least one year of experience as a legal secretary or legal assistant.

Law Clerk

U.S. District Court, Southern District of Florida—Miami

Salary: $59,557–$130,407 (2009)

The law clerk will be in charge of all aspects of criminal and civil cases in which he or she is assigned. Clerks will perform legal research, make recommendations to the U.S. district judge, and assist the judge in keeping up-to-date with relevant news and any changes in law. Candidates must have completed their law degree and must possess one of the following: graduation in the upper third of their class, service on the editorial board of their school's law review, graduation with an LLM degree, or demonstrated skill and ability in legal studies. The ideal candidate will have previous experience as a federal law clerk and one year of legal experience. The candidate must be responsible and mature, possessing exemplary writing and legal research skills.

There is a limit to the length of time one can serve as a law clerk. No one can hold a federal clerkship in the U.S. Courts for more than four years.

Where Can You Find and Apply for Judicial Jobs?

The U.S. courts website is a fantastic one-stop resource that posts many job openings across the nation. The simplest way to find out about current job opportunities is to search using the Court Locator page, uscourts.gov/courtlinks. From there, you can select the state or district in which you are interested in applying and contact the office. District contact information is posted online, so don't hesitate to use it.

For example, let's say that you want to search for judicial jobs in San Francisco. From the U.S. courts website's Court Locator page, click on the State of California. This will take you to links for the contact information of the Court of Appeals Clerk, Bankruptcy Court, District Court, Federal Public Defender's Office, and Probation and Pretrial Services Offices within the City of San Francisco. Use the posted contact information to inquire about any current openings that might not be listed online or search their individual website for job postings.

Top Secret

Any kind of legal or law-supportive position within the judiciary requires a law degree. However, most administrative positions, such as human resources specialist, investigator, or legal secretary, do not require a law degree. In these positions, knowledge and/or experience in law, criminal justice, government, or a related field is always a plus.

To find out what opportunities are currently available for probation and pretrial services officers, contact a probation or pretrial services representative within the district court where you would like to work. You can find their contact information on the U.S. courts website's Court Locator page.

Jobs at the Administrative Office of the U.S. Courts can be found on the U.S. courts website. Follow the Administrative Office link to learn more about working at the Administrative Office and where you can find career opportunities. The Federal Judicial Center posts jobs on its website, fjc.gov. Follow the General Information about the FJC link to the Employment Opportunities page. The U.S. Sentencing Commission also posts jobs on its website, ussc.gov.

At the bottom of each announcement on the U.S. courts job board are specific directions on how to apply. Some postings will direct you to apply on USAJOBS.com, while others provide the address where you can send your application.

USAJOBS.gov for Judicial Jobs

USAJOBS.gov also posts judicial jobs. Search under "U.S. Courts" or "Supreme Court" for a list of current vacancies. Here are some examples of judicial jobs you might find on USAJOBS.gov. You will notice that some of the salary ranges are fairly wide. This is generally dependent on the amount of experience you have when applying for the job.

U.S. Probation Officer

U.S. Probation Office, Northern District of California

Salary: $53,246–$103,722 (2009)

Investigate and supervise convicted criminals, develop individual plans, monitor assigned persons, provide counsel, and report violations. Candidates must have their Bachelor's degree in criminal justice, psychology, human resources, business administration, or a related field. At least two years of specialized experience as a probation or pretrial services officer, corrections or parole officer, or substance abuse treatment counselor are required.

Quality Assurance Clerk

U.S. District Court, Eastern District of Louisiana

Salary: $37,279–$60,643 (2009)

Maintain the official court records database with thoroughness and accuracy. The ideal candidate will have previous experience with automated systems, strong analytical and customer service skills, and attention to detail. Qualified applicants must have at least their high school diploma and at least three years of professional experience.

Judicial Support Specialist

U.S. Courts, Southern District of Texas

Salary: $30,493–$49,553 (2009)

The judicial support specialist will process new cases, facilitate each case from start to finish, record trials, gather a jury, and provide general case management support. Candidates must have at least their high school diploma (a Bachelor's degree is preferred), two years of clerical experience, and previous experience with automated systems.

Get Your OSCAR

The Online System for Clerkship Application and Review (OSCAR) is designed to link jobseekers to federal clerkships. The OSCAR website can be found at oscar.uscourts.gov. From there, jobseekers can locate current clerkship openings, select the judge they would like to work for, upload their resumé and application materials, and find employment information. Federal judges use the site to locate applicants and initiate contact.

The Supreme Court Fellows Program

This prestigious one-year program is designed to give high-achieving and experienced professionals a chance to explore the Supreme Court and its interbranch offices. Fellows come from a range of backgrounds, including law, social science, public administration, communications, technology, and more.

Fellows are placed in one of the following institutions: the Supreme Court, the Administrative Office of the U.S. Courts, the Federal Judicial Center, or the U.S. Sentencing Commission. Supreme Court Fellows must be professionally established with at least two years of experience and at least one postgraduate degree. They must also be familiar with the judicial process.

Federal Facts

The Supreme Court Fellows Program is extremely competitive: Only four fellows are chosen each year.

As fellows are already working in a professional field, they will typically take a leave of absence for the duration of the program and return to their profession upon program completion. Fellows are eligible for compensation at the GS-15 level and will receive competitive work benefits. (See Chapter 4 for details on salary associated with differing GS levels.)

Fellows must be driven, enthusiastic, and highly motivated thinkers, speakers, and writers. Eight finalists will be invited to attend a reception, where they will be oriented, interviewed further, and introduced to the commission. Afterward, the fellows will be chosen and notified of their acceptance. Applications can be completed online or by mail and include the application form, resumé, writing samples, personal statement, and candidate evaluations. For more information or to apply, visit fellows.supremecourtus.gov/selection.

Judicial Internship Program

Since its inception in 1972, more than 400 interns have served in the Judicial Internship Program. This program is offered to outstanding, advanced undergraduate students and graduating seniors. Judicial interns have the opportunity to network with prestigious federal officials, take part in research projects, and enjoy being a part of the highest court in the nation. Their responsibilities include conducting background research for speeches presented to foreign dignitaries, scanning news articles, and composing memoranda. Interns are also invited to participate in a range of research projects.

The program is unpaid, but a $1,000 scholarship may be offered upon completion of the program. The ideal candidate will be extraordinarily bright, motivated, and mature. Research and writing experience is crucial, as is some previous coursework in constitutional law. Interns must work closely with one another and be extremely trustworthy, with sound judgment.

The application includes a resumé, an unofficial transcript, three letters of recommendation, a personal statement, a writing sample, and an essay about the U.S. Constitution. Applications may be submitted online or by mail. Summer interns will work for a 12-week period and fall and spring interns for a 16-week period. For more information or to apply, visit supremecourtus.gov.

The Least You Need to Know

- About 32,000 people work in the federal judicial branch, as opposed to the roughly 2 million people who work in the executive branch.
- You don't necessarily need a law degree to work in the judicial branch, but knowledge and/or experience in law, criminal justice, government, or a related field is always a plus.
- Uscourts.gov and USAJOBS.gov are the main online resources for judicial job listings. Contact the district court, court of appeals, or bankruptcy court where you would like to apply, and inquire about current job openings.
- The Supreme Court Fellows Program and the Judicial Internship Program are both extremely competitive.

Chapter 17

Other Routes to Government Service

In This Chapter

- Looking in from the outside: government contracting
- Finding work as a grantee
- Getting appointed to a political position in government
- Seeking temporary or term employment in government

So far we've covered all three branches of government, which represent more than 2 million potential jobs. But with government being so big, there are still more ways you can get in on the government and government-related employment action.

Specifically, there are four additional paths to jobs that are either funded by the federal government or which are in the government: work as a government contractor, a grantee, or a political appointee, or in a temporary/term appointment. All four are distinctive, so we'll give you an overview of what they are and how you can find, apply for, and get these jobs.

Government Contracting

In addition to being our nation's largest employer, our government is the largest customer *in the world*, meaning that it purchases many, many items and uses outside contractors to help deliver services. In fact, federal agencies spend more than $500 billion on products and services each year. Companies across the country and around the world compete with each other to get the often-profitable business of our government.

Working for a government contractor is a great way to work with the government while still reaping the benefits of being in the private sector (or, in some cases, the nonprofit sector). This can include a shorter period of time from application to start date, a less complicated hiring process, and, depending on the company and the job, a higher salary. On the flip side, contracting does not always offer the same stability and job security that government offers and may not offer the same level of responsibility and ability to drive change and make a difference.

Top Secret

Depending on the job, working for or as a government contractor can also give you some insights into government operations and the opportunity to meet government employees and managers. This could lead to future opportunities for a job within government, and many people do move from contracting into government employment—and vice versa.

Many of the jobs in government contracting are found in the information technology, engineering, and health care fields. However, you can also find administrative, policy, and analyst jobs, among others.

There are literally thousands of government contractors. Here is a list of the 10 largest government contractors and what they do. If one seems like the right fit for you, visit its website to learn more about its job opportunities. Keep in mind that there are many other government contractors not listed here:

- **Lockheed Martin.** This global security company is principally engaged in the research, design, development, manufacture, integration, and sustainment of advanced technology systems, products, and services.

  Website for jobseekers: Lockheedmartinjobs.com

  Number of employees worldwide: 146,000

- **Boeing Company.** Boeing is a leading aerospace company and the largest manufacturer of commercial jetliners and military aircraft combined.

  Website for jobseekers: Boeing.com/employment

  Number of employees worldwide: approximately 160,000

- **Northrup Grumman Corporation.** This global security company provides systems, products, and solutions in aerospace, electronics, information systems, shipbuilding, and technical services to government and commercial customers worldwide.

  Website for jobseekers: careers.northrupgrumman.com

  Number of employees worldwide: 120,000

- **General Dynamics Corporation.** General Dynamics is engaged in business aviation; land and expeditionary combat vehicles and systems, armaments, and munitions; shipbuilding and marine systems; and mission-critical information systems and technologies.

  Website for jobseekers: Gdcareers.com

  Number of employees worldwide: approximately 92,000

- **Raytheon.** This technology company specializes in defense, homeland security, and other government markets throughout the world.

  Website for jobseekers: Rayjobs.com

  Number of employees worldwide: 73,000

- **KBR Inc.** KBR is a technology-driven engineering, procurement, and construction company.

  Website for jobseekers: KBR.com/careers

  Number of employees worldwide: 50,000

- **Science Applications International Corporation (SAIC).** SAIC's work includes medical research, testing next-generation robotics, deploying tsunami warning systems, and crime labs investigations.

  Website for jobseekers: SAIC.com/careers

  Number of employees worldwide: approximately 45,000

- **L-3 Communications, Inc.** This is a prime defense contractor in intelligence, surveillance, and reconnaissance (ISR); secure communications; government services; training and simulation; and aircraft modernization and maintenance.

  Website for jobseekers: L-3.com/careers

  Number of employees worldwide: approximately 66,000

- **Computer Sciences Corporation.** This is a global consulting, systems integration, and outsourcing company. Its mission is to provide customers in industry and government with solutions crafted to meet their strategic goals with advanced use of technology.

  Website for jobseekers: CSC.com/careers

  Number of employees worldwide: 92,000

- **Booz Allen Hamilton.** This is a strategy and technology consulting firm that does contractual work with the federal government, primarily on defense and homeland security matters.

  Website for jobseekers: Boozallen.com/careers

  Number of employees worldwide: 20,000

Grantees

The federal government awards grants (money) each year to a wide variety of state and local governments, educational institutions, public housing organizations, nonprofit organizations, and individuals. Grants are provided for a variety of purposes that benefit the public. Federal grants for individuals are limited and small businesses must typically employ at least 100 employees. The Small Business Administration (sba.gov) does have several loan programs for small businesses that are not eligible for federal grants.

There are 26 grant-making agencies in the federal government. All grant opportunities and eligibility information can be found on grants.gov, which has more than 2,000 grant listings at any given time.

The Fine Print

There's no such thing as a free lunch ... or a free grant. If you have seen ads for "making millions" by applying for grants and thought "cha ching!" think again. The government doesn't simply hand out money to people who want it. Grants are provided for specific works and tasks, and only certain organizations and individuals are eligible to apply.

Grants.gov provides information on the eligibility requirements and lists more than 20 categories of grants, including:

- Agriculture
- Arts
- Business and commerce
- Community development
- Consumer protection
- Disaster prevention and relief
- Education
- Employment, labor, and training
- Energy
- Environment
- Food and nutrition
- Health
- Housing
- Humanities
- Income security and social services
- Information and statistics
- Law, justice, and legal services
- Natural resources
- Regional development
- Science and technology
- Transportation

The downside? Getting a government grant takes a lot of preparation, work, and know-how, and nobody is guaranteed to receive one. To keep everyone honest, grants come with strings attached. These are rules and requirements that the grantee must follow (failure to do so can lead to messy legal situations). Once awarded the grant, grantees need to be sure they have the staff or structure in place to comply with the reporting requirements, which can be overwhelming, particularly for smaller organizations. Competition can also be tough: in fiscal year 2008, over 200,000 applications for grants were received.

So how do you benefit from all this grant money? This can be accomplished in several ways:

- You can work for an organization that receives grant funding (that is, a "grantee").
- You can become a grant writer. This is a highly sought-after skill and will allow you to get to know the grant process inside and out. You might also be helping worthy organizations receive money to do good things in our country and around the world.
- Some individuals can qualify for grants if they meet the criteria and have the qualifications needed to do the work. One can do a search on grants.gov for those grants for which individuals may apply.

Political Appointments

Giving advice on how to become a political appointee is kind of like giving advice on how to get someone to ask you on a date. We can steer you down the right path and give you advice on how to become an attractive candidate, but we can't guarantee you'll be picked.

Political appointees are just that—people who are appointed to a position within government by someone in the political party in charge. The biggest flood of political appointments comes right after a new President takes office, because that person has the legal authority to put his or her "people" in more than 4,000 positions in the executive branch, from cabinet secretaries to policy advisors to agency chiefs of staff to special assistants. Approximately 1,100 of these appointees must be confirmed by the U.S. Senate.

Staffing decisions don't just come from the President. After all, he (or she) has a country to run. The President's aides, the White House personnel office, and White House liaisons in the various federal departments and agencies all have a hand in placing staff in appointed positions (and, yes, most of the people helping to place new political appointees are also in appointed positions).

Federal Facts

Within three months after the November 2008 election, President Obama received more than 400,000 applications for approximately 4,000 appointed positions.

So who are the chosen ones for political appointments? Many of them come from the President's campaign staff, although there are typically many more campaign staff and volunteers than there are available political appointee positions, so there are no guarantees. If you choose to try this route, you will find that a stellar (and we mean *stellar*) job performance is just the first part of getting a job offer in the administration. Obviously, your candidate has to win the election. Then, it's a matter of who you know (and who they know), what skills you have, and what talents the administration needs. So go back to your networking roots from Chapter 6 and work it! Patience and persistence, especially if you are a lower-level staffer, will be key.

Other political appointees are experts in their field, especially at the higher levels of an agency. A few political appointees from an outgoing administration may be asked to stay on, but most are replaced by the incoming administration.

Political appointee positions are not the same as regular civil service jobs. They differ in three distinct ways:

- Appointees do not go through the regular hiring process—no USAJOBS.gov, no KSAs, no questionnaires. They do typically go through interviews and background checks, but this is much more like a typical hiring process in the private sector. For higher-level political positions, such as those requiring confirmation by the Senate, the background checks or the "vetting" process can be quite intensive and applicants must disclose detailed information about their finances and affiliations.
- By their very nature, political appointees do not have the job security that other civil servants enjoy. The average length of a political appointee's service is roughly 18 months to two years. They serve "at the pleasure of the President," meaning that they can be fired or replaced at any time. If they stick out a President's full term (or terms), they can still expect to get the boot once a new administration comes in (i.e., when the next President is inaugurated on January 20 after an election).
- No merit system is in place for political appointments. This isn't to say that the people appointed are not highly qualified. However, their route to employment goes through political connections and high-level references, which is not the case for your average civil servant. Ability and willingness to support a new President's agenda and policies are important considerations.

The process of a political appointment can be long and tedious or short and sweet. Some people get in right away (such as White House staffers, some of whom start the day of or the day after inauguration), while others can wait for months (and months … and months).

Top Secret

A great resource when looking at the political appointment process is the Plum Book (gpoaccess.gov/plumbook), which is a complete list of all political appointee positions in the executive and legislative branches and who currently holds those positions.

Don't think you're getting off too easy, though. In addition to undergoing the background checks, political appointees may face other roadblocks, even if the people in charge want to offer you the position that you want. For example, political appointees often have to wait until the head of the agency is confirmed before being placed. If that appointee needs to be confirmed by the Senate, you could wait several months with no definite start date.

Temporary and Term Appointments

Within the civil service in the executive branch, there are nonpermanent positions available where there is not a need to have a full-time, permanent employee. These are called temporary and term appointments.

Temporary appointments only last up to a year, and you will know ahead of time when your end date is, although once the year is up, the job can be extended for up to another year. Term appointments last between one and four years (the first year is considered a trial year, during which that employee can be let go).

The benefits package will differ depending on whether you are temporary or term. Temporary appointees can earn sick leave and vacation days, but receive no other benefits (meaning no health insurance). Term appointees have a better deal: They earn vacation and sick leave but also receive health insurance, life insurance, and access to retirement benefits.

The Fine Print

Due to the nonpermanent nature of temporary and term appointments, these employees cannot be promoted and do not get the competitive status that other civil servants are awarded, which means that they cannot apply for jobs through the internal merit promotion system.

Just about any position in the federal government can be filled on a temporary or term basis. Since many people searching for jobs apply only for "permanent" jobs, the competition for a temporary or term appointment is not as fierce and it may be easier to get hired as long as you still have the qualifications needed. Further, if you make a good impression in your temporary or term government job, this may give you an advantage in applying for permanent jobs in the same organization. Finally, the experience you gain may make you more competitive when applying for permanent jobs in other government organizations.

Examples of Temporary or Term Appointment Jobs

Following are some examples of federal jobs that have been advertised as temporary or term appointments. Keep in mind that it's not the job itself that determines whether it's going to be filled on a time-limited basis, but the fact that the job does not need to be filled on an ongoing basis. For example, a census taker (called an enumerator) is needed only while a census is actually being taken. Other jobs are filled this way when there is an increase in workload that is not expected to continue or to fill in behind another employee who will be gone from the job for an extended period but is expected to return.

The salary will vary according to the type of job and your level of experience.

Medical Instrument Technician (EKG)

Veteran's Health Administration—Wilkes Barre, PA

Salary: $30,772–$49,553

The medical instrument technician will operate medical equipment, carry out electrocardiogram procedures, consult with patients, and perform other duties as assigned. Candidates must possess the knowledge, skills, and abilities of a medical instrument technician and must have at least one year of specialized experience. This is a temporary appointment only—not to exceed 12 months.

Lead Survey Technician

USDA Forest Service—Multiple Locations

Salary: $14.24 hourly

The lead survey technician will work as a team leader and implement a range of surveying techniques to perform analyses. This employee will facilitate projects and coordinate with management to ensure that tasks are completed. Candidates must have one year of specialized experience. This is a temporary appointment only, not to exceed six months.

Associate Professor (Faculty Development)

U.S. Army Training and Doctrine Command—Monterey County, CA

Salary: $49,544–$89,068

The associate professor will determine, implement, and monitor faculty foreign-language education and training courses and will observe feedback and make necessary changes to the courses. This employee will also perform various administrative duties. Candidates must have a Master's degree in foreign-language education or a related field and two years of language teaching experience. This is a temporary appointment only, with multiple schedules.

Loan Review Specialist

Federal Deposit Insurance Corporation—Multiple Locations

Salary: $59,387–$94,023

The loan review specialist will perform duties related to the review and classification of credits in line with the FDIC's Risk Management Examination. He or she will perform various tasks, including the assessment of lending policies, analysis of financial information, and review of loan files. Candidates must have a doctoral degree or a Master of Laws degree in business, finance, accounting, or a related field. A combination of specialized experience and education may be substituted. This is a term appointment only, not to exceed two years.

Community Planner

U.S. Agency for International Development—Washington, D.C.

Salary: $102,721–$133,543

The community planner will perform tasks related to the design, implementation, and management of community planning projects and will determine mission-specific community planning programs. This employee will work with and maintain relationships with government, private sector, and academic stakeholders. Candidates must have a Bachelor's degree in community planning, architecture, engineering, sociology, geography, or a related field in addition to one year of specialized experience with community planning. This is a term appointment only, not to exceed two years.

IT Specialist (Internet)

U.S. Geological Survey—St. Petersburg, FL

Salary: $44,524–$69,204

The IT specialist will work with various Internet services to ensure compatibility, represent websites and projects at conferences and workshops, and create databases. This employee must work with managers, scientists, and other employees to obtain content for websites. Candidates must have a Bachelor's degree or a combination of education and specialized experience. This is a term appointment only, not to exceed 13 months.

Finding Temporary or Term Appointments

So how can you get a temporary or term appointment? Generally, you will want to apply through USAJOBS.gov, just like other civil service jobs. Simply go to the website and type in **temporary** or **term** into the keyword search box. Your search will yield thousands of temporary and term job openings across the country, so be sure to narrow it down to the region or city where you want to work. You can also directly contact the agency or agencies where you would like to work.

The Least You Need to Know

- Hundreds of thousands of jobs are available with government contractors.
- Contractors often go into government and vice versa, so government contracting could help you ultimately get into government if that is your goal.
- Only certain organizations and individuals can apply for and receive grants, which are given out for work and projects that benefit the public. Grants.gov is a good place to start.
- Political appointments are difficult to get and do not offer the same job security as other civil service jobs, but they can be exciting if you are one of the relatively lucky few to get one.
- Temporary appointments last up to one year, while term appointments last from one to four years. However, these types of appointments are a great way to get your foot in the door and can sometimes help you obtain a permanent job down the road.

Chapter 18

State Government Jobs

In This Chapter

- What types of jobs are available in state government
- How to find and apply for state government jobs
- How the process differs from applying for federal jobs
- Why you should work in state government
- Advice on getting the job you want

More than 3.7 million Americans have full-time jobs in state government, according to the 2008 U.S. Census Bureau. State government is a great option for employment if you want to broaden your job search beyond federal government or if you are simply interested in working for your state.

As in the federal government, there are literally thousands of occupational areas to choose from when applying for state government jobs. Plus, state governments hire all experience levels and educational backgrounds, so you are sure to find something to fit your employment needs.

Seeking employment in state government is unlike pursuing federal government jobs, where you can access and apply for virtually all jobs through USAJOBS.gov. Each of the 50 states (and D.C.) has a different hiring procedure and application process.

In this chapter, we will walk you through how to find and apply for state government jobs, fill you in on what kinds of jobs are available (and which are in most need of being filled), and the benefits of working in state government.

Occupational Areas for State Government

As with federal government jobs, state governments hire for full-time, part-time, temporary, and hourly positions.

Examples of jobs states are hiring for:

- Nurses
- Nursing assistants
- Other health care professionals
- Corrections officers
- Revenue-generating positions, such as auditors and debt collectors
- 24/7 institution personnel (psychologists, medical personnel, orderlies, etc.)
- Law enforcement officers
- Engineers
- State parks workers
- Community college and public university professors and administrative and support staff

Top Secret

Most states do not have a residency requirement, but there are some jobs (e.g., in law enforcement) that require you to live within a certain distance from your workplace. However, Pennsylvania is an example in which there is a residency requirement unless the agency can't find anyone in state to fill the job. Oklahoma and Nevada don't require you to be a resident, but do give preference to in-state residents.

The State of Wisconsin lists its jobs by the following categories:

- Accounting, budget, finance, purchasing
- Administrative support, clerical
- Agriculture
- Aviation
- Corrections
- Education
- Engineers, architects
- Food service
- General business
- Health care
- Human resources
- Information technology
- Inspectors, investigators
- Law enforcement, public safety
- Legal
- Librarians, archivists, curators
- Maintenance, general laborers
- Management
- Media, communications
- Natural resources, environmental sciences
- Psychologists
- Real estate
- Research
- Science
- Social services
- Trades, skilled crafts
- Unknown, other
- Warehouse, mailroom

On the Commonwealth of Virginia jobs site, for example, you might find hourly wage positions ranging from an "Art Model" for a community college to "Personal Care Aide" for the Department of Health to a "Certified Nurse Assistant" at the local veterans care center.

Where to Find State Government Jobs

Each state has its own website where you can find and apply for jobs. For a full listing of state government job sites, see Appendix E. Another great resource is the National Association of State Personnel Executives (NASPE.net), which has links to state government job openings.

Although the websites are the best place to go for a full listing of jobs, most states also host career fairs. States frequently advertise these job fairs on the state government website, through media press releases, and in public service announcements on local

> **Federal Facts**
>
> Although it is hard to say how many jobs are generally available in state government without calling and asking each state, South Carolina, for example, reports that it generally has between 500 to 1,000 job openings at any given time.

radio programs. They may also do some advertising in newspapers, magazines, and elsewhere for critical needs positions, such as engineers and health care professionals.

You may be surprised to hear that recruiting for state government jobs is also going the way of Web 2.0. Some states are using Twitter, Facebook, and LinkdIn to advertise jobs and recruit new employees, so be sure to check the Internet for out-of-the-box ways to connect with your state government through these social networking sites.

How to Apply for State Government Jobs

As we've mentioned, each state has its own application process. The good news is that many states are now using online systems that make it easy to apply and streamline the process for both the applicant and hiring personnel.

Most state government pages have employment links on their homepage. Look for the words "careers," "jobs," or "employment." This will connect you to all the job listings for the state.

As on USAJOBS.gov, you may be asked to create an account and upload your resumé (and/or enter information about your work history). Once you have entered your information, it should be easy to search and apply for jobs.

For many states, if you don't see anything you like, you can fill out a form to have them alert you when a job becomes available that is suited to your given criteria.

Let's walk through the application process using an example state and job that we want. For this instance, we are going to use the Lone Star state, Texas, as an example. The job we are looking for is structural engineer (although you could substitute virtually any job).

Here are the steps:

1. Go to www.workintexas.com.
2. Now you have a choice. Under "Looking for a Job" you could go straight to "search jobs." But since we really want to get into the system, let's go ahead and get registered with the site, so click on "Looking for a Job."

3. Under "New to Work in Texas," click "Register." Read the user agreement and then click "I Accept."

4. Create your login by filling out the personal information form, including your Social Security number.

5. Continue your registration by filling out contact information, additional information, job search preferences, and work history.

   Once you are done filling out all your information, there will be a box titled "Find Job Resources in Your Area." This has the name, location, and phone number where you can find out about job fairs, employers that are currently interviewing, new businesses opening in your area, and more through the Events Calendar for your nearest workforce center. Write this down (and definitely reach out to this person/place when you are done searching online) and then click "Next," which takes you to "My Portfolio."

6. Under "My Portfolio" you have the opportunity to completely fill out your resumé with all work history and education, fill out a State of Texas job application, and check the boxes that will help you find your perfect job match.

7. Once you have filled out all of this information, click "Match Jobs." This takes you to a list of available jobs that meet your experience and search criteria. From here, you can view the job listings to see if it's a job you like and are qualified for. At the bottom of the job description, you have the option of clicking "How to Apply," "Not Interested," "Not Qualified," or "Decide Later."

   If you choose "How to Apply," you will receive instructions of what to do next. Likely, you will be instructed to submit your application and/or resumé to an e-mail address that is provided.

Simply follow the instructions, and there you go—you've applied for a state government job!

Note that after you submit your application, you may be asked to answer questions, take relevant tests, submit to a background check, or provide more information.

How Is State Government Different from Federal Government?

Although every state has its own application process, there are many similarities between applying for state government jobs and applying for federal government jobs.

While states' hiring processes are not exactly the same as those of the federal government, you should be prepared to go through a process similar to the federal government's, wherein you will be asked to fill out questionnaires, submit lengthy resumés, take relevant exams, and be asked for further information.

Because state systems and processes can differ, there is no comprehensive data on how long the application process takes in state government, and it will vary from state to state. However, state human resources personnel (the people who process the job applications) have reported a significant increase in efficiency since they have gone to an electronic system for job applicants. Information technology has reportedly speeded up the process tremendously across the board.

Top Secret

If you have been discouraged by applying for state government jobs in the past, you might want to try again. The big move to electronic systems (meaning you apply online and human resources personnel can manage all applications in an online database) has made them quicker on the draw, so they can respond to and communicate with applicants more quickly after they apply.

As in federal government, for many of the most in-demand professions—especially in the health care field and engineering—some states offer recruitment and retention bonuses. Sometimes there's also flexibility to negotiate a higher salary (it never hurts to ask).

Also, most state governments give preference to veterans (and perhaps particularly to disabled veterans), similar to federal government policy, although the way this is done varies by state. Some states give preference for other backgrounds. For example, Montana offers residents of Native American reservations preference for state jobs within a reservation.

The Benefits of Working in State Government

The benefits of working in state government are similar to those of working in federal government. For example, working in state government is also a way to give back by serving the public interest, and you can move from job to job and agency to agency fairly easily, even if you end up in a position that's totally different from the state job you initially get. There are literally thousands of different job categories, so there's something for every background, major, and interest in state government.

While job stability is still a benefit in state government, it is reportedly not quite as stable as federal government work. In 2009, many states were forced to lay off workers (or cut back on hiring) due to budget constraints and economic hardship. For example, in 2009 South Carolina reported that because of an 18 percent budget reduction, it had to cut back on hiring, particularly in administrative positions. However, the state did not cut back on hiring critical needs positions, including public health positions and public safety personnel.

States often offer competitive salaries and benefits, particularly for locations outside major metropolitan areas (think Albany, not New York City, or Sacramento, not San Francisco or Los Angeles). In these locations, your dollar will go further due to lower cost of living. In other words, housing and other expenses are cheaper in those areas, saving you money.

Top Five Pieces of Advice from State HR Managers

According to state HR managers, there are several things an applicant can do to both find the right job and improve his or her chances of getting a job:

- To find the job you want, go online and monitor a state's job website continuously for updated options. Or, if the state offers this service, you can fill out a form with your job search criteria and have new job openings sent to you that meet that criteria.
- Submit a different resumé and application for each job you apply for if those jobs require different qualifications and duties. This is similar to tailoring your federal resumé (see Chapter 9): the point is to provide information about your background and experience that is relevant to the job for which you are applying. This takes time and is something that many applicants simply fail to do, possibly at the cost of a new job.

- Proofread. Typos and poor grammar are unfortunately all too common in job applications, according to state government hiring personnel. Proofread everything before you send it, or, better yet, have someone else proofread it for you to get a fresh perspective. This may sound simple, but it could be the difference between you getting a job and not getting a job.
- When attending job fairs or interviews, dress conservatively, look the part, and prepare your materials, such as your resumé, with the utmost care. Many state hiring personnel said they were appalled at the way many people dress (unprofessionally and unkempt) and at the way they presented their resumé (folded in half, crumpled in an old folder, etc.).
- Don't give up. Keep applying for jobs, keep following up, keep hope alive! As with the federal job search, persistence pays off in the end.

The Least You Need to Know

- There are thousands of job options in state government for people of all educational and experience backgrounds.
- To apply for state jobs, go to your state government's job website.
- State government work has many of the same benefits of federal government work: the satisfaction of public service, a level of job security, good pay and benefits, and more.
- Don't lose hope—persistence and diligence in your application(s) will pay off.

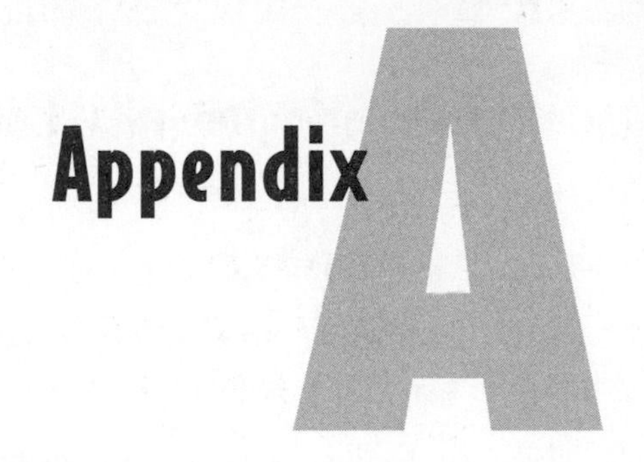

Federal Agency List

When we said the possibilities for government work were nearly limitless, we weren't kidding! As you can see from this comprehensive list of federal agencies and agency subcomponents, there's a place for jobseekers of virtually every interest and background.

If you're not quite sure which agency is the best fit for you, start by reading through the agency missions and checking out their websites to find your perfect match.

In cases where they apply for the agency, we've included information on other locations and subcomponents.

Administration for Children and Families (HHS) (ACF)

Website: www.acf.hhs.gov/

HQ: Washington, D.C.

Other locations: Boston, MA; Philadelphia, PA; Chicago, IL; Kansas City, KS; San Francisco, CA; New York City, NY; Atlanta, GA; Dallas, TX; Denver, CO; and Seattle, WA

Mission: To direct federal programs that promote the economic and social well-being of families, children, individuals, and communities.

Administration on Aging (HHS) (AOA)

Website: www.aoa.gov/

HQ: Washington, D.C.

Other locations: New York, NY; Boston, MA; Atlanta, GA; Chicago, IL; Dallas, TX; Kansas City, MO; Denver, CO; Seattle, WA; and San Francisco, CA

Mission: To develop a comprehensive, coordinated, and cost-effective system of long-term care that helps elderly individuals to maintain their dignity in their homes and communities.

Agency for Healthcare Research and Quality (HHS) (AHRQ)

Website: www.ahrq.gov/

HQ: Rockville, MD

Mission: To improve the quality, safety, effectiveness, and cost-effectiveness of health care for all Americans.

Agency for International Development (USAID)

Website: www.usaid.gov

HQ: Washington, D.C.

Other locations: More than 80 international missions

Mission: To promote economic growth, development, and humanitarian assistance around the world in support of U.S. foreign policy. In collaboration with foreign governments, businesses, and nongovernmental organizations, the Agency for International Development operates health, democracy, agriculture, and conflict prevention programs.

Agricultural Research Service (USDA) (ARS)

Website: www.ars.usda.gov/main/main.htm

HQ: Washington, D.C.

Other locations: Numerous offices throughout the United States

Mission: To act as the primary research center for U.S. Department of Agriculture.

Alcohol and Tobacco Tax and Trade Bureau (USDT) (TTB)

Website: www.ttb.gov/

HQ: Washington, D.C.

Mission: To collect alcohol, tobacco, firearms, and ammunition excise taxes, to ensure that these products are labeled, advertised, and marketed in accordance with the law, and to administer the laws and regulations in a manner that protects the consumer and the revenue, and promotes voluntary compliance.

Ames Research Center (NASA) (ARC)

Website: www.arc.nasa.gov/

HQ: Moffet Field, CA

Mission: To research, develop, and transfer leading-edge aeronautical technologies through the utilization of computations, simulations, ground and flight experimentation, and information services.

Antitrust Division (DOJ)

Website: www.usdoj.gov/atr/index.html

HQ: Washington, D.C.

Other locations: Atlanta, GA; Chicago, IL; Cleveland, OH; Dallas, TX; New York, NY; Philadelphia, PA; and San Francisco, CA

Mission: To promote and protect the competitive process, and the American economy, through the enforcement of the antitrust laws.

Bonneville Power Administration (DOE) (BPA)

Website: www.bpa.gov/corporate/

HQ: Portland, OR

Other locations: Various regional offices in the Pacific Northwest

Mission: To create and deliver the best value for our customers and constituents as we act in concert with others to assure the Pacific Northwest an adequate, efficient, economical, and reliable power supply; a transmission system that maintains electrical reliability and stability; and mitigation of the Federal Columbia River Power System's impact on fish and wildlife.

Broadcasting Board of Governors (BBG)

Website: www.bbg.gov/

HQ: Washington, D.C.

Mission: To serve as an example of a free and professional press, reaching a worldwide audience with news, information, and relevant discussions.

Bureau of Alcohol, Tobacco, Firearms, and Explosives (DOJ) (ATF)

Website: www.atf.gov

HQ: Washington, D.C.

Other locations: Boston, MA; Baltimore, MD; Philadelphia, PA; New York, NY; Charlotte, NC; Chicago, IL; Columbus, OH; Dallas and Houston, TX; Detroit, MI; Kansas City, KS; Louisville, KY; New Orleans, LA; Seattle, WA; Los Angeles and San Francisco, CA; Phoenix, AZ; Atlanta, GA; Miami and Tampa, FL; Nashville, TN; and St. Paul, MN

Mission: To enforce and administer laws regulating firearms and explosives and the production, taxation, and distribution of alcohol and tobacco products.

Bureau of the Census (DOC) (Census)

Website: www.census.gov/

HQ: Washington, D.C.

Other locations: Various offices in all United States territories

Mission: To serve as the leading source of quality data about the nation's people and economy. The Census Bureau honors privacy, protects confidentiality, shares its expertise globally, and conducts its work openly.

Bureau of Citizenship and Immigration Services (DHS) (USCIS)

Website: www.uscis.gov/graphics/index.htm

HQ: Washington, D.C.

Other locations: Various offices throughout the United States

Mission: To oversee lawful immigration to the United States. USCIS establishes immigration services, policies, and priorities to preserve America's legacy as a nation of immigrants while ensuring that no one is admitted who is a threat to public safety.

Bureau of Customs and Border Protection (DHS) (CBP)

Website: www.cbp.gov/xp/cgov/border_security/border_patrol/

HQ: Washington, D.C.

Other locations: Various offices throughout the United States

Mission: To secure the homeland by preventing the illegal entry of people and goods while facilitating legitimate travel and trade.

Bureau of Engraving and Printing (USDT) (BEP)

Website: www.moneyfactory.gov/

HQ: Washington, D.C.

Other locations: Fort Worth, TX

Mission: To design and manufacture high quality security documents that deter counterfeiting and meet customer requirements for quality, quantity, and performance.

Bureau of Immigration and Customs Enforcement (DHS) (ICE)

Website: www.ice.gov/

HQ: Washington, D.C.

Other locations: Various offices throughout the United States

Mission: To protect national security by enforcing our nation's customs and immigration laws.

Bureau of Indian Affairs (DOI) (BIA)

Website: www.doi.gov/bia/

HQ: n/a

Mission: To administer and manage 55.7 million acres of land held in trust by the United States for American Indians, Indian tribes, and Alaska Natives. Responsibilities include developing forestlands, leasing assets on these lands, directing agricultural programs, protecting water and land rights, developing and maintaining infrastructure, providing for health and human services, and economic development.

Bureau of Labor Statistics (DOL) (BLS)

Website: www.bls.gov/

HQ: Washington, D.C.

Other locations: Seven regional offices in San Francisco, Dallas, Chicago, Atlanta, Philadelphia, Boston, and New York. Additional economists/staff stationed in 95 cities across the United States.

Mission: To serve as the principal fact-finding agency for the federal government in the broad field of labor economics and statistics. The Bureau of Labor Statistics provides and disseminates timely, accurate, and relevant information about the economy using state-of-the-art statistical techniques, economic concepts, technology, and management processes.

Bureau of Land Management (DOI) (BLM)

Website: www.blm.gov/nhp/

HQ: Washington, D.C.

Other locations: Centers and field offices located in AK; AZ; CA; CO; ID; MT; NV; NM; OR; UT; WY; Jackson, MS; Milwaukee, WI; and Springfield, VA

Mission: To manage the surface resources and subsurface minerals of 12 percent of the U.S.'s public land (mostly in the West) with a commitment to sustain the health, diversity, and productivity of the lands for the use and enjoyment of present and future generations.

Bureau of Prisons/Federal Prison System (DOJ) (BOP)

Website: www.bop.gov/

HQ: Washington, D.C.

Other locations: Offices located throughout the United States

Mission: To attend to the custody and care of federal offenders. The Bureau of Prisons also works to ensure that its facilities are safe, humane, cost-efficient, and appropriately secure.

Bureau of the Public Debt (USDT) (BPD)

Website: www.publicdebt.treas.gov/

HQ: Washington, D.C.

Other locations: Parkersburg, WV

Mission: To borrow the money needed to operate the federal government, account for the resulting debt, issue Treasury securities to refund maturing debt, and raise new money.

Bureau of Reclamation (DOI) (USBR)

Website: www.usbr.gov/

HQ: Washington, D.C.

Other locations: Denver, Loveland, and Grand Junction, CO; Billings, MT; Grand Island, NE; Mills, WY; Austin, TX; Bismarck, ND; Yuma and Phoenix, AZ; Shasta Lake, Folsom, Temecula, Sacramento, and Fresno, CA; Carson City and Boulder City, NV; Klamath Falls, OR; Boise, ID; Yakima and Grand Coulee, WA; Salt Lake City and Provo, UT; and Farmington and Albuquerque, NM

Mission: To manage, develop, and protect water sources throughout the United States, including dams, canals, and reservoirs. It also produces hydroelectric power and manages 58 power plants in the U.S.

Centers for Disease Control and Prevention (HHS) (CDC)

Website: www.cdc.gov/

HQ: Atlanta, GA

Other locations: Centers, facilities, quarantine offices, and state and local health agencies located across the United States and abroad. Sites include Anchorage, AK; Cincinnati, OH; Fort Collins, CO; Morgantown, WV; Pittsburgh, PA; Research Triangle Park, NC; San Juan, PR; Spokane, WA; and Washington, D.C.

Mission: To protect the health and safety of people at home and abroad by providing information on health issues and promoting disease prevention and control, environmental health, and educational activities.

Centers for Medicare and Medicaid Services (HHS) (CMS)

Website: www.cms.hhs.gov/

HQ: Baltimore, MD, and Washington, D.C.

Other locations: Boston, New York, Philadelphia, Atlanta, Dallas, Kansas City, Chicago, Denver, San Francisco, and Seattle

Mission: To assure health care security for the general public through the management of programs that include Medicare, Medicaid, State Children's Health Insurance Program, and the Health Insurance Portability and Accountability Act, and provide leadership in the broader health care marketplace to improve the health of all citizens.

Civil Division (DOJ)

Website: www.usdoj.gov/civil/home.html

HQ: Washington, D.C.

Mission: To represent the United States, its departments and agencies, Members of Congress, Cabinet officers, and other federal employees. The Civil Division's litigation reflects the diversity of government activities, involving, for example, the defense of challenges to Presidential actions; national security issues; benefit programs; energy policies; commercial issues such as contract disputes, banking insurance, patents, fraud, and debt collection; all manner of accident and liability claims; and criminal violations of the immigration and consumer protection laws.

Civil Rights Division (DOJ)

Website: www.usdoj.gov/crt/crt-home.html

HQ: Washington, D.C.

Mission: To enforce federal statutes prohibiting discrimination on the basis of race, sex, handicap, religion, and national origin.

Combined Research, Education, Economic Services (USDA)

Website: www.ree.usda.gov/

HQ: Washington, D.C.

Mission: To create a safe, sustainable, competitive U.S. food and fiber system and strong, healthy communities, families, and youth through integrated research, analysis, and education.

Commander, Navy Installations (DON) (CNI)

Website: www.cni.navy.mil/

HQ: Washington, D.C.

Other locations: Various domestic and international regional offices

Mission: To provide shore support for naval installations.

Commodity Futures Trading Commission (CFTC)

Website: www.cftc.gov/cftc/cftchome.htm

HQ: Washington, D.C.

Other locations: Chicago, Kansas City, and New York

Mission: To protect market users and the public from abusive practices related to the sale of commodity and financial futures and options.

Congressional Budget Office

Website: www.cbo.gov/

HQ: Washington, D.C.

Mission: To provide the Congress with the objective, timely, nonpartisan analyses needed for economic and budget decisions and with the information and estimates required for the Congressional budget process.

Consumer Product Safety Commission (CPSC)

Website: www.cpsc.gov/

HQ: Bethesda, MD

Other locations: New York, Chicago, and Oakland

Mission: To protect the public from harm associated with manufactured products.

Corporation for National and Community Service (CNCS)

Website: www.nationalservice.org/

HQ: Washington, D.C.

Other locations: Numerous offices throughout the United States

Mission: To improve lives, strengthen communities, and foster civic engagement through service and volunteering. The Corporation's three major programs include Senior Corps, AmeriCorps, and Learn and Serve America.

Court Services and Offender Supervision Agency (CSOSA)

Website: www.csosa.gov/

HQ: Washington, D.C.

Mission: To provide supervisory and treatment services to over 26,000 individuals on pretrial release, probation, and parole and to assist federal and local courts in determining eligibility for release.

Criminal Division (DOJ)

Website: www.usdoj.gov/criminal/index.html

HQ: Washington, D.C.

Mission: To develop, enforce, and supervise the application of all federal criminal laws except those specifically assigned to other divisions.

Defense Commissary Agency (DOD) (DECA)

Website: www.commissaries.com/

HQ: Fort Lee, VA

Other locations: Main regional offices in Fort Lee, VA; McClellan, CA; and Kapaun Air Station, Germany, which manage nearly 280 commissaries in the United States, the Pacific, and Europe

Mission: To provide an efficient and effective worldwide system of commissaries for the resale of groceries and household supplies to members of the military services, their families, and other authorized patrons.

Defense Contract Audit Agency (DOD) (DCAA)

Website: www.dcaa.mil/

HQ: Fort Belvoir, VA

Other locations: Regional offices in Irving, TX; Smyrna, GA; Philadelphia, PA; Lowell, MA; and La Miranda, CA; more than 300 field audit offices and sub-offices throughout the United States, Europe, and the Pacific

Mission: To provide standardized contract audit services to the DOD and several other government agencies. The Defense Contract Audit Agency also provides accounting and financial advisory services regarding contracts and subcontracts to all DOD offices responsible for procurement and contract administration.

Defense Contract Management Agency (DOD) (DCMA)

Website: www.dcma.mil/

HQ: Alexandria, VA

Other locations: 65 major office locations worldwide

Mission: To provide contract management services to the DOD to ensure that federal acquisition programs, supplies, and services are delivered on time, within cost, and meet performance requirements.

Defense Finance and Accounting Service (DOD) (DFAS)

Website: www.dod.mil/dfas/

HQ: Main offices in Cleveland, OH; Columbus, OH; Denver, CO; Indianapolis, IN; Kansas City, KS

Other locations: Limestone, ME; Rome, NY; and in Europe and Asia

Mission: To provide accounting services to the DOD and information concerning payment to DOD vendors.

Defense Information Systems Agency (DOD) (DISA)

Website: www.disa.mil/

HQ: Falls Church, VA

Other locations: Directorates in Falls Church and Arlington, VA. Field offices in Washington, D.C.; Annapolis, MD; Norfolk and Fort Belvoir, VA; Fort Huachuca, AZ; Miami and MacDill Air Force Base, FL; Peterson Air Force Base, CO; Scott Air Force Base, IL; Offutt Air Force Base, NE; Wheeler Army Airfield, HI; and Vaihingen, Germany.

Mission: To plan, develop, field, operate, and support command, control, communications, and information systems that serve the needs of the President, Vice President, Secretary of Defense, Joint Chiefs of Staff, Combatant Commanders, and other DOD components.

Defense Logistics Agency (DOD) (DLA)

Website: www.dla.mil/

HQ: Fort Belvoir, VA

Other locations: Over 500 sites in 28 countries, including the United States. Lead centers/offices located in Richmond, VA; Philadelphia, PA; Mechanicsburg, PA; Columbus, OH; Wright-Patterson Air Force Base, OH; Battle Creek, MI; Wiesbaden, Germany; and Taegu, Korea.

Mission: To provide supplies and services to America's military forces worldwide.

Department of Agriculture (USDA)

Website: www.usda.gov/

HQ: Washington, D.C.

Other locations: Administrative offices in Alexandria, VA, and Beltsville, MD, plus state and county offices nationwide

Subcomponents: Agricultural Marketing Service (USDA); Agricultural Research Service (USDA); Rural Housing Service (USDA); Risk Management Agency (USDA); Foreign Agricultural Service (USDA); Forest Service (USDA); Natural Resources Conservation Service (USDA); National Agricultural Statistics Service (USDA); Office of the Inspector General (USDA); Food and Nutrition Service (USDA); Animal and Plant Health Inspection Service (USDA); Grain Inspection, Packers and Stockyards Administration (USDA); Food Safety and Inspection Service (USDA); Office of the Chief Financial Officer (USDA); Combined Rural Development Services (USDA); Combined Research, Education, Economic Services (USDA); All Other Components (USDA); Departmental Administration (USDA); Farm Service Agency (USDA)

Mission: To promote U.S. agriculture domestically and internationally and to set standards governing the quality, quantity, safety, and labeling of food sold in the United States. The Department of Agriculture's broad range of responsibilities also include the food stamp program, anti-poverty programs, conservation and natural resource protection, and an array of rural development programs.

Department of the Air Force (USAF)

Website: www.af.mil/

HQ: Arlington, VA, at the Pentagon

Other locations: Go to www.airforce.com/baselocator.php

Subcomponents: U.S. Air Force Academy (Air Force); U.S. Air Forces, Europe (Air Force); Air Education and Training Command (Air Force); Headquarters, Air Force Reserve (Air Force); Pacific Air Forces (Air Force); Headquarters Air Intelligence Agency (Air Force); Air Combat Command (Air Force); Air Mobility Command (Air Force); U.S. Air Force Materiel Command (Air Force); Space Command (Air Force); All Other Components (Air Force); Air National Guard Units (Air Force)

Mission: To deliver sovereign options for the defense of the United States of America and its global interests. To fly and fight in air, space, and cyberspace.

Department of the Army (DA)

Website: www.army.mil/

HQ: Arlington, VA, at the Pentagon

Other locations: Go to www.army.mil/institution/organization/

Subcomponents: All Other Components (Army); U.S. Army Contracting Agency (Army); U.S. Army Acquisition Support Center (Army); U.S. Army Intelligence and Security Command (Army); U.S. Army Test and Evaluation Command (Army); U.S. Army Installation Management Agency (Army); U.S. Army Corps of Engineers (Army); U.S. Army Forces Command (Army); U.S. Army Netcom/9th Army Signal Command (Army); U.S. Army Reserve Command (Army); U.S. Army Medical Command (Army); U.S. Army Materiel Command (Army); U.S. Army Human Resources Command (Army); U.S. Army National Guard Units (Army); Field Operating Agencies of the Army Staff Resourced Through OA-22 (Army); U.S. Army Accessions Command (Army); U.S. Army Training and Doctrine Command (Army)

Mission: To provide expeditionary land forces wherever and whenever they are required. Working in conjunction with the U.S. Department of Defense, the U.S. Army trains and equips soldiers and creates leaders among them to rapidly respond when they are called upon to serve our nation.

Department of Commerce (DOC)

Website: www.commerce.gov

HQ: Washington, D.C.

Other locations: NOAA, Census, and ITA offices nationwide

Subcomponents: National Oceanic and Atmospheric Administration (Commerce); International Trade Administration (Commerce); Patent and Trademark Office (Commerce); National Institute of Standards and Technology (Commerce); Bureau of the Census (Commerce); All Other Components (Commerce)

Mission: To promote economic growth and security in the United States through the development of technology, promotion of exports, and gathering of economic information and analysis. The Department of Commerce compiles economic statistics, conducts the census, regulates patents and trademarks, forecasts the weather, charts the oceans, and encourages international trade.

Department of Defense (DOD)

Website: www.defenselink.mil/

HQ: Arlington, VA, at the Pentagon

Other locations: Installations in every state in the country and in 146 countries around the world

Subcomponents: Office of the Secretary of Defense (DOD); Defense Information Systems Agency (DOD); Defense Logistics Agency (DOD); Defense Contract Audit Agency (DOD); Department of Defense Education Activity (DOD); Washington Headquarters Services (DOD); Defense Commissary Agency (DOD); Defense Finance and Accounting Service (DOD); Defense Contract Management Agency (DOD); All Other Components (DOD)

Mission: To protect and advance the security and interests of the United States, to deter aggressors and, if deterrence fails, to defeat any adversary.

Department of Defense Education Activity (DOD) (DoDEA)

Website: www.dodea.edu/

HQ: Arlington, VA

Other locations: DoDEA operates 192 schools in 14 districts located in 12 foreign countries, seven states, Guam, and Puerto Rico.

Mission: To manage a worldwide school system for the children of enlisted military personnel (which comprise 80 percent of its student body) and DOD civilian employees.

Department of Education (ED)

Website: www.ed.gov/index.jsp

HQ: Washington, D.C.

Other locations: Boston, MA; New York, NY; Philadelphia, PA; Atlanta, GA; Chicago, IL; Dallas, TX; Kansas City, MO; Denver, CO; San Francisco, CA; and Seattle, WA

Subcomponents: All Other Components (ED); Office for Civil Rights (ED); Office of Inspector General (ED); Office of Special Education and Rehabilitative Services (ED); Office of the Chief Financial Officer (ED); Federal Student Aid (ED); Office of Postsecondary Education (ED)

Mission: To promote equal access to education and educational excellence. The Department of Education establishes policies on and manages the funds for federal financial aid programs, collects and disseminates data on America's schools, and focuses national attention on educational issues.

Department of Energy (DOE)

Website: www.energy.gov/index.htm

HQ: Washington, D.C.

Other locations: Nuclear security operations offices in Oakland, CA; Albuquerque, NM; and Nevada; plus nine site offices nationwide. Regional power administrations in Portland, OR; Elberton, GA; Tulsa, OK; and Lakewood, CO. Field offices in Albuquerque, NM; Chicago, IL; Idaho Falls, ID; Las Vegas, NV; Oakland, CA; Oak Ridge, TN; Springdale, OH; Hanford, WA; and Aiken, SC; plus 20 laboratories and technology centers.

Subcomponents: Bonneville Power Administration (DOE); Headquarters Program Offices (DOE); Headquarters Staff Offices (DOE); Field Locations (DOE); National Nuclear Security Administration Headquarters Offices (DOE); National Nuclear Security Administration Field Sites (DOE); Power Marketing Administrations–Southeastern, Southwestern, and Western Areas (DOE)

Mission: To advance the national, economic, and energy security of the United States, to promote scientific and technological innovation in support of that mission, and to ensure the environmental cleanup of the national nuclear weapons complex.

Department of Health and Human Services (HHS)

Website: www.hhs.gov/

HQ: Washington, D.C.

Other locations: Major sub-units in Baltimore, MD; Bethesda, MD; Rockville, MD; and Atlanta, GA. HHS regional offices in Seattle, WA; San Francisco, CA; Denver, CO; Dallas, TX; Kansas City, MO; Chicago, IL; Atlanta, GA; Philadelphia, PA; New York, NY; and Boston, MA.

Subcomponents: Office of the Secretary of Health and Human Services (HHS); Program Support Center (HHS); Administration On Aging (HHS); Substance Abuse and Mental Health Services Administration (HHS); Agency for Healthcare Research and Quality (HHS); Health Resources and Services Administration (HHS); Food and Drug Administration (HHS); Indian Health Service (HHS); National Institutes of Health (HHS); Centers for Disease Control and Prevention (HHS); Centers for Medicare and Medicaid Services (HHS); Administration for Children and Families (HHS); All Other Components (HHS)

Mission: To protect the health of all Americans and provide essential human services, especially to those with the greatest need. The Department of Health and Human Services sponsors medical and social science research, approves the use of new drugs and medical devices, manages infectious disease prevention and response programs, administers Medicare, Medicaid, and other programs that provide financial assistance and services to low-income families.

Department of Homeland Security (DHS)

Website: www.dhs.gov

HQ: Washington, D.C.

Other locations: Offices nationwide and overseas

Subcomponents: Headquarters (DHS); Bureau of Customs and Border Protection (DHS); Bureau of Immigration and Customs Enforcement (DHS); Transportation Security Administration (DHS); United States Coast Guard (DHS); Secret Service (DHS); Office of the Inspector General (DHS); U.S. Visit (DHS); Bureau of Citizenship and Immigration Services (DHS); Federal Emergency Management Agency (DHS); Federal Law Enforcement Training Center (DHS); Defense Nuclear Detection Office (DHS); Office of the Under Secretary for Science and Technology (DHS)

Mission: To protect the nation against terrorist attacks and coordinate defense of the homeland. The Department of Homeland Security analyzes threats and intelligence, guards the nation's borders and airports, protects critical national infrastructure, and coordinates the nation's emergency response.

Department of Housing and Urban Development (HUD)

Website: www.hud.gov/

HQ: Washington, D.C.

Other locations: Seattle, WA; Atlanta, GA; Ft. Worth, TX; San Francisco, CA; Denver, CO; Boston, MA; Philadelphia, PA; Kansas City, KS; Chicago, IL; and New York, NY

Subcomponents: All Other Components (HUD); Assistant Secretary for Housing—Federal Housing Commissioner (HUD)

Mission: To ensure decent, safe, and affordable housing for all Americans. The Department of Housing and Urban Development funds public housing projects, enforces equal housing laws, and insures and finances mortgages.

Department of the Interior (DOI)

Website: www.doi.gov/

HQ: Washington, D.C.

Other locations: Anchorage, AK; Omaha, NE; Denver, CO; Oakland, CA; Philadelphia, PA; and Atlanta, GA

Subcomponents: Office of the Secretary of the Interior (Interior); Bureau of Land Management (Interior); Bureau of Indian Affairs (Interior); Bureau of Reclamation (Interior); U.S. Geological Survey (Interior); National Park Service (Interior); U.S. Fish and Wildlife Service (Interior); Office of the Solicitor (Interior); Office of Surface Mining, Reclamation and Enforcement (Interior); Mineral Management Service (Interior); Office of the Inspector General (Interior); Office of Special Trustee (Interior)

Mission: To protect and provide access to our nation's natural and cultural heritage and to honor the country's responsibilities to Indian tribes and island communities. The Department of the Interior's duties include managing federal lands, such as national parks and forests, running hydroelectric power systems, and promoting the conservation of natural resources.

Department of Justice (DOJ)

Website: www.usdoj.gov/

HQ: Washington, D.C.

Other locations: Offices for FBI, DEA, U.S. Marshals, ATF, Federal Prison System, and U.S. Attorneys nationwide

Subcomponents: Federal Bureau of Investigation (DOJ); Bureau of Prisons/Federal Prison System (DOJ); Office of Justice Programs (DOJ); U.S. Marshals Service (DOJ); Executive Office of U.S. Attorneys and U.S. Attorneys (DOJ); Office of the Inspector General (DOJ); U.S. Trustees Program (DOJ); Executive Office for Immigration Review (DOJ); Bureau of Alcohol, Tobacco, Firearms, and Explosives (DOJ); All Other Components (DOJ); Drug Enforcement Administration (DOJ); Justice Management Division (DOJ); Anti Trust Division (DOJ); Civil Division (DOJ); Civil Rights Division (DOJ); Criminal Division (DOJ); Environment and Natural Resources Division (DOJ); Tax Division (DOJ); National Drug Intelligence Center (DOJ)

Mission: To protect the security of Americans by enforcing federal laws and assuring fair and impartial administration of justice. The Department of Justice administers and enforces immigration laws, conducts criminal prosecutions in federal courts, and manages the federal prison system.

Department of Labor (DOL)

Website: www.dol.gov/

HQ: Washington, D.C.

Other locations: ETA, BLS, OSHA, and ESA offices nationwide, including Boston, MA; New York, NY; Philadelphia, PA; Atlanta, GA; Dallas, TX; Chicago, IL; and San Francisco, CA. MSHA in 11 district offices.

Subcomponents: All Other Components (DOL); Office of the Assistant Secretary for Administration and Management (DOL); Employment Standards Administration (DOL); Employment and Training Administration (DOL); Bureau of Labor Statistics (DOL); Mine Safety and Health Administration (DOL); Employee Benefits Security Administration (DOL); Occupational Safety and Health Administration (DOL)

Mission: To foster and promote the welfare of American workers by enforcing laws guaranteeing fair pay, safe working conditions, and equal job opportunities. The Department of Labor also administers unemployment insurance, regulates pension funds and collects and analyzes relevant economic data.

Department of the Navy (DON)

Website: www.navy.mil/

HQ: Arlington, VA, at the Pentagon

Subcomponents: Marine Corps (Navy); Immediate Office of the Secretary of the Navy (Navy); Assistant for Administration, Under Secretary of the Navy (Navy); Office of Naval Research (Navy); Naval Medical Command (Navy); Naval Air Systems Command (Navy); Naval Supply Systems Command (Navy); Naval Sea Systems Command (Navy); Naval Facilities Engineering Command (Navy); Military Sealift Command (Navy); Space and Naval Warfare Systems Command (Navy); Commander, Navy Installations (Navy); U.S. Atlantic Fleet, Commander In Chief (Navy); U.S. Pacific Fleet, Commander In Chief (Navy); Naval Education and Training Command (Navy); All Other Components (Navy)

Mission: To maintain, train, and equip combat-ready Naval forces capable of winning wars, deterring aggression, and maintaining freedom of the seas.

Department of State (DOS)

Website: www.state.gov/

HQ: Washington, D.C.

Other locations: Administrative offices nationwide and 250 post locations internationally

Mission: To conduct the nation's foreign affairs and diplomatic initiatives. To oversee embassies and consulates, issue passports, monitor U.S. interests abroad, and represent the U.S. before international organizations.

Department of Transportation (DOT)

Website: www.dot.gov/

HQ: Washington, D.C.

Other locations: FAA and FHWA offices nationwide

Subcomponents: Federal Aviation Administration (DOT); Federal Highway Administration (DOT); All Other Components (DOT)

Mission: To ensure a fast, safe, efficient, accessible, and convenient transportation system. The Department of Transportation's duties include setting national transportation policy, planning and funding the construction of highways and mass transit systems, and regulating aviation, maritime, and railroad operations.

Department of the Treasury (USDT)

Website: www.ustreas.gov/

HQ: Washington, D.C.

Other locations: 400 local IRS offices nationwide. Mints in Washington, D.C.; Philadelphia, PA; Denver, CO; San Francisco, CA; and West Point, NY.

Subcomponents: Office of Thrift Supervision (Treasury); Alcohol and Tobacco Tax and Trade Bureau (Treasury); Departmental Offices (Treasury); Internal Revenue Service (Treasury); Office of Inspector General (Treasury); Financial Management Service (Treasury); Bureau of the Public Debt (Treasury); U.S. Mint (Treasury); Financial Crimes Enforcement Network (Treasury); Bureau of Engraving and Printing (Treasury); Office of the Comptroller of the Currency (Treasury); Office of the Inspector General for Tax Administration (Treasury)

Mission: To print national currency, set domestic financial, economic, and tax policy, regulate banks and other financial institutions, manage the public debt, collect federal income taxes, and enforce the law in the areas of counterfeit and tax violation.

Department of Veterans Affairs (VA)

Website: www.va.gov/

HQ: Washington, D.C.

Other locations: 160 hospitals and 850 clinics nationwide, 58 benefits regional offices

Subcomponents: All Other Components (VA); Veterans Benefits Administration (VA); National Cemetery Administration (VA); Veterans Health Administration (VA)

Mission: To administer programs involving health care, pensions, benefits, and employment to aid U.S. veterans and their families. The Department of Veterans Affairs also operates the veterans' hospital system and national cemeteries.

Departmental Administration (USDA) (DA)

Website: www.usda.gov/da/

HQ: Washington, D.C.

Mission: To serve as the U.S. Department of Agriculture's central administrative management office. Departmental Administration provides support to the Department officials, directs and coordinates the Department's administrative programs and services, manages the Headquarters Complex, and provides direct customer service to Washington, D.C. employees.

Drug Enforcement Administration (DOJ) (DEA)

Website: www.dea.gov/

HQ: Alexandria, VA

Other locations: Seattle, WA; San Diego, San Francisco, and Los Angeles, CA; Phoenix, AZ; Denver, CO; Chicago, IL; Detroit, MI; El Paso, Houston, and Dallas, TX; Atlanta, GA; New Orleans, LA; Miami, FL; St. Louis, MO; Boston, MA; Philadelphia, PA; New York, NY; Newark, NJ; Washington, D.C.; and the Caribbean

Mission: To enforce controlled substances laws and regulations of the U.S. and support programs aimed at reducing the availability of illicit controlled substances on the domestic and international markets.

Dryden Flight Research Center (NASA)

Website: www.nasa.gov/centers/dryden/home/index.html

HQ: Edwards, CA

Mission: To advance technology and science through flight. Dryden Flight Research Center is NASA's primary flight research center.

Employee Benefits Security Administration (DOL) (PWBA)

Website: www.dol.gov/ebsa/

HQ: Washington, D.C.

Other locations: Offices located throughout the United States

Mission: To assist workers in getting the information they need to protect their benefits (pensions, health plans, etc.). The Pension and Welfare Benefits Administration helps officials understand the requirements of relevant statutes and develops policies and laws that encourage the growth of employment-based benefits.

Employment and Training Administration (DOL) (ETA)

Website: www.doleta.gov/

HQ: Washington, D.C.

Other locations: San Francisco, Dallas, Chicago, Atlanta, Philadelphia, Boston, and New York

Mission: To contribute to the efficient functioning of the U.S. labor market by providing job training, employment, labor market information, and income maintenance services primarily through state and local workforce development systems.

Employment Standards Administration (DOL) (ESA)

Website: www.dol.gov/esa/

HQ: Washington, D.C.

Other locations: Offices located in every state across the United States

Mission: To administer and enforce numerous labor laws and mandates that protect the rights and working conditions of U.S. workers. Includes programs dealing with minimum wage, overtime standards, and workers' compensation programs for federal and certain private employees and employers.

Environment and Natural Resources Division (DOJ) (ENRD)

Website: www.usdoj.gov/enrd/

HQ: Washington, D.C.

Mission: To represent the United States in matters concerning the stewardship of the nation's natural resources and public lands.

Environmental Protection Agency (EPA)

Website: www.epa.gov/

HQ: Washington, D.C.

Other locations: Regional offices in Boston, MA; New York, NY; Philadelphia, PA; Atlanta, GA; Chicago, IL; Dallas, TX; Kansas City, MO; Denver, CO; San Francisco, CA; and Seattle, WA; plus 16 laboratories nationwide

Subcomponents: Office of the Administrator (EPA); Office of Enforcement Compliance Assurance (EPA); OGC, OIG, CFO, Offices of International Affairs and Environmental Information (EPA); Office of Administration and Resources Management (EPA); Office of Water (EPA); Office of Solid Waste and Emergency Response (EPA); Office of Air and Radiation (EPA); Office for Prevention, Pesticides and Toxic Substances (EPA); Office of Research and Development (EPA); Region 1—Boston (EPA); Region 2—New York (EPA); Region 3—Philadelphia (EPA); Region 4—Atlanta (EPA); Region 5—Chicago (EPA); Region 6—Dallas (EPA); Region 7—Kansas City (EPA); Region 8—Denver (EPA); Region 9—San Francisco (EPA); Region 10—Seattle (EPA)

Mission: To protect human health and the environment. The Environmental Protection Agency leads the nation's environmental science, research, education, and assessment efforts, runs programs to control and reduce pollution, and works with other federal agencies, state and local governments, and Native American tribal nations to conduct environmental research and set environmental standards.

EPA Region 1—Boston

Website: www.epa.gov/region1/

HQ: Boston, MA

Mission: To work with the state, local, and tribal governments of Connecticut, Maine, Massachusetts, New Hampshire, Rhode Island, and Vermont to carry out U.S. environmental laws. Develops, proposes, and implements an approved regional program for comprehensive and integrated environmental protection activities.

EPA Region 2—New York

Website: www.epa.gov/region2/

HQ: New York, NY

Other locations: Edison, NJ; Niagara Falls, NY; and Santurce, Puerto Rico

Mission: To work with the state, local, and tribal governments of New Jersey, New York, Puerto Rico, and the U.S. Virgin Islands to carry out U.S. environmental laws. Develops, proposes, and implements an approved regional program for comprehensive and integrated environmental protection activities.

EPA Region 3—Philadelphia

Website: www.epa.gov/region3/

HQ: Philadelphia, PA

Other locations: Field operations and laboratories in Wheeling, WV; Annapolis, MD; Fort George G. Meade, MD; and Pittsburgh, PA

Mission: To work with the state, local, and tribal governments of Delaware, D.C., Maryland, Pennsylvania, Virginia, and West Virginia to carry out U.S. environmental laws. Develops, proposes, and implements an approved regional program for comprehensive and integrated environmental protection activities.

EPA Region 4—Atlanta

Website: www.epa.gov/region4/

HQ: Atlanta, GA

Mission: To work with the state, local, and tribal governments of Alabama, Florida, Georgia, Kentucky, Mississippi, North Carolina, South Carolina, and Tennessee to carry out U.S. environmental laws. Develops, proposes, and implements an approved regional program for comprehensive and integrated environmental protection activities.

EPA Region 5—Chicago

Website: www.epa.gov/region5/

HQ: Chicago, IL

Mission: To work with the state, local, and tribal governments of Illinois, Indiana, Michigan, Minnesota, Ohio, and Wisconsin to carry out U.S. environmental laws. Develops, proposes, and implements an approved regional program for comprehensive and integrated environmental protection activities.

EPA Region 6—Dallas

Website: www.epa.gov/region6/

HQ: Dallas, TX

Mission: To work with the state, local, and tribal governments of Louisiana, Arkansas, Oklahoma, New Mexico, and Texas to carry out U.S. environmental laws. Develops, proposes, and implements an approved regional program for comprehensive and integrated environmental protection activities.

EPA Region 7—Kansas City

Website: www.epa.gov/region7/

HQ: Kansas City, KS

Mission: To work with the state, local, and tribal governments of Iowa, Kansas, Missouri, and Nebraska to carry out U.S. environmental laws. Develops, proposes, and implements an approved regional program for comprehensive and integrated environmental protection activities.

EPA Region 8–Denver

Website: www.epa.gov/region8/

HQ: Denver, CO

Other locations: Montana operations facility in Helena, MT, and regional laboratory in Golden, CO

Mission: To work with the state, local, and tribal governments of Colorado, Montana, North Dakota, South Dakota, Utah, and Wyoming to carry out U.S. environmental laws. Develops, proposes, and implements an approved regional program for comprehensive and integrated environmental protection activities.

EPA Region 9–San Francisco

Website: www.epa.gov/region9/

HQ: San Francisco, CA

Other locations: Laboratory in Richmond, CA; outreach offices in San Diego, CA, and Honolulu, HI; and a field office in Los Angeles, CA

Mission: To work with the state, local, and tribal governments of Arizona, California, Hawaii, Nevada, and the Pacific Islands to carry out U.S. environmental laws. Develops, proposes, and implements an approved regional program for comprehensive and integrated environmental protection activities.

EPA Region 10–Seattle

Website: www.epa.gov/region10/

HQ: Seattle, WA

Mission: To work with the state, local, and tribal governments of Alaska, Idaho, Oregon, and Washington to carry out U.S. environmental laws. Develops, proposes, and implements an approved regional program for comprehensive and integrated environmental protection activities.

Equal Employment Opportunity Commission (EEOC)

Website: www.eeoc.gov

HQ: Washington, D.C.

Mission: To prevent discrimination in public and private work places.

Executive Office for Immigration Review (DOJ) (EOIR)

Website: www.usdoj.gov/eoir/

HQ: Falls Church, VA

Mission: To adjudicate immigration cases in a careful and timely manner, including cases involving detained aliens, criminal aliens, and aliens seeking asylum as a form of relief from removal, while ensuring the standards of due process and fair treatment for all parties involved.

Executive Office of U.S. Attorneys (DOJ) (EOUSA)

Website: www.usdoj.gov/usao/eousa/

HQ: Washington, D.C.

Other locations: 94 U.S. Attorneys' offices located throughout the 50 states, the District of Columbia, Guam, the Marianas Islands, Puerto Rico, and the U.S. Virgin Islands

Mission: The U.S. Attorney's office conducts most of the trial work in which the United States is a party, including prosecuting criminal cases brought by the federal government (including all criminal cases in the District of Columbia), and represents the government in both prosecution and defense of civil cases. The executive office facilitates coordination between the Offices of the U.S. Attorneys and other units of DOJ.

Export-Import Bank of the United States (Ex-Im)

Website: www.exim.gov/

HQ: Washington, D.C.

Other locations: New York, Miami, Chicago, Houston, Dallas, Orange County, San Diego, and San Francisco

Mission: To assist in financing the export of U.S. goods and services to international markets. Ex-Im Bank does not compete with private sector lenders but provides export financing products that fill gaps in trade financing.

Farm Credit Administration (FCA)

Website: www.fca.gov/FCA-HomePage.htm

HQ: McLean, VA

Mission: To regulate credit institutions that support U.S. agriculture.

Farm Service Agency (USDA) (FSA)

Website: www.fsa.usda.gov/pas/

HQ: Washington, D.C.

Other locations: Offices in every state across the United States

Mission: To stabilize farm income, assist farmers in conserving land and water resources, provide credit to new or disadvantaged farmers and ranchers, and help farm operations recover from the effects of disaster.

Federal Acquisition Service (FAS)

Website: gsa.gov/fas

Mission: To deliver available adaptable, secure, and cost effective technology services to the Department of Veterans Affairs (VA) and act as a steward for all VA's IT assets and resources.

Federal Aviation Administration (DOT) (FAA)

Website: www.faa.gov/

HQ: Washington, D.C.

Other locations: Located in nine geographical regions and two major centers (in Oklahoma City, OK, and Atlantic City International Airport, NJ)

Mission: To ensure the safety of civil aviation. The Federal Aviation Administration also encourages research and development with respect to the National Airspace

System and civil aeronautics; develops and operates a common system of air traffic control and navigation for both civilian and military aircraft; develops and implements programs to control aircraft noise and other environmental effects of civilian aviation; and regulates U.S. commercial space transportation.

Federal Bureau of Investigation (DOJ) (FBI)

Website: www.fbi.gov/

HQ: Washington, D.C.

Other locations: 56 field offices located in major cities throughout the United States, 400+ resident agencies in smaller cities and towns across the nation, and more than 50 international offices called "Legal Attaches" in United States embassies worldwide

Mission: To protect and defend the United States against terrorist and foreign intelligence threats, to uphold and enforce the criminal laws of the United States, and to provide leadership and criminal justice services to federal, state, municipal, and international agencies and partners.

Federal Communications Commission (FCC)

Website: www.fcc.gov/

HQ: Washington, D.C.

Other locations: The FCC's three regional offices, covering the Northeast, South Central, and Western regions of the nation, are located in Chicago, IL, Kansas City, MO, and San Francisco, CA, respectively. The 16 district offices are located in Atlanta, GA: Boston, MA; Chicago, IL; Columbia, MD; Dallas, TX; Denver, CO; Detroit, MI; Kansas City, MO; Los Angeles, CA; New Orleans, LA; New York, NY; Philadelphia, PA; San Diego, CA; San Francisco, CA; Seattle, WA; and Tampa, FL

Mission: To ensure that the American people have available—at reasonable costs and without discrimination—rapid, efficient, nationwide, and worldwide communication services whether by radio, television, wire, wireless, satellite, or cable. FCC is responsible for ensuring that an orderly framework exists within which communications products and services can be quickly and reasonably provided to consumers and businesses. FCC also addresses the communications aspects of public safety, health, and emergency operations; universal availability of basic telecommunications service; accessibility of communications services to all people; and consumer protection.

Federal Deposit Insurance Corporation (FDIC)

Website: www.fdic.gov

HQ: Washington, D.C.

Other locations: Atlanta, Boston, Chicago, Kansas City, San Francisco, New York City, Dallas, and Memphis

Mission: To maintain stability and public confidence in the nation's financial system by insuring deposits, examining and supervising financial institutions for safety and soundness and consumer protection, and managing receiverships.

Federal Election Commission (FEC)

Website: www.fec.gov/

HQ: Washington, D.C.

Mission: To disclose campaign finance information, to enforce the provisions of the law such as the limits and prohibitions on contributions and to oversee the public funding of Presidential elections.

Federal Emergency Management Agency (DHS) (FEMA)

Website: www.fema.gov/

HQ: Washington, D.C.

Mission: To reduce the loss of life and property and protect the nation from all hazards, including natural disasters, acts of terrorism, and other man-made disasters, by leading and supporting the Nation in a risk-based, comprehensive emergency management system of preparedness, protection, response, recovery, and mitigation.

Federal Energy Regulatory Commission (FERC)

Website: www.ferc.gov/

HQ: Washington, D.C.

Other locations: Atlanta, Chicago, New York City, Portland, and San Francisco

Mission: To regulate and oversee energy industries in the economic, environmental, and safety interests of the American public.

Federal Highway Administration (DOT) (FHWA)

Website: www.fhwa.dot.gov/

HQ: Washington, D.C.

Other locations: 5 resource centers, 52 operating federal-aid division offices, and 3 federal lands highway divisions across the United States

Mission: To provide technical expertise, financial resources, and information to continually improve the quality of the nation's highway system and intermodal connections. It also develops regulations, policies, and guidelines to achieve safety, access, and economic development.

Federal Housing Finance Board (FHFB)

Website: www.fhfb.gov/

HQ: Washington, D.C.

Other locations: Stationed in each of the 12 FHLBank districts

Mission: To ensure that the FHLBanks are safe and sound so they serve as a reliable source of liquidity and funding for the nation's housing finance and community investment needs.

Federal Investigative Service (OPM) (FISD)

Website: www.opm.gov/extra/investigate/

HQ: Boyers, PA

Other locations: Tucson, AZ; Washington, D.C; Orlando, FL; Boston, MA; Ft. Meade, MD; and Arlington, VA

Mission: To provide background investigations and services, supporting over 90 Federal agencies' personnel security programs.

Federal Labor Relations Authority (FLRA)

Website: www.flra.gov/

HQ: n/a

Other locations: Seven regional offices

Mission: To resolve complaints of unfair federal labor practices, to determine the appropriateness of units for Labor organization representation, to adjudicate exceptions to arbitrator's awards, and to adjudicate legal issues relating to duty, bargain, and resolve impasses during negotiations.

Federal Law Enforcement Training Center (DHS) (FLETC)

Website: www.fletc.gov/

HQ: Glynco, GA

Other locations: The FLETC operates two other residential training sites in Artesia, NM, and Charleston, SC. The FLETC also operates an in-service re-qualification training facility in Cheltenham, MD, for use by agencies with large concentrations of personnel in the Washington, D.C., area.

Mission: To serve as an interagency law enforcement training organization for more than 80 federal agencies. FLETC also provides services to state, local, and international law enforcement agencies.

Federal Maritime Commission (FMC)

Website: www.fmc.gov/

HQ: Washington, D.C.

Mission: To regulate oceanborne transportation in the foreign commerce of the U.S.

Federal Mediation and Conciliation Services (FMCS)

Website: www.fmcs.gov/internet/

HQ: Washington, D.C.

Other locations: Numerous offices throughout the United States

Mission: To mediate labor management disputes.

Federal Student Aid (ED) (FSA)

Website: www.ed.gov/about/offices/list/fsa/index.html

HQ: Washington, D.C.

Other locations: Offices located throughout the United States

Mission: To provide financial aid (e.g., grants, loans, work-study assistance) to college students enrolled in eligible programs at participating schools, to make education beyond high school financially possible.

Federal Trade Commission (FTC)

Website: www.ftc.gov/

HQ: Washington, D.C.

Other locations: New York City, Cleveland, Atlanta, Chicago, Dallas, Seattle, San Francisco, and Los Angeles

Mission: To administer antitrust and consumer protection laws and the federal Do Not Call List.

Financial Crimes Enforcement Network (USDT) (FinCen)

Website: www.fincen.gov/index.html

HQ: Washington, D.C.

Mission: To safeguard the financial system from the abuses of financial crime, including terrorist financing, money laundering, and other illicit activity.

Financial Management Service (USDT) (FMS)

Website: www.fms.treas.gov/

HQ: Washington, D.C.

Other locations: Hyattsville, MD; Austin, TX; Kansas City, MO; Philadelphia, PA; and San Francisco, CA

Mission: To serve as the U.S.'s money manager, providing centralized payment, collection, and reporting services for the federal government.

Food and Drug Administration (HHS) (FDA)

Website: www.fda.gov/

HQ: Rockville, MD

Other locations: Several regional and district offices, and district office program area specialists and project monitors located throughout the United States

Mission: To protect public health by assuring the safety, efficacy, and security of human and veterinary drugs, biological products, medical devices, cosmetics, radioactive materials, and the U.S. food supply.

Food and Nutrition Service (USDA) (FNS)

Website: www.fns.usda.gov/fns/

HQ: Alexandria, VA

Other locations: Offices across the United States and Puerto Rico

Mission: To provide children and needy families with better access to food and a more healthful diet through food assistance programs and comprehensive nutrition education efforts.

Food Safety and Inspection Service (USDA) (FSIS)

Website: www.fsis.usda.gov/

HQ: Washington, D.C.

Other locations: Springdale, AR; Raleigh, NC; Philadelphia, PA; Minneapolis, MN; Madison, WI; Lawrence, KS; Ridgeland, MS; Des Moines, IA; Dallas, TX; Pickerington, OH; Lombard, IL; Boulder, CO; Salem, OR; Beltsville, MD; Atlanta, GA; Alameda, CA; and Albany, NY

Mission: To improve the safety of U.S. meat, poultry, and egg products in order to better protect public health.

Foreign Agricultural Service (USDA) (FAS)

Website: www.fas.usda.gov/

HQ: Washington, D.C.

Other locations: Offices worldwide

Mission: To operate programs for building new markets and improving the competitive position of U.S. agriculture in the global marketplace.

Forest Service (USDA) (FS)

Website: www.fs.fed.us/

HQ: Washington, D.C.

Other locations: Nine regional offices across the United States

Mission: To protect and manage national forests and grasslands. The Forest Service also provides technical and financial assistance to state and private forest landowners, cities, and urban communities, and develops and provides scientific and technical knowledge.

General Services Administration (GSA)

Website: www.gsa.gov

HQ: Washington, D.C.

Other locations: Boston, MA; New York, NY; Philadelphia, PA; Atlanta, GA; Chicago, IL; Kansas City, MO; Fort Worth, TX; Denver, CO; San Francisco, CA; and Auburn, WA

Subcomponents: Public Buildings Service (GSA); Office of the Chief Financial Officer (GSA); Federal Supply Service (GSA); Federal Technology Service (GSA); All Other Components (GSA)

Mission: To leverage the buying power of the federal government to acquire best value for taxpayers and federal customers. GSA exercises responsible asset management; delivers superior workplaces, quality acquisition services, and expert business solutions; and develops innovative and effective management policies.

George C. Marshall Space Flight Center (NASA) (MSFC)

Website: www.msfc.nasa.gov/

HQ: Huntsville, AL

Mission: To develop transportation systems, conduct microgravity research, and develop optics manufacturing technology. George C. Marshall Space Flight Center is the lead space propulsion center and supports the Johnson Space Center in developing the International Space Station facilities.

Goddard Space Flight Center (NASA) (GSFC)

Website: www.nasa.gov/centers/goddard/home/index.html

HQ: Greenbelt, MD

Mission: To expand the knowledge on the Earth and its environment, the solar system, and the universe through observations from space. Goddard Space Flight Center develops and operates unmanned scientific spacecraft and manages many of NASA's earth observation, astronomy, and space physics missions.

Government Accountability Office (GAO)

Website: www.gao.gov

HQ: Washington, D.C.

Other locations: Atlanta, Boston, Chicago, Dallas, Dayton, Denver, Huntsville, Los Angeles, Norfolk, Seattle, and San Francisco

Mission: To support the Congress in meeting its constitutional responsibilities and to help improve the performance and ensure the accountability of the federal government for the benefit of the American people. GAO provides Congress with timely information that is objective, fact-based, nonpartisan, nonideological, fair, and balanced.

Headquarters Air Intelligence Agency (Air Force) (AIA)

Website: www.afisr.af.mil/

HQ: Lackland Air Force Base, TX

Other locations: Fort George G. Meade, MD; Patrick Air Force Base, FL; Wright-Patterson Air Force Base, OH; and Langley Air Force Base, VA

Mission: To provide intelligence services to support Air Force operations through flexible collection, tailored air and space intelligence, weapons monitoring, and information warfare products and services.

Health Resources and Services Administration (HHS) (HRSA)

Website: www.hrsa.gov/

HQ: Rockville, MD

Other locations: Boston, New York, Philadelphia, Atlanta, Chicago, Dallas, Kansas City, Denver, San Francisco, and Seattle

Mission: To provide national leadership, program resources, and services needed to improve access to culturally competent, quality health care.

Human Capital Leadership and Merit System Accountability (OPM) (ESC)

Website: www.opm.gov/

HQ: Washington, D.C.

Other locations: Atlanta, GA; Chicago, IL; Denver, CO; Kansas City, MO; Norfolk, VA; Philadelphia, PA; Raleigh, NC; San Francisco, CA; San Antonio, TX; and Honolulu, HI

Mission: To provide advice and assistance in all areas of staffing and human resource management—such as examining for internal and external selection, workforce restructuring and downsizing, and assistance in recruiting and employment information.

Human Resources Products and Services (OPM) (HRPS)

Website: www.opm.gov/Products_and_Services/

HQ: Washington, D.C.

Mission: To assist federal agencies in building high-performing organizations by providing cost-effective, results-oriented services and products that help to recruit, develop, and retain the best workforce and leadership talent.

Indian Health Service (HHS) (HIS)

Website: www.ihs.gov/

HQ: Rockville, MD

Other locations: Offices located throughout the United States

Mission: To ensure that comprehensive and culturally acceptable personal and public health services are available and accessible to all American Indian and Alaska Native people. To provide a comprehensive health services delivery system and work with tribes to develop and manage programs to meet their health needs.

Internal Revenue Service (USDT) (IRS)

Website: www.irs.ustreas.gov/

HQ: Primarily located in the Washington Metropolitan area

Other locations: Offices located in every state across the United States

Mission: To help U.S. taxpayers understand and meet their tax responsibilities and apply tax law with integrity and fairness.

International Boundary and Water Commission (USIBWC)

Website: www.ibwc.state.gov/home.html

HQ: El Paso, TX

Other locations: Eleven other affiliated field offices located throughout the United States/Mexico border region

Mission: To provide binational solutions to issues that arise during the application of United States—Mexico treaties regarding boundary demarcation, national ownership of waters, sanitation, water quality, and flood control in the border region.

International Trade Administration (DOC) (ITA)

Website: www.ita.doc.gov/

HQ: Washington, D.C.

Other locations: Various offices in all United States territories

Mission: To create prosperity by strengthening the competitiveness of U.S. industry, promoting trade and investment, and ensuring fair trade and compliance with trade laws and agreements.

John C. Stennis Space Center (NASA) (SSC)

Website: www.nasa.gov/centers/stennis/home/index.html

HQ: Hancock County, MS

Mission: To act as the primary center for rocket propulsion testing and home to NASA's applied sciences directorate.

John Glenn Research Center at Lewis Field (NASA) (GRC)

Website: www.nasa.gov/centers/glenn/home/index.html

HQ: Cleveland, OH

Mission: To develop and transfer critical technologies in aeropropulsion and space applications. John Glenn Research Center provides research, technology development, and systems development for new aeropropulsion technologies, aerospace power, microgravity science, electric propulsion, and communications technologies for aeronautics, space, and aerospace applications.

John F. Kennedy Space Center (NASA) (KSC)

Website: www.ksc.nasa.gov/

HQ: Kennedy Space Center, FL

Mission: As the only launch complex for manned operations in the U.S., John F. Kennedy Space Center handles multiple space shuttles, military and commercial launches for missions around the Earth and beyond.

Justice Management Division (DOJ)

Website: www.usdoj.gov/jmd/

HQ: Washington, D.C.

Other locations: Other offices in Washington, D.C.

Mission: To provide assistance to senior management officials relating to basic DOJ policy for evaluation, budget, and financial management, personnel management and training, equal opportunity programs, ethics training, and advice, automatic data processing and telecommunications, security, records management, procurement, real property, and material management, and for all other matters pertaining to organization, management, and administration.

Langley Research Center (NASA) (LARC)

Website: www.larc.nasa.gov/

HQ: Hampton, VA

Mission: To conduct aviation and space research for aerospace, atmospheric sciences, and technology commercialization. Langley Research Center is also committed to improving U.S. civilian and military aircraft.

Lyndon B. Johnson Space Center (NASA) (JSC)

Website: www.nasa.gov/centers/johnson/home/index.html

HQ: Houston, TX

Mission: To lead NASA's effort in human space exploration. Johnson Space Center serves as the lead NASA center for the International Space Station, a U.S.-led collaborative effort of 16 nations, and is responsible for the leadership in the field of astromaterials.

Management Services (OPM) (MSD)

Website: www.opm.gov/index.asp

HQ: n/a

Mission: n/a

Marine Corps (DON) (USMC)

Website: www.usmc.mil/

HQ: Quantico, VA

Mission: To recruit, train, and equip marine forces for operations worldwide. It is the only service specifically tasked by Congress to be able to fight in the air, on land, and at sea.

Marketing and Regulatory Programs (USDA)

Website: www.aphis.usda.gov/mrpbs/

HQ: n/a

Mission: To facilitate domestic and international marketing of U.S. agricultural products and to ensure the health and care of animals and plants. MRP agencies are active participants in setting national and international standards.

Merit Systems Protection Board (MSPB)

Website: www.mspb.gov/

HQ: Washington, D.C.

Other locations: Various regional offices

Mission: To protect federal merit systems and the rights of individuals within those systems.

Military Sealift Command (DON) (MSC)

Website: www.msc.navy.mil/

HQ: Washington, D.C.

Other locations: Afloat and shoreside jobs along the East and West coasts and abroad. Additional engineering shoreside opportunities located at key U.S. ports; various U.S. shipyards; and offices in Washington, D.C., Japan, and Italy.

Mission: To transport military supplies and equipment, supply sea-going platforms to support special at-sea missions, and provide logistical support to U.S. Navy ships at sea.

Millennium Challenge Corporation (MCC)

Website: www.mcc.gov/

HQ: Washington, D.C.

Mission: To reduce global poverty through the promotion of sustainable economic growth.

Mineral Management Service (DOI) (MMS)

Website: www.mms.gov/

HQ: Washington, D.C.

Other locations: Offshore program offices located in Alaska, Gulf of Mexico, and the Pacific. Minerals revenue program offices operationally based in Denver, CO.

Mission: To manage the U.S.'s natural gas, oil, and other mineral resources on the outer continental shelf. The Minerals Management Service also collects, accounts for, and disburses revenues from federal offshore and onshore mineral leases on federal and Indian lands.

National Aeronautics and Space Administration (NASA)

Website: www.nasa.gov

HQ: Washington, D.C.

Other locations: Moffet Field, CA; Edwards Air Force Base, CA; Cleveland, OH; Greenbelt, MD; Houston, TX; Kennedy Space Center, FL; Hampton, VA; Huntsville, AL; Pasadena, CA; New York, NY; Fairmont, WV; Baltimore, MD; Stennis Space Center, MS; Wallops Island, VA; and White Sands, NM

Subcomponents: Headquarters (NASA); Ames Research Center (NASA); John Glenn Research Center at Lewis Field (NASA); Langley Research Center (NASA); Dryden Flight Research Center (NASA); Goddard Space Flight Center (NASA); George C. Marshall Space Flight Center (NASA); John C. Stennis Space Center (NASA); Lyndon B. Johnson Space Center (NASA); John F. Kennedy Space Center (NASA)

Mission: To understand and protect the Earth, explore the universe, and inspire the next generation of explorers. The National Aeronautics and Space Administration oversees aviation research and conducts exploration and research beyond the Earth's atmosphere.

National Agricultural Statistics Service (USDA) (NASS)

Website: www.nass.usda.gov/index.asp

HQ: Washington, D.C.

Other locations: 45 field offices across the United States

Mission: To provide timely, accurate, and useful statistics in service to U.S. agriculture.

National Archives and Records Administration (NARA)

Website: www.archives.gov

HQ: College Park, MD

Other locations: Alaska, Arkansas, California, Colorado, District of Columbia, Georgia, Illinois, Iowa, Kansas, Maryland, Massachusetts, Michigan, Missouri, New Mexico, New York, Ohio, Oklahoma, Pennsylvania, Washington, and Wyoming

Mission: To administer a nationwide network of archives, including the presidential libraries.

National Credit Union Administration (NCUA)

Website: www.ncua.gov/

HQ: Alexandria, VA

Mission: To charter and supervise federal credit unions and insure savings in federal and most state-chartered credit unions across the country.

National Drug Intelligence Center (DOJ) (NDIC)

Website: www.usdoj.gov/ndic/

HQ: Johnstown, PA

Other locations: Washington, D.C.

Mission: To support national policymakers and law enforcement decision makers with strategic domestic drug intelligence, to support Intelligence Community counter drug efforts, and to produce national, regional, and state drug threat assessments.

National Endowment for the Arts (NEA)

Website: www.nea.gov/

HQ: Washington, D.C.

Mission: To support excellence in the arts, both new and established; to bring the arts to all Americans; and to provide leadership in arts education.

National Endowment for the Humanities (NEH)

Website: www.neh.gov/

HQ: Washington, D.C.

Mission: To serve and strengthen our nation by promoting excellence in the humanities and to convey the lessons of history to all Americans.

National Institute of Standards and Technology (DOC) (NIST)

Website: www.nist.gov/

HQ: Washington, D.C.

Other locations: Various offices in all United States territories

Mission: To develop and promote measurement, standards, and technology to enhance productivity, facilitate trade, and improve the quality of life.

National Institutes of Health (HHS) (NIH)

Website: www.nih.gov/

HQ: Bethesda, MD

Other locations: 27 institutes and centers throughout MD; Research Triangle Park, NC; New York, NY; Boston, MA; Hamilton, MT; and Phoenix, AZ

Mission: To serve as the steward of medical and behavioral research for the United States. NIH acquires new knowledge to help prevent, detect, diagnose, and treat disease and disability. It conducts supportive and innovative laboratory research, trains research investigators, and disseminates medical and health sciences information.

National Labor Relations Board (NLRB)

Website: www.nlrb.gov/index.aspx

HQ: Washington, D.C.

Other locations: San Francisco, New York, and Atlanta

Mission: To administer the National Labor Relations Act, the primary law governing relations between unions and employers in the private sector.

National Nuclear Security Administration Field Sites (DOE) (NNSA)

Website: http://nnsa.energy.gov/

HQ: n/a

Other locations: Livermore, CA; Kansas City, MO; Las Vegas, NV; Albuquerque, NM; Los Alamos, NM; Aiken, SC; and Amarillo, TX

Mission: To direct the management and security of the nation's nuclear weapons, nuclear nonproliferation, and naval reactor programs.

National Nuclear Security Administration Headquarters Offices (DOE) (NNSA)

Website: http://nnsa.energy.gov/

HQ: Washington, D.C.

Mission: To direct the management and security of the nation's nuclear weapons, nuclear nonproliferation, and naval reactor programs.

National Oceanic and Atmospheric Administration (DOC) (NOAA)

Website: www.noaa.gov/

HQ: Washington, D.C.

Other locations: Various offices in all United States territories

Mission: To understand and predict changes in the Earth's environment and conserve and manage coastal and marine resources to meet our nation's economic, social, and environmental needs.

National Park Service (DOI) (NPS)

Website: www.nps.gov/

HQ: Washington, D.C.

Other locations: Maintains seven regional offices; an interpretive design center in Harpers Ferry, WV; and a service center in Denver, CO, for park design and construction of facilities. Encompasses more than 380 sites across the United States, Guam, Saipan, Samoa, Puerto Rico, and the Virgin Islands.

Mission: To promote and regulate the use of national parks in order to conserve scenery, natural and cultural resources, historic objects and wildlife for the enjoyment, education, and inspiration of this and future generations.

National Regulatory Commission (NRC)

Website: www.nrc.gov

HQ: Rockville, MD

Other locations: King of Prussia, PA; Chattanooga, TN; Las Vegas, NV; Lisle, IL; Atlanta, GA; and Arlington, TX

Mission: To ensure the safe handling of nuclear materials and to oversee nuclear facilities.

National Science Foundation (NSF)

Website: www.nsf.gov/

HQ: Arlington, VA

Other locations: Small international offices

Mission: To promote the progress of science and engineering through the support of research and education programs. The National Science Foundation primarily focuses on research and aims to improve the understanding of the fundamental laws of nature.

National Transportation Safety Board (NTSB)

Website: www.ntsb.gov

HQ: Washington, D.C.

Other locations: Numerous offices throughout the United States

Mission: To investigate every civil aviation accident in the United States and significant accidents in the other modes of transportation, conduct special investigations and safety studies, and issue safety recommendations to prevent future accidents.

Natural Resources Conservation Service (USDA) (NRCS)

Website: www.nrcs.usda.gov/

HQ: Washington, D.C.

Other locations: Beltsville, MD

Mission: To conserve, maintain, and improve our natural resources and environment. The Natural Resources Conservation Service works with farmers, ranchers, and other private landowners to develop and carry out voluntary conservation efforts.

Naval Air Systems Command (DON) (NAVAIR)

Website: www.navair.navy.mil/

HQ: Patuxent River, MD

Other locations: North Island, Point Mugu, and China Lake, CA; Orlando and Jacksonville, FL; Cherry Point, NC; and Lakehurst, NJ

Mission: To provide material support to the Navy and Marine Corps for aircraft, airborne weapon systems, avionics, related photographic and support equipment, ranges, and targets.

Naval Education and Training Command (DON) (NETC)

Website: https://www.netc.navy.mil/

HQ: Pensacola, FL

Other locations: Various installations throughout the United States

Mission: To educate and train naval personnel.

Naval Facilities Engineering Command (DON) (NAVFAC)

Website: https://portal.navfac.navy.mil/portal/page/portal/navfac/

HQ: Washington Navy Yard, D.C.

Other locations: Specialty units, public works centers, and 11 engineering field divisions and engineering field activities in Norfolk, VA; Charleston, SC; Lester, PA; Jacksonville and Pensacola, FL; Great Lakes, IL; Poulsbo, WA; San Diego, Daly City, and Port Hueneme, CA; Pearl Harbor, HI; Guam; Yokosuka, Japan; and Naples, Italy

Mission: To manage the planning, design, and construction of shore facilities for U.S. Navy activities around the world. Naval Facilities Engineering Command provides engineering support, scientific and technical products and services, global/program/equipment/materiel management, procurement, and evaluation.

Naval Medical Command (DON) (NAVMEDCOM)

Website: www.navy.mil/

HQ: Bethesda, MD

Other locations: Eight geographic direct health care commands and seven special mission commands

Mission: To ensure the highest level of health for Navy personnel through the promotion of physical fitness, the prevention and control of diseases and injuries, and the treatment and care of the sick and injured.

Naval Sea Systems Command (DON) (NAVSEA)

Website: www.navsea.navy.mil/

HQ: Washington Navy Yard, D.C.

Other locations: Groton, CT; Panama City, FL; Indian Head, MD; Portsmouth, NH; Mechanicsburg, PA; Newport News, Portsmouth, and Wallops Island, VA; Pearl Harbor, HI; Bath and Kittery, ME; Bremerton, WA

Mission: To engineer, build, and support the U.S. fleet of ships and combat systems.

Naval Supply Systems Command (DON) (NAVSUP)

Website: https://www.navsup.navy.mil/navsup

HQ: Mechanicsburg, PA

Other locations: Philadelphia, PA; Norfolk, VA; Jacksonville, FL; San Diego, CA; Puget Sound, WA; Pearl Harbor, HI; and Yokosuka, Japan

Mission: To deliver combat capability through logistics, supporting the Navy, Marine Corps, Joint and Allied Forces with high-quality supplies and services whenever and wherever those supplies and services are needed.

Occupational Safety and Health Administration (DOL) (OSHA)

Website: www.osha.gov/

HQ: Washington, D.C.

Other locations: Offices located throughout the United States

Mission: To determine and enforce workplace safety and health standards and assist employers in complying with those standards.

Office for Civil Rights (ED) (OCR)

Website: www.ed.gov/about/offices/list/ocr/index.html

HQ: Washington, D.C.

Other locations: Offices located throughout the United States

Mission: To resolve complaints of discrimination and to provide technical assistance to help institutions achieve compliance with the civil rights laws that the Department of Education enforces.

Office of Administration and Resources Management (EPA) (OARM)

Website: www.epa.gov/oarm/

HQ: Washington, D.C.

Other locations: Cincinnati, OH; Research Triangle Park, NC

Mission: To perform a number of key support functions for the EPA, including human resource management, acquisition activities, grants management, and facility maintenance and management.

Office of Air and Radiation (EPA) (OAR)

Website: www.epa.gov/oar/

HQ: Washington, D.C.

Other locations: Research Triangle Park, NC; Ann Arbor, MI; and Glen Allen, VA

Mission: To develop national programs, technical policies, and regulations for controlling air pollution and radiation exposure.

Office of Enforcement Compliance Assurance (EPA) (OECA)

Website: www.epa.gov/compliance/

HQ: Washington, D.C.

Other locations: Ten regional offices across the United States, Puerto Rico, and Guam

Mission: To maximize compliance with U.S. environmental laws and reduce threats to public health and the environment by employing an integrated approach of compliance assistance, compliance incentives, and innovative civil and criminal enforcement.

Office of Federal Housing Enterprise Oversight

Website: www.fhfa.gov/

Mission: The Federal Housing Finance Agency (FHFA) was formed by a legislative merger of the Office of Federal Housing Enterprise Oversight (OFHEO), the Federal Housing Finance Board (FHFB), and the U.S. Department of Housing and Urban Development (HUD) government-sponsored enterprise (GSE) mission team. FHFA regulates Fannie Mae, Freddie Mac, and the 12 Federal Home Loan Banks.

Office of Justice Programs (DOJ) (OJP)

Website: www.ojp.usdoj.gov/

HQ: Washington, D.C.

Mission: To provide federal leadership in developing the nation's capacity to prevent and control crime, improve the criminal and juvenile justice systems, increase knowledge about crime and related issues, and assist crime victims.

Office of Management and Budget (OMB)

Website: www.whitehouse.gov/omb/

HQ: Washington, D.C.

Mission: To evaluate, formulate, and coordinate management procedures and program objectives across the federal government. It also controls the federal budget and advises the President on budget proposals and legislation.

Office of Naval Research (DON) (ONR)

Website: www.onr.navy.mil/default.asp

HQ: Arlington, VA

Other locations: International field office in London, England. Science and Technology Reserve Program Units in Washington, D.C.; Aberdeen, MD; Norfolk, VA; Raleigh, NC; Newport, RI; Chicago, IL; Albuquerque, NM; Chattanooga, TN; Seattle, WA; Houston, TX; San Diego, and San Jose and Monterey, CA. Naval Research Laboratory located in Washington, D.C., with field sites in MS; Monterey, CA; Lexington Park, MD; Chesapeake Beach, MD; and Mobile Bay, AL.

Mission: To coordinate, execute, and promote the science and technology programs of the U.S. Navy and Marine Corps through schools, universities, government laboratories, and non-profit and for-profit organizations. The Office of Naval Research provides technical advice to the Chief of Naval Operations and the Secretary of the Navy and works with industry to improve technology manufacturing processes.

Office of Personnel Management (OPM)

Website: www.opm.gov/

HQ: Washington, D.C.

Other locations: California, Georgia, Illinois, Missouri, and Pennsylvania

Subcomponents: Human Capital Leadership and Merit System Accountability (OPM); Strategic Human Resources Policy (OPM); Human Resources Products and Services (OPM); Office of the Chief Financial Officer (OPM); Management Services (OPM); Office of the Inspector General (OPM); Federal Investigative Service (OPM); Executive Staff Offices (OPM)

Mission: To build a high quality and diverse federal workforce, based on merit system principles, that America needs to guarantee freedom, promote prosperity, and ensure the security of this great nation.

Office of Postsecondary Education (ED) (OPE)

Website: www.ed.gov/about/offices/list/ope/index.html

HQ: Washington, D.C.

Mission: To formulate federal postsecondary education policy and administer programs that address critical national needs in support of our mission to increase access to quality postsecondary education.

Office for Prevention, Pesticides and Toxic Substances (EPA) (OPPTS)

Website: www.epa.gov/oppts/

HQ: Washington, D.C.

Mission: To protect public health and the environment from potential risk from toxic chemicals by promoting pollution prevention, support the public's right to know about chemical risks, and evaluate pesticides and chemicals.

Office of Research and Development (EPA) (ORD)

Website: www.epa.gov/ord/

HQ: Washington, D.C.

Other locations: Cincinnati, OH; Ada, OK; and Las Vegas, NV

Mission: To serve as the scientific research arm of EPA, conducting research on ways to prevent pollution, protect human health, and reduce risk.

Office of the Secretary of Defense (OSD)

Website: www.defenselink.mil/osd/

HQ: Washington, D.C.

Mission: To support the Secretary of Defense in the formulation and execution of general defense policy. Its responsibilities include policy development, fiscal and resource management, and program evaluation.

Office of Solid Waste and Emergency Response (EPA) (OSWER)

Website: www.epa.gov/oswer/

HQ: Washington, D.C.

Other locations: Crystal City, VA; plus additional facilities and 10 regional offices across the United States, Puerto Rico, and Guam

Mission: To provide policy, guidance, and direction for EPA's solid waste and emergency response programs. Develops guidelines for the land disposal of hazardous waste and underground storage tanks; provides technical assistance to all levels of government to establish safe practices in waste management; supports state and local governments in redeveloping and reusing potentially contaminated sites; and responds to abandoned and active hazardous waste sites and accidental oil and chemical releases.

Office of Special Education and Rehabilitative Services (ED) (OSERS)

Website: www.ed.gov/about/offices/list/osers/index.html

HQ: Washington, D.C.

Mission: To improve educational outcomes for people with disabilities by providing information, technical, and financial assistance to parents, individuals, school districts, and states in special education, vocational rehabilitation, and research.

Office of Special Trustee (DOI) (OST)

Website: www.doi.gov/ost/

HQ: Washington, D.C.

Mission: To provide oversight, reform, and coordination of the policies, procedures, systems, and practices used by various agencies to manage Indian trust assets. This mission is integrally related to the Department of the Interior's goal of meeting its responsibilities to American Indians.

Office of Surface Mining, Reclamation and Enforcement (DOI) (OSMRE)

Website: www.osmre.gov/

HQ: Washington, D.C.

Other locations: Birmingham, AL; Denver, CO; Alton, IL; Indianapolis, IN; Lexington, London, Madisonville, and Pikeville, KY; Albuquerque and Farmington, NM; Columbus, OH; Tulsa, OK; Harrisburg, Johnstown, Pittsburgh, and Wilkes-Barre, PA; Knoxville, TN; Big Stone Gap, VA; Olympia, WA; Beckley, Charleston, and Morgantown, WV; and Casper, WY

Mission: To carry out the requirements of the Surface Mining Control and Reclamation Act in cooperation with states and Indian tribes. The Office of Surface Mining, Reclamation and Enforcement ensures that coal mines are operated in a manner that protects citizens and the environment, assures that the land is restored to beneficial use following mining, and pursues reclamation of abandoned coal mines.

Office of Thrift Supervision (USDT) (OTS)

Website: www.ots.treas.gov/

HQ: Washington, D.C.

Other locations: Jersey City, Atlanta, Dallas, and San Francisco

Mission: To supervise savings associations and their holding companies in order to maintain their safety and soundness and compliance with consumer laws and to encourage a competitive industry that meets America's financial services needs.

Office of the U.S. Trade Representative

Website: www.ustr.gov/

HQ: n/a

Other locations: Washington, Geneva, and Brussels

Mission: To develop and coordinate U.S. international trade, commodity, and direct investment policy and oversee negotiations with other countries. The head of USTR is the U.S. Trade Representative, a Cabinet member who serves as the president's principal trade adviser, negotiator, and spokesperson on trade issues.

Office of Water (EPA) (OW)

Website: www.epa.gov/ow/

HQ: Washington, D.C.

Mission: To implement the Clean Water Act and Safe Drinking Water Act. The agency targets activities on preventing pollution wherever possible and reducing risk for people and ecosystems in the most cost-effective way.

Overseas Private Investment Corporation

Website: www.opic.gov/

HQ: Washington, D.C.

Other locations: Works in over 150 countries

Mission: To mobilize and facilitate the participation of United States private capital and skills in the economic and social development of less developed areas and countries in transition from nonmarket to market economies.

Patent and Trademark Office (DOC) (PTO)

Website: www.uspto.gov/

HQ: Washington, D.C.

Other locations: Various offices in all United States territories

Mission: To promote the progress of science and the useful arts by securing for limited times to inventors the exclusive right to their respective discoveries.

Pension Benefit Guaranty Corporation (PBGC)

Website: www.pbgc.gov/

HQ: Washington, D.C.

Mission: To protect the retirement incomes of nearly 44 million American workers in more than 29,000 private-sector defined benefit pension plans.

Power Marketing Administrations–Southeastern, Southwestern, and Western Areas (DOE)

Website: www.energy.gov/organization/powermarketingadmin.htm

HQ: n/a

Mission: To market and deliver reliable, cost-based hydroelectric power and related service.

Public Buildings Service (GSA) (PBS)

Website: www.gsa.gov/Portal/gsa/ep/channelView.do?pageTypeId=8199&channelId=-13303

HQ: Washington, D.C.

Other locations: Eleven regional offices located in major metropolitan centers across the country

Mission: To deliver comprehensive real estate services to the federal government and to provide a superior workplace for the federal worker. The Public Buildings Service oversees the design, construction, maintenance, and security of government facilities, including office buildings, laboratories, border stations, child care centers, data processing centers, courthouses, and historic properties.

Railroad Retirement Board (RRB)

Website: www.rrb.gov/

HQ: Chicago, IL

Other locations: Field offices throughout the United States

Mission: To oversee all issues pertaining to the benefits of retired railroad workers.

Risk Management Agency (USDA) (RMA)

Website: www.rma.usda.gov/

HQ: Washington, D.C.

Other locations: Regional and compliance offices located throughout the United States

Mission: To assist farmers in managing their business risks through effective, market-based risk management solutions, thereby preserving and strengthening the economic stability of U.S. agricultural producers.

Rural Housing Service (USDA) (RHS)

Website: www.rurdev.usda.gov/rhs/

HQ: Washington, D.C.

Other locations: Offices in every state across the United States, and Puerto Rico

Mission: To assist rural communities and individuals by providing loans and grants for housing and community facilities.

Secret Service (DHS)

Website: www.secretservice.gov/

HQ: Washington, D.C.

Other locations: Various offices in all United States territories

Mission: To safeguard the nation's financial infrastructure and payment systems to preserve the integrity of the economy, and to protect national leaders, visiting heads of state and government, designated sites and National Special Security Events.

Securities and Exchange Commission (SEC)

Website: www.sec.gov/

HQ: Washington, D.C.

Other locations: New York City, Boston, Philadelphia, Atlanta, Chicago, Denver, Fort Worth, Salt Lake City, San Francisco, and Los Angeles

Mission: To protect investors, maintain fair, orderly and efficient markets, and facilitate capital formation.

Selective Service System (SSS)

Website: www.sss.gov/

HQ: Arlington, VA

Mission: To provide manpower to the armed forces in an emergency and to run an Alternative Service Program for men classified as conscientious objectors during a draft.

Small Business Administration (SBA)

Website: www.sbaonline.sba.gov/

HQ: Washington, D.C.

Other locations: Boston, MA; New York, NY; Philadelphia, PA; Atlanta, GA; Chicago, IL; Fort Worth, TX; Kansas City, MO; Denver, CO; San Francisco, CA; and Seattle, WA

Mission: To aid, counsel, assist, and protect the interests of small business concerns, to preserve free competitive enterprise, and to maintain and strengthen the overall economy of our nation.

Social Security Administration (SSA)

Website: www.ssa.gov/

HQ: Baltimore, MD

Other locations: Main regional offices in Boston, MA; New York, NY; Philadelphia, PA; Atlanta, GA; Chicago, IL; Kansas City, MO; Dallas, TX; Denver, CO; San Francisco, CA; and Seattle, WA; plus 1,500 field offices, teleservice centers (800 number), program service centers, and hearings offices nationwide.

Mission: To manage the nation's social insurance program (retirement, survivors, and disability insurance programs). The agency's responsibilities include assigning Social Security numbers to U.S. citizens, maintaining earnings records for workers under their Social Security numbers, and administering the Supplemental Security Income program for the aged, blind, and disabled.

Space Command (Air Force) (AFSPC)

Website: www.afspc.af.mil/

HQ: Peterson Air Force Base, CO

Other locations: Bases in F.E. Warren Air Force Base, WY; Malmstrom Air Force Base, MT; Minot Air Force Base, ND; Buckley Air Force Base, Peterson Air Force Base, and Schriever Air Force Base, CO; Los Angeles Air Force Base and Vandenberg Air Force Base, CA; Patrick Air Force Base, FL; and many geographically separated units around the globe

Mission: To operate space and ballistic missile systems, including ballistic missile warning, space control, spacelift, and satellite operations.

Space and Naval Warfare Systems Command (DON) (SPAWAR)

Website: http://enterprise.spawar.navy.mil/

HQ: San Diego, CA

Other locations: Field offices in Charleston, SC; New Orleans, LA; and Norfolk, VA

Mission: To provide technical and material support to the Navy for space systems, command, control, communications, computer, intelligence systems, electronic warfare, and undersea surveillance.

Strategic Human Resources Policy (OPM) (SHRP)

Website: www.opm.gov/insure/

HQ: Washington, D.C.

Mission: To design, develop, and implement innovative, flexible, merit-based HR policies.

Substance Abuse and Mental Health Services Administration (HHS) (SAMHSA)

Website: www.samhsa.gov/

HQ: Rockville, MD

Mission: To focus attention, programs, and funding on improving the lives of people with or at risk for mental and substance abuse disorders.

Surface Transportation Board

Website: www.stb.dot.gov/

HQ: Washington, D.C.

Mission: To resolve railroad rate and service disputes and review proposed railroad mergers. The STB serves as both an adjudicatory and a regulatory body. The agency has jurisdiction over railroad rate and service issues and rail restructuring transactions (mergers, line sales, line construction, and line abandonments); certain trucking company, moving van, and non-contiguous ocean shipping company rate matters; certain intercity passenger bus company structure, financial, and operational matters; and rates and services of certain pipelines not regulated by the Federal Energy Regulatory Commission.

Tax Division (DOJ)

Website: www.usdoj.gov/tax/

HQ: Washington, D.C.

Mission: To handle or supervise civil and criminal matters that arise under the internal revenue laws.

Transportation Security Administration (DHS) (TSA)

Website: www.tsa.gov/index.shtm

HQ: Arlington, VA

Other locations: Various offices throughout the United States

Mission: To protect the nation's transportation systems by ensuring the freedom of movement for people and commerce.

United States Army Accessions Command (DA) (USAAC)

Website: www.usaac.army.mil/index.html

HQ: Fort Monroe, VA

Mission: To transform volunteers into quality soldiers, leaders, and team members for America's Army. To imbue them with a warrior and winning spirit and to meet the Army's manpower and readiness requirements and standards.

United States Army Acquisition Support Center (DA) (ASC)

Website: http://asc.army.mil/default.cfm

HQ: Fort Belvoir, VA

Other locations: Several regional offices

Mission: To support soldiers by continually improving the U.S. Army's combat capability and by developing critical systems and services used in battle.

United States Army Contracting Agency (DA) (ACA)

Website: http://aca.saalt.army.mil/ACA/index.htm

HQ: Arlington, VA

Other locations: Regional offices throughout the United States, Europe, and Asia

Mission: To provide contracting services to the U.S. Army, especially NETCOM.

United States Army Corps of Engineers (DA) (USACE)

Website: www.usace.army.mil/

HQ: Washington, D.C.

Other locations: Cincinnati, OH; Fort Hamilton, Brooklyn, NY; Portland, OR; Omaha, NE; Atlanta, GA; San Francisco, CA; Dallas, TX; Vicksburg, MS; and Fort Shafter, HI

Mission: To provide engineering, construction management, and environmental services in peace and war. The U.S. Army Corps of Engineers' civil works program includes flood damage reduction, hydropower and environmental regulation, and its military program includes construction of U.S. Army and Air Force facilities.

United States Army Forces Command (DA) (FORSCOM)

Website: www.forscom.army.mil/default.htm

HQ: Fort McPherson, GA

Other locations: 11 major installations (including the National Training Center at Fort Irwin, CA, and the Joint Readiness Training Center at Fort Polk, LA) and 11 sub-installations

Mission: To train, mobilize, deploy, and sustain combat ready forces capable of responding rapidly to crises world-wide.

United States Army Intelligence and Security Command (DA) (INSCOM)

Website: www.inscom.army.mil/

HQ: Fort Belvoir, VA

Other locations: 180 locations worldwide

Mission: To conduct intelligence, security, and information operations for military commanders and national decision makers.

United States Army Materiel Command (DA) (AMC)

Website: www.army.mil/institution/organization/unitsandcommands/commandstructure/amc/

HQ: Fort Belvoir, VA

Other locations: Alexandria, VA

Mission: To develop weapon systems, advance research on future technologies, and maintain and distribute spare parts and equipment.

United States Army Medical Command (DA) (MEDCOM)

Website: www.armymedicine.army.mil/

HQ: Fort Sam Houston, TX

Other locations: 39 facilities across the United States and Europe

Mission: To provide humanitarian assistance, peacekeeping, and other stability and support operations by sending trained medical specialists to the Army's combat medical units. The U.S. Army Medical Command also maintains day-to-day health care for soldiers, retired soldiers, and their families.

United States Army Netcom/9th Army Signal Command (DA) (NETCOM)

Website: www.netcom.army.mil/

Mission: To execute global communications capabilities to the U.S. Army. NETCOM is the U.S. military radio station.

United States Army Reserve Command (DA) (USARC)

Website: www.goarmy.com/reserve/nps/index.jsp

HQ: Atlanta, GA

Other locations: Locations worldwide

Mission: To provide combat support and combat service support specialties, such as medical, civil affairs, transportation, maintenance, and supply.

United States Army Test and Evaluation Command (DA) (ATEC)

Website: www.atec.army.mil/

HQ: Alexandria, VA

Other locations: Locations throughout the United States

Mission: To plan, conduct, and integrate developmental testing, independent operational testing, independent evaluations, assessments, and experiments in order to provide essential information to decision makers and ensure that war-fighters have the capability for success.

United States Army Training and Doctrine Command (DA) (TRADOC)

Website: www-tradoc.army.mil/

HQ: Fort Monroe, VA

Other locations: 26 training schools located across the United States

Mission: To support the recruiting, training, education, and development of U.S. Army soldiers. The U.S. Army Training Command cultivates leaders, supports training in units, develops doctrine, establishes standards, and builds the future U.S. Army.

United States Coast Guard (DHS) (USCG)

Website: www.uscg.mil/default.asp

HQ: Washington, D.C.

Other locations: Locations across the United States; training facility in Cape May, NJ

Mission: To protect the public, the environment, and the United States economic and security interests in any maritime region in which those interests may be at risk, including international waters and America's coasts, ports, and inland waterways.

United States Fish and Wildlife Service (DOI) (FWS)

Website: www.fws.gov/

HQ: Washington, D.C.

Other locations: 8 regional offices and 700 field units across the United States

Mission: To protect fish, wildlife, and plants and their habitats with a particular focus on migratory birds, endangered species, certain marine mammals, and freshwater and anadromous fish.

United States Geological Survey (DOI) (USGS)

Website: www.usgs.gov/

HQ: Reston, VA

Other locations: 400 offices across the United States and in several foreign countries

Mission: To provide a better scientific understanding of natural resource conditions and concerns. The Geological Survey carries out studies on a national scale and sustains long-term monitoring and assessment of natural resources.

United States Holocaust Memorial Museum

Website: www.ushmm.org/

HQ: Washington, D.C.

Mission: To stimulate leaders and citizens to confront hatred, prevent genocide, promote human dignity, and strengthen democracy.

United States International Trade Commission (USITC)

Website: www.usitc.gov/

HQ: Washington, D.C.

Mission: To administer U.S. trade remedy laws within its mandate in a fair and objective manner; provide the President, USTR, and Congress with independent analysis, information, and support on matters of tariffs, international trade, and U.S. competitiveness; and maintain the Harmonized Tariff Schedule of the United States (HTS).

United States Marshals Service (DOJ) (USMS)

Website: www.usdoj.gov/marshals/

HQ: Arlington, VA

Other locations: 94 district offices and 300 sub-offices nationwide

Mission: To protect the federal courts and ensure the effective operation of the judicial system. The U.S. Marshals Service's other duties include transporting federal prisoners, protecting endangered federal witnesses, managing assets seized from criminal enterprises, and capturing federal fugitives.

United States Mint (USDT) (USM)

Website: www.usmint.gov/

HQ: Washington, D.C.

Other locations: Production facilities in Denver, Philadelphia, San Francisco, and West Point, as well as the U.S. Bullion Depository at Fort Knox, KY

Mission: To protect the U.S.'s $100 billion of gold and silver assets and produce and distribute an adequate volume of circulating U.S. coinage to conduct trade and commerce.

United States Trustees Program (DOJ) (USTP)

Website: www.usdoj.gov/ust/

HQ: Washington, D.C

Other locations: Boston, MA; New York, NY; Philadelphia, PA; Columbia, SC; New Orleans, LA; Dallas, TX; Houston, TX; Memphis, TN; Cleveland, OH; Indianapolis, IN; Chicago, IL; Cedar Rapids, IA; Kansas City, MO; Phoenix, AZ; San Diego, CA; Los Angeles, CA; San Francisco, CA; Seattle, WA; Denver, CO; Wichita, KS; and Atlanta, GA

Mission: To promote integrity and efficiency in the nation's bankruptcy system by enforcing bankruptcy laws, providing oversight of private trustees, and maintaining operational excellence.

Veterans Benefits Administration (VA) (VBA)

Website: www.vba.va.gov/

HQ: Washington, D.C.

Other locations: 57 regional offices across the United States, Puerto Rico, and the Philippines

Mission: To administer benefit programs (including education and health services) that provide compensation to the U.S.'s eligible or disabled veterans and their families.

Veterans Health Administration (VA) (VHA)

Website: http://www1.va.gov/health/index.asp

HQ: VA

Other locations: Facilities located in every state across the United States

Mission: To provide primary care, specialized care, and related medical and social support services to U.S. veterans.

Washington Headquarters Services (DOD) (WHS)

Website: www.whs.mil

HQ: Washington, D.C.

Mission: To provide a broad variety of operational and support services to the Office of the Secretary of Defense, other specified DOD offices and the general public. Services include financial, human resources, record, and facilities management; information technology and data systems support; and legal services.

Appendix B

Glossary

ability The capacity to perform a task; for example, the ability to use laboratory equipment or prepare and deliver speeches.

adjudication The decision process that produces a judgment for whether or not you are suitable for the security clearance required by your position.

Agency Employees Only Title under "Who May Apply" on USAJOBS.gov, referring to employees already working at that agency.

All Groups of Qualified Individuals Title under "Who May Apply" on USAJOBS.gov, referring to qualified candidates, status candidates, and agency employees.

application questionnaires Questionnaires commonly used by federal agencies to select top candidates. They vary in length, but may have anywhere from 50 to 100 questions in a varied combination of multiple-choice and short-answer format.

appointment term Section within each job description on USAJOBS.gov. The appointment term tells you how long the job will last. Permanent, long-term appointments are the most common, followed by temporary and term appointments, which are shorter.

banded system A type of government pay system that combines grades from the GS system into a wider "band," or "cluster," of simpler pay grades.

blue-collar worker Employee who is paid by the hour, usually performing various manual labor jobs.

career appointment A professional position that a government employee achieves after working as a career-conditional appointment for three consecutive years within government. As a career appointment, the individual gains competitive status and greater job stability.

career ladder positions Positions that let you come into the government at one GS level and then move up to higher GS levels while staying in the same position (with no additional competition required for a promotion).

Career Transition Assistance Program (CTAP) Program intended for federal employees who are being laid off and have been given special preference to find another position in a different part of their agency.

career-conditional appointment In the competitive service (not exempted service or as a temporary or term appointment), a professional position that a new federal employee holds for three years before reaching career appointment. After serving in a career-conditional appointment for 90 days, an individual is eligible for competitive status. *See also* competitive service; competitive status.

case examining A technique used by employers to categorize job applicants. Jobseekers are ranked according to their level of competency, often by examining KSAs.

category rating A method of categorizing job applicants and selecting the most qualified individuals based on their set of knowledge, skills, and abilities (KSAs). This alternative rating system does not rely on a numerical rating system and does not have to follow the rule of three (only contacting the top three candidates), thus increasing the number of top candidates an agency has to choose from.

CCAR method A method used to organize one's thoughts by using the words Context, Challenge, Action, and Result (CCAR) to create a coherent response. Federal agencies often recommend the CCAR method to answer KSAs.

civil service A category of employment that includes all employees in the executive, judicial, and legislative branches of the United States government, excluding military employees, political appointees, and elected officials.

closing date The final date you can submit your application for a vacancy announcement on USAJOBS.gov. If you don't apply by the closing date, you will not be considered for the position.

competency The possession of important characteristics, skills, and knowledge that an individual needs in order to perform successfully on the job.

competitive appointment An appointment given to an employee hired to fill a permanent, full-time position in government. Agencies can hire candidates within government or outside of government. Competitive appointments are given to the most qualified candidate after he or she completes the full application process, including an application and interview.

competitive service A category of employment that includes the majority of federal civilian positions. Competitive service employees are hired through the regular application and hiring process outlined by the Office of Personnel Management. Competitive service announcements are open to the general public and must be posted on USAJOBS.gov.

competitive status Status held by a federal employee who does not have to compete with applicants from the general public but can be hired in a streamlined process. This status is given to employees with career appointment or those holding a career-conditional appointment for at least 90 days.

congressional committees Subcomponents of the House and Senate that handle major issues such as agriculture, education, labor, foreign affairs, natural resources, and taxation. These committees are comprised of members of Congress and also require their own staff, which averages about 40 non-elected employees.

Cost of Living Allowance (COLA) A federal monetary allowance given to even out differences in the cost of living for workers residing in Alaska, Hawaii, and the territories of the U.S. Virgin Islands, Puerto Rico, Guam, and the Northern Mariana Islands.

critical hiring need The need to fill one or more positions that are crucial to the overall mission of the agency. A critical hiring need could be brought about by emergencies, unpredictable circumstances, new presidential authorization, or federal law.

direct hire authority (dha) Hiring managers' authorization to make job offers to applicants without having to go through the full application process. Direct hire authority can be used for permanent, nonpermanent, or group positions for grades GS-1 through GS-15.

eligible Able to demonstrate that one meets the basic requirements for a job and is deemed qualified.

encore career A career that a retiree begins when he or she rejoins the workforce. This can also be when someone with a full career in one field or sector moves to another job in another field or sector. Such employees often begin encore careers to find meaning through continuing work, to get or maintain benefits, to make a difference and give back, or all of the above.

entry-level Under the General Schedule (GS), this term refers to jobs listed under GS-1 through GS-7 pay scales. Most jobs from the GS-1 to GS-4 levels are clerical and administrative. GS-5 is reserved for those with a Bachelor's degree and GS-7 for those with some graduate education or superior academic achievement.

equal opportunity employment Laws protecting individuals from discrimination based on race, color, national origin, sex, religion, age, disability, marital status, political affiliation, or sexual orientation.

excepted service A category of employment for which agencies can use a streamlined hiring process rather than the regular competitive process to meet a special or critical hiring need. Agencies use this process to hire individuals with specific backgrounds or for hard-to-recruit occupations, such as attorneys, chaplains, and medical doctors. Excepted service positions are not always posted on USAJOBS.gov. Schedule A, B, and C appointments are considered a part of the excepted service.

Federal Flexible Spending Account Program (FSAFEDS) Benefits program allowing federal employees to use pretax dollars to pay for health care and dependent care costs. This can result in a discount of up to 40 percent. The three types of plans within the FSAFEDS are the Health Care Flexible Spending Account, the Limited Expense Health Care Spending Account, and the Dependent Care Flexible Spending Account.

Federal Wage System (FWS) A pay system regulating the wages of blue-collar federal employees. The FWS ensures that federal employees who perform similar jobs within the same wage area receive equal pay. The FWS also ensures that federal employees are awarded pay equal to that of private-sector employees who perform a similar job within the same wage area. *See* wage area.

federal resumé A resumé altered specifically for federal jobs that contains information required by federal agencies. A federal resumé is longer than a general resumé, ranging from one to five pages. Individuals can expand information on their general resumé and go into greater depth about their skills, duties, and accomplishments.

fiscal year The government operates on a fiscal year, which goes from October 1 through September 30 of the following year.

Foreign Service Exam An exam required for employment within the Foreign Service of the State Department. The exam is given several times a year in multiple locations throughout the world. It's widely known to be difficult to pass, and a great deal of study is strongly recommended. The exam includes a written test, personal narrative, oral assessment, and final review.

Foreign Service Officer (FSO) Positions within the State Department and the U.S. Agency for International Development (USAID). FSOs are responsible for supporting international development and the agency mission, promoting peace and prosperity, and protecting American citizens internationally. Both the State Department and USAID require rigorous application processes for these highly sought-after positions.

Foreign Service Specialist An employee of the State Department who has a specialized skill that our government needs overseas. These skills include areas of administration, construction engineering, information technology, international information, English language programs, medical and health, office management, and security.

general experience Experience that is not directly related to the duties of the job at hand. What constitutes general experience depends on the position, but generally refers to any progressively responsible work experience. An example of general experience required for an entry-level program assistant position might be previous administrative and clerical experience.

General Schedule (GS) A federal pay system geared toward white-collar jobs. This system consists of 15 levels, beginning with GS-1 and continuing up to GS-15. Your GS level will depend on a number of factors, from your education and experience to the job itself.

government contractor A private company that conducts government work and projects under contract.

grant Financial assistance awarded to selected recipients that does not have to be repaid.

grantees Government, education, housing, nonprofit, for-profit, small businesses, and selected individuals who apply for and receive federal grants. Grants are not to be used for personal expenses but for specific charitable or organizational purposes or work benefiting the public.

hiring managers Individuals who work to fill open positions at the department or office they oversee. Hiring new employees isn't their sole function, but rather a duty added to their regular job, which could be anything from botanist to accountant. Often the hiring manager will be the direct supervisor of the new employee.

Individual Development Plan (IDP) A tool used by many agencies to highlight the needs and goals of their employees. It is the responsibility of employees to document their own IDP and review it with their supervisor. IDPs are a powerful motivator for employees and help set professional development as a priority.

informational interview An informal opportunity to speak with a more experienced person or employee. Such an interview gives individuals who would like to explore a new career the chance to ask for advice and expand their professional network.

Interagency Career Transition Assistance Program (ICTAP) Program intended for federal employees who are being laid off from and have been given special preference to find another position at an agency that isn't downsizing the same type of position.

invitational travel Expenses covered by an agency for a top candidate to travel to the job location for an in-person interview.

job status Section within each vacancy announcement on USAJOBS.gov specifying whether the position is full-time (40 hours per week) or part-time (typically between 16 and 32 hours per week).

job/vacancy announcement Job opening posted on the USAJOBS.gov website to give notice to the public. Like a want-ad, the job/vacancy announcement lists the conditions specific to the position and explains how to apply.

judicial branch One of the three coequal branches of the U.S. government. Also known as the judiciary, this branch is responsible for interpreting the Constitution, reviewing and administering laws, and deciding cases. The judiciary is comprised of the U.S. Court System, which includes the Supreme Court, the courts of appeals, and the district and bankruptcy courts.

keyword search Function on USAJOBS.gov that helps narrow your search to include only positions fitting your specifications. For example, if you're looking for a job with a specific title (e.g., engineer or writer), you can enter it into the keyword search box to yield only jobs with that title.

knowledge The understanding of facts and information needed to perform a certain task; for example, knowledge of engineering principles and concepts.

Knowledge, Skills, and Abilities (KSAs) Set of questions designed to establish a job candidate's combination of knowledge, skills, and abilities related to the job for which he or she is applying. KSAs require several short-answer responses, or essays, to prompts that range from assessing soft skills, such as the "ability to communicate in writing," to hard technical skills, such as the "knowledge of Microsoft Office Suite." KSAs help agencies select top candidates. Not all applications use KSAs, but those that do average about three to five essays.

legislate To create, consider, and enact laws.

legislative branch One of the three coequal branches of the U.S. government. This branch includes the Senate and House of Representatives, which together make up the U.S. Congress. Congress is responsible for establishing laws and making amendments to current laws.

locality pay scales Scales that maintain a standard rate of government pay that is then used to scale salaries according to various regions in all 50 states.

merit system Process by which the federal government hires employees based on their ability to perform a specific job rather than their political affiliation.

minimum qualifications The basic set of requirements that a jobseeker must possess to qualify for a job. Minimum qualifications depend on the job in which you are applying and are specified on the USAJOBS.gov vacancy announcement.

mission-critical job A position that must be filled for the agency to be able to meet its obligations to the American people. These positions are considered critical by the agency and vary based on the agency's mission.

name request A way for hiring managers to choose you for the job once you have made it into the pool of qualified applicants.

non-competitive appointment A job open to select candidates—typically those who have been a federal employee for at least three years. Under this authority, hiring managers may hire candidates without having to go through the full application process. Non-competitive appointment may be achieved through promotions, demotions, transfers, reinstatements, or reassignments. USAJOBS.gov vacancy announcements specify whether a position is competitive or non-competitive under the "Who May Apply" title. Non-competitive status candidates are not guaranteed federal employment, but are eligible to apply for jobs categorized as "non-competitive" (these jobs are not open to the general public). *See also* special hiring authority.

on-the-spot interview An interview that takes place at career fairs or other public events for which the interviewers do not give previous notice. Agencies must have permission to conduct on-the-spot interviews for specific jobs. These are generally one-on-one interviews.

one-on-one interview An interview between one jobseeker and one hiring manager or decision maker. Jobseekers may be required to have one-on-one interviews with numerous people in an agency or department before receiving a job offer.

Online System for Clerkship Application and Review (OSCAR) A website designed to link jobseekers to federal clerkships. Jobseekers can locate current clerkship openings, select judges for whom they would like to work, upload their resumé and application materials, and locate employment information. Federal judges use the site to locate applicants and initiate contact.

open period Title on USAJOBS.gov specifying the time period during which jobseekers may apply for a position.

open season Specific time of year where both current and former federal employees can enroll in or change their benefit plans. These plans include the Federal Employees Dental and Vision Insurance Program (FEDVIP), the Federal Employees Health Benefits Program (FEHBP), and the Federal Flexible Spending Account Program (FSAFEDS).

opening date Title on USAJOBS.gov designating the day a position was posted.

panel interview A popular federal interview style in which multiple team members interview top candidates. This style allows agencies to make informed decisions about candidates, since a number of employees can provide their perspective and opinion.

pay for performance (P4P) Method of payment in which employees are given raises when they meet targeted goals and contribute to the mission of the agency. The P4P method provides a powerful incentive for employees to focus on work quality.

pay plan Section on USAJOBS.gov describing what pay system is being used for the job (pay for performance, GS, banded, etc.).

political appointee Individual hired by the political party holding office. Political appointees do not go through the regular hiring process and do not have the same job security as permanent federal employees.

preference-eligible The ability of a veteran and selected family member of veterans to qualify to have 5 to 10 extra points added to his or her total job application score. Preference-eligible candidates are appointed through the excepted service, not the competitive service.

prompt Within a USAJOBS.gov vacancy announcement, a word or phrase that can help guide candidates in writing a KSA response.

Public Service Loan Forgiveness Program A program providing student loan forgiveness to selected federal, public service, and nonprofit employees. Employees who still have outstanding federal student loan debt after working in an approved occupation for 10 years and making 120 monthly payments are eligible for forgiveness of the remaining amount. Some eligible occupations include government employment, military service, law enforcement, public health, public education, social work, public legal service, public librarians, and nonprofit 501 (c)(3) organizations.

public Under "Who May Apply" on USAJOBS.gov, the title given to all U.S. citizens.

reinstatement Process allowing former federal employees to return to federal employment through a streamlined application process. Reinstatement eligibility extends to three years after the date of separation. There is no time limit on reinstatement eligibility for those who either have veterans' preference or career tenure.

rule of three A strategy within the federal hiring process, where only the top three candidates with the highest number of application points are considered for employment.

salary range Title under each USAJOBS.gov job description, outlining the potential salary range for the position. Agencies typically hire toward the bottom or middle of the range.

Schedule A appointment A special hiring authority under the excepted service for positions requiring a streamlined hiring process. Positions such as attorneys, chaplains, interpreters, doctors, dentists, and others are filled under this appointment type. Individuals with disabilities or mental handicaps frequently apply for Schedule A appointment. Other instances where this appointment is used include a critical hiring need, a temporary or term job in a remote location, cases where a commission must be rapidly established, or an instance where only non-citizens are available to fill the position. *See also* excepted service; special hiring authority.

Schedule B appointment A special hiring authority under the excepted service, used for candidates who fit the qualification requirements for the position but are not required to complete the regular application process. For example, students under the STEP and SCEP programs and the Federal Career Intern Program are eligible for this appointment type.

Schedule C appointment A special hiring authority under the excepted service, for the use of hiring political appointees, when deemed appropriate by the Office of Personnel Management.

Senior Executive Service (SES) Positions beyond the highest level of the General Schedule, GS-15. Such positions involve heightened managerial and policy-making skills and responsibility and are set apart from most other positions in the competitive service.

severe shortage of candidates A situation wherein an agency cannot find a candidate with the basic requirements needed to perform a specific job. The shortage is considered severe when an agency recruited specifically for the position, kept the vacancy announcement open longer than necessary, and/or attempted to offer recruitment and relocation bonuses, yet is still unable to fill the position.

skills The proficiency to perform a certain task based on knowledge or experience; for example, skill in directing and supervising staff to meet organizational objectives.

special hiring authority Special permission given to federal hiring managers to bypass the regular hiring process for certain qualified applicants. Qualified applicants include those hired through the Federal Career Intern Program, STEP, or SCEP; those with veterans' preference; AmeriCorps or Peace Corps alumni; and individuals with disabilities. This list is not all-inclusive, and other special hiring authorities may be used at the agency's discretion. *See also* excepted service; Schedule A appointment; Schedule B appointment; Schedule C appointment.

specialized experience Work experience directly related to duties performed on the job at hand. An example of this for a medical technician position might be that the jobseeker should have direct experience working with medical equipment, caring for patients, and supporting health care professionals with tests and procedures.

status candidates Title under "Who May Apply" on USAJOBS.gov referring to current or former federal employees who hold or held permanent competitive appointments (not appointments in the excepted service). Selected veterans under the Veterans Employment Opportunities Act are also considered status candidates. *See also* Veterans Employment Opportunities Act (VEOA).

Studentjobs.gov Official government website that posts federal student opportunities with a focus on entry-level and temporary jobs and internships.

subject-matter expert Individual with extensive knowledge of a specific occupation.

superior academic achievement Provision that allows applicants with a Bachelor's degree to advance from a GS-5 to at least a GS-7 level. If you graduated in the upper third of your class, maintained at least a 3.0 overall GPA or 3.5 GPA within your major, or held membership with a national scholastic honor society, you are considered eligible for superior academic achievement.

telework To work from home or a remote location.

temporary appointment Nonpermanent position generally lasting for one year but possibly extending to two years. Temporary appointees can earn vacation days and sick leave but do not qualify for other benefits, such as health insurance. Due to the nonpermanent nature of temporary appointments, these employees cannot be promoted and cannot achieve competitive status.

term appointment Nonpermanent position similar to a temporary appointment. Term appointments begin with a trial year during which the employee can be let go. After the trial year, the position can last up to four years beyond the initial start date. Term employees earn vacation days, sick leave, health insurance, life insurance, and retirement benefits. Like temporary employees, term employees cannot be promoted and do not achieve competitive status.

Thrift Savings Plan (TSP) Savings plan for federal employees equivalent to the private sector's 401(k) program. The TSP allows federal employees to control part of their own salary by investing it toward retirement savings.

U.S. citizens Title under "Who May Apply" on USAJOBS.gov, describing U.S. citizenship by birth or naturalization. Generally, individuals holding dual citizenship are eligible for federal employment, but Green Card holders and permanent U.S. residents are not.

USAJOBS.gov Official government website that posts virtually all government job openings. Jobseekers can post up to five federal resumés and apply for jobs directly from the site.

vacancy announcement *See* job/vacancy announcement.

Veterans Employment Opportunities Act (VEOA) Act designed to increase job opportunities for veterans. VOEA allows preference-eligible veterans to apply for positions open to candidates outside of the hiring agency. Selected veterans are given career or career-conditional appointments. To be eligible, veterans must have been employed continuously for three years of active service. *See* preference-eligible.

veterans' preference Special hiring authority established for veterans who served on active duty for at least two years during a time of war or who were disabled as a result of their time in service. Under veterans' preference, candidates receive an additional 5 to 10 points on their total application score—5 points for preference-eligible veterans and 10 points for veterans who were disabled as a result of their service. Veterans' preference does not guarantee federal employment. *See* preference-eligible.

video interview An interview conducted by webcam or similar video telecommunications technology. Agencies with the technological capability may choose to conduct video interviews rather than offering invitational travel if the candidate does not reside near the job location.

wage area Geographic boundaries defined by the Office of Personnel Management that regulate the hourly pay awarded to blue-collar workers by all agencies within the same wage area.

well-qualified employee An applicant with qualifications that exceed the basic requirements for a position and who demonstrates his or her ability through KSAs responses and other competency factors.

white-collar worker An employee who is paid by yearly salary. These employees typically hold office-related professional, administrative, and managerial positions.

Appendix

Resources

The following websites and publications can help give you additional guidance beyond the information in this book.

Publications

A Golden Opportunity: Recruiting Baby Boomers into Government
www.ourpublicservice.org/goldenopportunity

Discusses encore careers and the need to recruit older, experienced employees into top-level government positions. Available online.

Foreign Service Officer Test Study Guide
www.act.org/fsot

Recommended by State Department as a way to prepare for the rigorous Foreign Service Exam. Available online.

Partnership for Public Service Annual Report 2008
www.ourpublicservice.org/ar08

Read about the Partnership for Public Service, its mission to revitalize our federal workforce, and what the future holds for the organization. Available online.

United States Government Policy and Supporting Positions (Plum Book)
www.gpoaccess.gov/plumbook

The Plum Book is released every four years, defining presidentially appointed positions in the executive and legislative branches of government. You can access past and present Plum Books on the site. Available online.

Websites

AARP
www.aarp.org

AARP is a nonprofit membership organization that works to improve the lives of individuals aged 50 and older. The site posts career and internship opportunities.

American University Washington Internships for Native Students (WINS)
www.american.edu/wins

Official site for the WINS program at American University. Application forms and general program information can be found here.

Best Places to Work in the Federal Government
www.bestplacestowork.org

Ranks federal agencies in terms of employee satisfaction. Site shows data trends for agency pay and benefits, work/life balance, demographics, and more. The site also provides tips for jobseekers.

Boeing Company
www.boeing.com/employment

You can register at the Boeing Company employment site to build and submit your resumé and monitor applications.

Booz Allen Hamilton
www.boozallen.com/careers

Career site for Booz Allen Hamilton, a technology consulting firm. Search for a range of analysis, technology, engineering, accounting, consulting, and administrative positions.

Call to Serve
www.calltoserve.org

The Call to Serve initiative equips students and campuses with information about federal service and employment.

Career Voyages
www.careervoyages.gov

This career exploration resource site provides information on in-demand jobs and the training and education that they require.

Computer Sciences Corporation
www.csc.com/careers

Career site for the Computer Sciences Corporation, an international consulting, systems integration, and outsourcing company. Register with the site to build a user profile, search for jobs, and apply for them.

Electronic Questionnaires for Investigations Processing (e-QIP)
www.opm.gov/e-QIP

Office of Personnel Management website that allows applicants to enter, update, and transmit personal data to send to the hiring agency for review. The site is used to help applicants and hiring agencies meet security requirements.

Federal Bureau of Investigation Careers
www.fbijobs.gov

Official FBI job site. Learn more about FBI careers, student opportunities, and life at the FBI.

Federal Judicial Center
www.fjc.gov

This site posts Federal Judicial Center research findings, educational materials, and employment opportunities.

Federal Players
www.washingtonpost.com/wp-srv/politics/fedpage/players

Federal players is a weekly *Washington Post* publication. Highlights extraordinary federal employees, their achievements, and the impact they have on our nation.

General Dynamics Corporation
www.gdcareers.com

Career site for General Dynamics, an international contractor of the defense industry. General Dynamics hires for many different occupations, including accounting, information technology (IT), law, health care, research, manufacturing, and more.

Government Support Jobs
www.governmentsupportjobs.com

An online career service that connects jobseekers to government contracting jobs.

Grants.gov
www.grants.gov

U.S. government site designed for users to find and apply for federal grants.

Hispanic Association of Colleges and Universities (HACU)
www.hacu.net

Official site for the HACU, a network of colleges and universities that support Hispanic higher education. The site includes information about HACU jobs, scholarships, and internships.

KBR Inc.
www.kbr.com/careers

Career site for KBR, an international U.S. contractor for engineering, construction, and other services. The site offers job searches for different regions around the world.

L-3 Communications, Inc.
www.l-3com.com/careers

Career site for L-3 Communications, a U.S. defense contractor. Search for jobs in different locations around the nation. The site also posts information about internships and student opportunities.

Lockheed Martin Jobs
www.lockheedmartinjobs.com

Career site for Lockheed Martin, an international security company headquartered in Bethesda, Maryland. The site allows you to search for jobs and upload resumés and cover letters for immediate or future use.

Making the Difference
www.makingthedifference.org

Site produced by the Partnership for Public Service. It offers information about federal jobs and internships as well as a Federal Internship Directory.

National Helping Individuals with criminal records Re-enter through Employment (H.I.R.E.) Network
www.hirenetwork.org

Website for the National H.I.R.E. Network, an organization that works to improve public policy and opinion regarding individuals with criminal backgrounds and helps them gain employment. The site has resources for jobseekers and employers.

Northrup Grumman Corporation
www.careers.northrupgrumman.com

Career site for the Northrup Grumman Corporation, an international defense company headquartered in Los Angeles, California. You can register with the site and create a candidate profile.

Office of Defender Services
www.fd.org

Site posts employment opportunities with federal public and community defender offices.

Office of Personnel Management
www.opm.gov

The government's human resources website is a great place for jobseekers to find information on everything from salary information to veterans' preferences. Download security clearance forms and learn more about benefits of working for the federal government.

Online System for Clerkship Application and Review (OSCAR)
www.oscar.uscourts.gov

One-stop source for clerkship openings and application information. Applicants can register and build their applications online.

Park Ranger Careers
www.rangercareers.com

Information on jobs with the National Park Service.

Raytheon
www.rayjobs.com

Career site for Raytheon, a U.S. defense contractor. It posts a diverse mixture of job opportunities worldwide.

RetirementJobs.com, Inc.
www.retirementjobs.com

Online career resource for individuals age 50 and older. The site posts a wide range of job opportunities with age-friendly employers.

Science Applications International Corporation (SAIC)
www.saic.com/careers

Career site for the SAIC, a U.S. science, technology, and engineering corporation. The site posts many different positions available worldwide.

Security Clearance Forms
www.opm.gov/forms/html/sf.asp

This website gives you access to security clearance forms, in addition to other standard forms from the Office of Personnel Management (OPM).

Senior Community Service Employment Program (SCSEP)
www.doleta.gov/seniors

Run by the Department of Labor, this training-based community service program supports older Americans (over the age of 55) who are in financial need in securing part-time, subsidized employment. For more information or to apply for this program, visit the website. Preference is given to seniors over the age of 60, veterans, spouses of veterans, minorities, those with the greatest financial need, and those with limited English language skills.

Studentjobs.gov
www.studentjobs.gov

Official federal job site for students. The site provides student employment information and allows users to search for entry-level and summer jobs and student internships. Students can also use the site to build their federal resumé.

Students.gov
www.students.gov

This site is a student resource center, with links to jobs, internships, scholarships, career exploration, and more.

Supreme Court Fellows Program
www.fellows.supremecourtus.gov

This site provides information about the Supreme Court Fellows Program and how to apply.

Supreme Court of the United States
www.supremecourtus.gov

General information about the Supreme Court. The site features links to court rulings, bar admissions, and opinions. It also has links to the Supreme Court Fellows Program and the Judicial Internship Program.

United Negro College Fund, Inc.
www.uncf.org

The UNCF provides promising African American students with financial assistance, scholarships, and internships. Their goal is to increase the number of African Americans who graduate from college.

United States Courts
www.uscourts.gov

Official site for the United States Courts. The site posts information about the judicial branch, job openings at the U.S. Courts, and provides a court locator resource.

United States Marshals Service
www.usmarshals.gov

Official website for the U.S. Marshals Service. Career opportunities can be found at usmarshals.gov/careers.

United States Sentencing Commission
www.ussc.gov

Posts education and training materials, publications, and employment opportunities.

USA.gov
www.usa.gov

Your one-stop portal for information and services within the U.S. government. This collaborative search engine is kept up-to-date and is accessible to the public.

USAJOBS.gov
www.usajobs.gov

Official job site of the U.S. government. The site provides employment information and allows users to search for federal jobs by location, agency, occupation, series, and pay grade. Users can build their federal resumé on the site.

Washington Center, The
www.twc.edu

Website for the Washington Center, an independent, nonprofit organization offering student opportunities in the Washington, D.C., area. The site also posts current career opportunities at the Washington Center.

Where the Jobs Are: Mission Critical Opportunities for America
www.wherethejobsare.org

Identifies mission-critical federal hiring needs by agency and links directly to current openings on USAJOBS.gov. The site also has a section for jobseekers with tips and information for optimizing a federal job search.

Who Runs Gov
www.whorunsgov.com

Provides bios and information about federal employees, including White House staff, state governors, members of Congress, and more.

Workforce Recruitment Program
www.wrp.gov

Provides information about the federal Workforce Recruitment Program tailored to students, schools, and employers.

Appendix D

Application Checklist

Now that you've learned everything there is to know about getting government jobs, here's a handy yet thorough checklist that puts what you've learned into action items.

1. Research federal agencies.

   - ❏ Use Appendix A to learn agency missions, and decide which agencies interest you most.

2. Plan your career path.

   - ❏ Determine which career path best fits your short- and long-term goals.

   - ❏ If you are interested in working abroad, remember that there are thousands of overseas jobs, not including the Peace Corps.

3. Register with USAJOBS.gov.

   - ❏ From the USAJOBS home page, follow the USAJOBS First Stop link.

   - ❏ Create your user account.

4. Build Your federal resumé.

   ❑ From the USAJOBS home page, click the My Resumes tab, and follow the link to Build New Resume.

   ❑ Complete up to five resumés. Tailor your resumé to each job for which you apply.

   ❑ See Chapter 9 for an example of a good versus a bad federal resumé.

5. Network.

   ❑ Compile a list of contacts who may be helpful.

   ❑ Call or e-mail your contacts, asking them if they would be willing to chat or meet with you.

   ❑ If you are conducting an informational interview, plan your questions ahead of time. See Chapter 6 for more on informational interviewing.

   ❑ Reach out to your campus career center or any alumni or professional associations of which you are a member.

6. Determine your GS level and eligibility.

   ❑ Read the Qualifications and Evaluations tab on each vacancy announcement carefully.

   ❑ Refer to the table under "Qualifying Education or Training" at www.opm.gov/qualifications/policy/ApplicationOfStds-04.asp. This resource will help you decipher your GS-level based on your level of education and experience.

7. Search for jobs online.

   ❑ From USAJOBS.gov, follow the Search for Jobs link. Enter your search criteria to yield specific announcements.

   ❑ Visit agency websites.

   ❑ For Federal Career Intern Program openings, contact the agency directly (by phone or e-mail).

8. Search for jobs offline.

   ❑ Attend job fairs.

   ❑ Check newspapers.

   ❑ Use the Blue Pages: Use these pages in your phone book to see which agencies are located near you. Call or e-mail them directly.

9. Write your KSAs.

   ❑ Use the CCAR method: Context, Challenge, Action, and Result.

   ❑ As much as possible, use exact words from the "Qualifications and Evaluations" section of the vacancy announcement that apply to your education, experience, and skills.

   ❑ Refer to "A Guide to KSA Writing," from makingthedifference.org. You can access the guide here: www.ourpublicservice.org/OPS/programs/calltoserve/toolkit/KSAs.pdf.

10. Complete questionnaires and required forms.

    ❑ Complete all multiple-choice questionnaire assessments in the online application.

    ❑ Read the vacancy announcement carefully to see which forms are required.

    ❑ Download all required forms from the "forms" tab on USAJOBS.gov

11. Monitor your application status.

    ❑ Log on to your USAJOBS.gov user profile.

    ❑ Click on the My Applications tab to view your application status.

12. Follow up with agencies.

    ❑ If you haven't heard from an agency within a reasonable period of time (three weeks to a month), call to follow up.

    ❑ Use the contact information located at the bottom-right of the vacancy announcement or call the agency's human resources department. Contact information for agencies can be found on their websites.

13. Follow up with a thank you note.

    ❑ Send a brief thank you to the contact person on the vacancy announcement if he or she spoke with you and was helpful.

14. When contacted for an interview, gather the following information:

    ❏ Name of caller.

    ❏ Return phone number.

    ❏ Confirmation of job title.

    ❏ Time and date of interview.

    ❏ Exact location of the interview.

    ❏ Name(s) of interviewer(s).

    ❏ Interview format.

    ❏ Security/access requirements for location.

    ❏ Parking or transportation instructions.

    ❏ Approximate interview length.

15. Lay everything out the night before and arrange the details:

    ❏ Government-issued ID.

    ❏ Directions.

    ❏ Extra resumé used to apply to this job.

    ❏ Attire.

    ❏ List of names of interviewers (if provided in advance).

    ❏ Review answers to standard questions or, if possible, prepare with a mock interview.

    ❏ Dress appropriately: refer to Chapter 11 for gender-appropriate attire.

    ❏ Bring a map or use a GPS device on the day of the interview, if you are unfamiliar with the area.

    ❏ Phone interview? Use a landline, if possible, and make sure that you are in a quiet area.

16. Send the interviewer(s) a thank you note.

    ❏ Send a quick thank you to everyone who met with you. A handwritten note mailed to the primary interviewer or selecting official is a nice touch.

17. Submit required information for your background check. Compile the following information:

    - ❑ Past home addresses.
    - ❑ Past jobs.
    - ❑ Contacts who knew you in all locations in which you have lived or worked.
    - ❑ All foreign contacts.
    - ❑ All dates of travel.
    - ❑ Complete all required forms and questionnaires.
    - ❑ Follow up with the agency (after about a month). Let them know if any of your information has changed.
    - ❑ Write legibly.
    - ❑ Provide your full name.
    - ❑ Don't leave any gaps in time unaccounted for.

18. Prepare for a possible wait while your background check is completed.
19. Start your government job!

Appendix E

State Government Websites for Jobseekers

Alabama
personnel.state.al.us

Alaska
jobs.state.ak.us/statejobs.html

Arizona
Azstatejobs.gov

Arkansas
www.ark.org/arstatejobs

California
spb.ca.gov

Colorado
www.gssa.state.co.us/announce/Job+Announcements.nsf

Connecticut
www.das.state.ct.us/exam

Delaware
delawarestatejobs.com

Florida
jobs.myflorida.com/joblist.html

Georgia
careers.ga.gov

Hawaii
agency.governmentjobs.com/Hawaii

Idaho
www.dhr.idaho.gov/StateJobs/tabid/970/Default.aspx

Illinois
state.il.us/cms

Indiana
in.gov/spd

Iowa
das.hre.iowa.gov/state_jobs.html

Kansas
da.ks.gov/ps/aaa/recruitment

Kentucky
personnel.ky.gov/employment

Louisiana
civilservice.la.gov

Maine
maine.gov/bhr/state_jobs

Maryland
dbm.maryland.gov/Pages/home.aspx

Massachusetts
https://jobs.hrd.state.ma.us/recruit/public/3111/index.do

Michigan
michigan.gov/mdcs

Minnesota
www.careers.state.mn.us

Mississippi
www.spb.ms.gov

Missouri
www.oacentral.oa.mo.gov/dopweb/joa.aspx

Montana
www.mt.gov/statejobs

Nebraska
www.das.state.ne.us/personnel/nejobs/per.htm

Nevada
dop.nv.gov/fshome.html

New Hampshire
admin.state.nh.us/hr

New Jersey
www.state.nj.us/csc

New Mexico
www.spo.state.nm.us

New York
www.cs.state.ny.us

North Carolina
www.osp.state.nc.us/jobs

North Dakota
nd.gov/hrms/jobs/announcements.asp

Ohio
careers.ohio.gov

Oklahoma
ok.gov/opm

Oregon
oregonjobs.org

Pennsylvania
www.scsc.state.pa.us

Rhode Island
www.dlt.state.ri.us/webdev/JobsRI/statejobs.htm

South Carolina
Jobs.sc.gov

South Dakota
bop.sd.gov/workforus

Tennessee
tn.gov/dohr/employment/career.html

Texas
Workintexas.com

Utah
statejobs.utah.gov

Vermont
www.vermontpersonnel.org/jobapplicant

Virginia
jobs.state.va.us

Washington
www.dop.wa.gov/Pages/JobSeekers.aspx

West Virginia
www.state.wv.us/admin/personnel/jobs

Wisconsin
Wisc.jobs

Wyoming
personnel.state.wy.us/stjobs

Index

A

B

C

D

E

F

G

H

I

J

K

L

M

N

O

P

Q

R

S

T

U

V

W-X-Y-Z